OFF THE BEATEN PATH®
UPSTATE NEW YORK →

Help Us Keep This Guide Up to Date

We would love to hear from you concerning your experiences with this guide and how you feel it could be improved and kept up to date. Please send your comments and suggestions to:

editorial@GlobePequot.com

Thanks for your input, and happy travels!

FIRST EDITION

OFF THE BEATEN PATH®
UPSTATE NEW YORK →

A GUIDE TO UNIQUE PLACES

SUSAN FINCH

gpp®
travel
Guilford, Connecticut

All the information in this guidebook is subject to change. We recommend that you call ahead to obtain current information before traveling.

Editor: Kevin Sirois
Project Editor: Lynn Zelem
Layout: Joanna Beyer
Text design: Linda R. Loiewski
Maps: Equator Graphics © Morris Book Publishing, LLC

Library of Congress Cataloging-in-Publication Data is available on file.
ISBN 978-0-7627-5945-3

Printed in the United States of America
10 9 8 7 6 5 4 3 2 1

About the Author

Susan Finch is a freelance travel and lifestyle writer living in Brooklyn, New York, with an affinity for offbeat attractions. She's the author of *Metro New York Off the Beaten Path*, *Best Easy Day Hikes: Long Island*, and *Best Easy Day Hikes: Columbus*.

Acknowledgments

I want to extend my endless appreciation to my husband and travel partner, Drew Padrutt. Without your support, friendship, patience, and stubbornness, I would have never known just how much there is to love about New York. I wouldn't want to explore it with anyone else. Thanks to Katie Mantell and all my friends who contributed their expert insight and enthusiasm to this guide, I couldn't have done this without you. I'd also like to thank everyone at Family TravelForum.com for believing in me and giving me a start with something I hold dear, travel writing. And a big thanks to Globe Pequot Press, New York State Tourism, The New York State Office of Parks, Recreation, and Historic Preservation, and all the men and women who keep this state up and running.

Contents

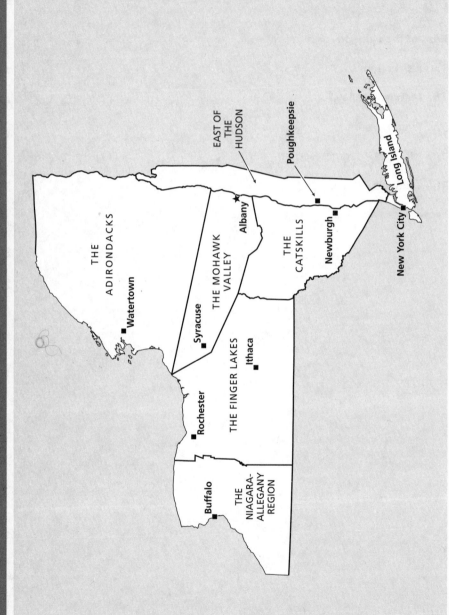

Introduction

In 1784 George Washington declared New York as the "Seat of the Empire," and centuries later we still call it "the Empire State." Yet up until the 1780s, most of New York was an encroaching frontier country, with the exception of the Dutch settlements at New Amsterdam and in the Hudson Valley. Most of the state was settled not just by new arrivals from Europe, but also by migrating New Englanders, setting the pattern for the next hundred years of westward expansion—and making New York a transitional place between "old" coastal America and the horizons of the West.

More than that, New York became a staging area for the people, ideas, and physical changes that would transform the United States in the nineteenth century. Its geographic position between the harbors of the Atlantic Coast and the Great Lakes ensured an early leadership position in the development of canals and, later, of railroads. New York's vast resources made it a powerhouse of industrial power, while its size and the fertility of its soil guaranteed its importance as an agricultural state.

As growth came early in New York, westward expansion created an infrastructure of small towns connected by back roads, rivers, and canals. The coming of the railroads in the nineteenth century gave rise to great cities.

Fast Facts

- With an area of 54,471 square miles, New York ranks twenty-seventh in size among the fifty states.

- With over nineteen million residents, it ranks third in population.

- The state has four mountain ranges: Adirondack, Catskill, Shawangunk, and Taconic.

- New York has 70,000 miles of rivers and streams, 127 miles of Atlantic Ocean coastline, and, including lake, bay, and oceanfront, 9,767 miles of shoreline.

- The state flower is the rose.

- The state bird is the eastern bluebird.

- The state freshwater fish is the brook trout; the saltwater fish is the striped bass.

- The state tree is the sugar maple.

- The state motto is "Excelsior," and the state song is, of course, "I Love New York."

The intellectual and spiritual atmosphere of New York was equally responsive and enthusiastic to change. The Empire State is where the Quakers played out much of their experiment in simple living, where Washington Irving proclaimed an indigenous American literature, where the artists of the Hudson River School painted nature in America as it had never been painted before, and where Elbert Hubbard helped introduce the Arts and Crafts movement to the United States.

This book explores the tangible associations left behind by the state's s history and creativity. New York is plentiful, as are few other states, with the homes, libraries, and workshops of its distinguished locals; with the remnants of historic canals; with museums chronicling pursuits as divergent as horse racing, gunsmithing, and winemaking.

EAST OF THE HUDSON

Named for the English navigator who first explored its waters in 1609, the Hudson River has been the lifeline of New York from its earliest days as a royal colony to its emergence as a world center of commerce and culture.

Today, railroads and highways handle the bulk of commercial traffic, and the river is less of a thoroughfare and more of a welcoming escape for recreation and reflection, a way to savor the enduring beauty of the Hudson Valley. It's not difficult to see how this majestic landscape inspired the artists of the Hudson River School of painting, who portrayed a vision of the pristine American landscape as the new Garden of Eden. In addition to artists like Jasper Cropsey and Fredric Church, the area east of the Hudson has plenty of famous names to drop—Roosevelt, Vanderbilt, and Rockefeller among them.

Over the years, many of the writers, artists, inventors, political leaders, and business tycoons who shaped this state—and the nation—have called this area home. The grand and historic country estates they left behind make a drive along the scenic Taconic Parkway a weekender's delight.

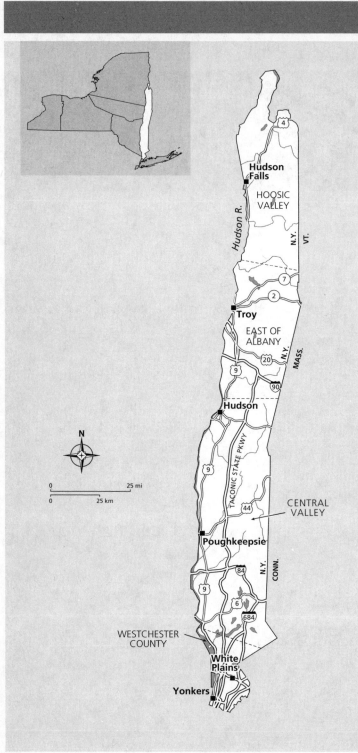

This chapter starts in the crowded bedroom communities of Westchester County. From there, like the Friday-night weekenders looking for a refuge upstate, we'll travel north.

Westchester County

Just beyond the New York City limits, in Yonkers, the ***Hudson River Museum*** occupies the magnificent 1876 ***Glenview Mansion.*** As the preeminent cultural institution of Westchester County and the lower Hudson Valley, the museum's resources reflect the natural, social, and artistic history of the area.

A visit to the Hudson River Museum includes a walk through the four meticulously restored rooms on the first floor of the mansion itself. You'll hardly find a better introduction to the short-lived but influential phase of Victorian taste known as the Eastlake style, marked by precise geometric carving and ornamentation—the traceries in the Persian carpets almost seem to be echoed in the furniture and ceiling details.

Aside from the furnishings and personal objects that relate to the period when the Trevor family lived in the mansion, the museum's collections have grown to include impressive holdings of Hudson River landscape paintings, including works by Jasper Cropsey and Albert Bierstadt.

In contrast to the period settings and historical emphases of the older parts of the museum, the state-of-the-art ***Andrus Planetarium*** features the Zeiss M1015 star projector, the only one of its kind in the Northeast. A contemporary orientation is also furthered by special art, science, and history exhibitions each year, centered on the work of American artists of the nineteenth and twentieth centuries. There is a Victorian Holiday celebration each December.

The Hudson River Museum, 511 Warburton Ave., Yonkers (914-963-4550; www.hrm.org), is open Wednesday through Sunday noon to 5 p.m., Friday

AUTHOR'S FAVORITES—EAST OF THE HUDSON

Chuang Yen Monastery	Old Drovers Inn
Donald M. Kendall Sculpture Gardens	Old Rhinebeck Aerodrome
FASNY Museum of Firefighting	Rodgers Book Barn
Locust Grove	Sunnyside
Olana	Walkway Over the Hudson

The Real "FDR Drive"

The Taconic Parkway offers motorists the most scenic of several routes along the east side of the Hudson River. Started in 1927, the road was originally planned as an offshoot of the Bronx Parkway, but a major extension was already under consideration even before ground was broken. In 1924 the Taconic State Park Commission was formed, and its commissioner, Franklin D. Roosevelt, was eager to push the parkway north as far as Albany. It didn't get quite that far—in 1963 the Taconic eventually reached its northernmost point at the intersection with Interstate 90 in Chatham. It was FDR, however, who insisted on the road's scenic path through some of the most majestic portions of his beloved Hudson Valley. He even prescribed the rustic, thickly mortared stone bridges that help make the Taconic such a handsome rural thoroughfare.

until 7:30 p.m. Admission to the museum galleries is $5 for adults, $3 for senior citizens and youth 5 to 16. Admission to the planetarium is $2 for adults, $1 for senior citizens and youth 5 to 16. There is a free planetarium star show Friday at 6:30 p.m. Other planetarium shows are held Saturday and Sunday on the half-hour from 12:30 to 3:30 p.m. Admission for both museum and star show is $7 for adults and $4 for seniors and youth 5 to 16.

Hundreds of years before Glenview Mansion was built, the Philipse family assembled a Westchester estate that makes Glenview's twenty-seven acres seem puny by comparison. Frederick Philipse I came to what was then New Amsterdam in the 1650s and began using his sharp trader's instincts. By the 1690s his lands had grown into an enormous, oversized estate, including a 52,500-acre tract that encompassed one-third of what is now Westchester County.

In 1716 Philipse's grandson Frederick Philipse II assumed the title of Lord of the Manor of Philipsborough, greatly enlarged the cottage built by his grandfather, and used Philipse Manor Hall as a summer residence. Col. Frederick Philipse (III) rebuilt and further enlarged the Georgian manor house, planted elaborate gardens, and imported the finest furnishings for the hall. His tenure as Lord of the Manor ended when he decided to side with the Tory cause at the beginning of the American Revolution.

Confiscated along with the rest of its owner's properties after the war, Philipse Manor Hall was auctioned by the State of New York and passed through the hands of a succession of owners until 1908, when the state bought the property back. The state has since maintained the mansion as a museum of history, art, and architecture. Home to the finest papier-mâché rococo ceiling in the United States, inside and out it remains one of the most perfectly preserved examples of Georgian style in the Northeast.

Philipse Manor Hall State Historic Site, 29 Warburton Ave., Yonkers (914-965-4027; www.nysparks.state.ny.us/historic-sites), is open year-round for tours and special programs only. April through October, tours are offered Tuesday through Sunday at noon, 2 p.m., and 3 p.m.; November through March, tours are noon to 2 p.m. on the hour; or by appointment. Admission is $4 for adults, $3 for seniors and students, and free for children 12 and under. Group tours are available by appointment.

Fans of the nineteenth-century New York–born Hudson River School painter and architect Jasper F. Cropsey flock to ***Ever Rest,*** his Gothic home and studio, and the ***Newington Cropsey Foundation Gallery of Art*** (www .newingtoncropsey.com). Ever Rest is preserved as it appeared when the artist lived there and exhibits his paintings, watercolors, and sketches. The handsome Gallery of Art, with its octagonal gallery built to resemble "Aladdin," Cropsey's studio in Hastings-on-Hudson, New York, houses the world's largest collection of the artist's works.

They're both in Hastings-on-Hudson: his home and studio, 49 Washington Ave. (914-478-1372), is open for tours by appointment only, Monday through Friday 10 a.m. to 1 p.m.; closed January and August. The gallery, 25 Cropsey Lane (914-478-7990), offers forty-five-minute tours of the permanent collection by appointment only (at least a week in advance) weekdays from 1 to 5 p.m. Visitors are welcome to tour the grounds weekdays from 1 to 5 p.m. without an appointment.

Donald M. Kendall, former chairman of the board and chief executive officer of PepsiCo, Inc., had a dream that extended far beyond bubbly soft drinks. He wanted to create a garden where the atmosphere of stability, creativity, and experimentation would reflect his vision of the company. In 1965 he began collecting sculptures; today more than forty works by major twentieth-century artists are displayed on 168 acres of magnificent gardens—many created by internationally renowned designers Russell Page and François Goffinet, who picked up where Mr. Page left off.

Happy Holidays East of the Hudson

The holiday season is a perfect time to explore the great houses of the region, which are decked out in festive finery throughout the month of December. Sunnyside, Philipsburg, Lyndhurst, Boscobel, Van Cortlandt Manor, and others offer such events as candlelight tours, bonfires, carols, storytelling, and dancing. Check www.hudson valley.org/calendar and the individual Web sites of the manor houses for information on specific events.

ANNUAL EVENTS EAST OF THE HUDSON

JANUARY

Ice Festival
Hillsdale
(518) 325-3200
www.catamountski.com

FEBRUARY

Black History Month Events
Poughkeepsie
(845) 454-1702
www.pokchamb.org

MARCH

Annual HVP String Competition
Vassar College
Poughkeepsie
(845) 473-5288
www.bardavon.org

Annual Maple Weekend
Various locations
(585) 591-1190
www.mapleweekend.com

APRIL

Annual Movable Feast
Hudson Opera House
Hudson
(518) 822-1438
www.hudsonoperahouse.org

Great Poughkeepsie Easter Egg Hunt
Waryas Park
Poughkeepsie
(845) 471-7565

MAY

Rhinebeck Antiques Fair
Duchess County Fairgrounds
Rhinebeck
(845) 876-1989
www.rhinebeckantiquesfair.com

JUNE

Caramoor International Music Festival
Katonah
(914) 232-5035
www.caramoor.org

Clearwater Festival
Croton Point
(800) 677-5667
www.clearwaterfestival.org

Crafts at Rhinebeck
Duchess County Fairgrounds
(845) 876-4001
www.dutchessfair.com

Alexander Calder, Jean Dubuffet, Marino Marini, Alberto Giacometti, Auguste Rodin, Henry Moore, and Louise Nevelson are just a few of the artists whose works are displayed in the *Donald M. Kendall Sculpture Gardens.* Mr. Kendall's artistic vision has truly been realized.

The Donald M. Kendall Sculpture Gardens, PepsiCo World Headquarters, 700 Anderson Hill Rd., Purchase (914-253-2000), is open daily year-round from 9 a.m. to dusk. There is no admission fee.

In 1838 the great Gothic Revival architect Alexander Jackson Davis designed *Lyndhurst* for former New York City mayor William Paulding. Overlooking the broad expanse of the Tappan Zee from the east, this beautiful

Hudson Valley Shakespeare Festival
(through August)
(845) 265-7858
www.hvshakespeare.org

Riverfront Arts Festival
Troy
(518) 273-0552

JULY

Falcon Ridge Folk Festival
Hillsdale
(860) 364-0366
www.falconridgefolk.com

AUGUST

Bard Music Festival
Annandale-on-Hudson
(845) 758-7410
www.bard.edu/bmf

SEPTEMBER

Battle of Saratoga Encampment
Stillwater
(518) 664-6148
www.stillwaterny.org

OCTOBER

Legend Weekend
Sunnyside and Philipsburg Manor
(914) 631-8200
www.sleepyhollowhalloween.com

NOVEMBER

Thanksgiving Weekend
Sunnyside and Philipsburg Manor
(914) 631-8200
www.hudsonvalley.org

DECEMBER

Great Estates Candlelight Tours
Hudson River Valley
(914) 631-8200
www.hudsonvalley.org

stone mansion and its landscaped grounds represented the full American flowering of the neo-Gothic aesthetic that had been sweeping England since the closing years of the eighteenth century.

Lyndhurst remained in the Paulding family until 1864, when it was purchased by wealthy New York merchant George Merritt. Merritt had Davis enlarge the house and add its landmark stone tower, a large greenhouse, and several outbuildings. He also laid out the romantic English-style gardens to complement the Gothic architecture of the main house.

One of the most notorious of America's railroad barons, Jay Gould, acquired Lyndhurst in 1880 and maintained it as a country estate. Upon his death in 1892, Lyndhurst became the property of his oldest daughter, Helen, who left it in turn to her younger sister Anna, duchess of Talleyrand-Périgord, in 1938. The duchess died in 1961, leaving instructions that the estate become the property of the National Trust for Historic Preservation.

Lyndhurst, 635 South Broadway (Route 9 just south of the Tappan Zee Bridge), Tarrytown (914-631-4481; www.lyndhurst.org), is open mid-April through October, Tuesday through Sunday 10 a.m. to 5 p.m., and November through mid-April, Saturday and Sunday 10 a.m. to 4 p.m. Open on Monday holidays. Closed Thanksgiving, Christmas, and New Year's. Guided tours and cell phone tours are available. Admission is $12 for adults, $11 for senior citizens, $6 for children 6 to 16, and under 6 free with paying adult.

If a visit to Lyndhurst leaves you wanting to live like a robber baron, book yourself some luxurious lodgings at the **Castle on the Hudson** at 400 Benedict Ave., Tarrytown (914-631-1980; www.castleonthehudson.com). Built between 1900 and 1910, this Norman-style mansion stands imposingly on ten acres overlooking the Hudson River. Surrounded by a stone wall and a magnificent arboretum, the castle features a 40-foot Grand Room with a vaulted ceiling, stained-glass windows, and a musicians' balcony. One of the dining rooms has paneling taken from a house outside Paris that had been given to the exiled King James II of England by Louis XIV of France. Breakfast, lunch, dinner, and Sunday brunch are served in the elegant Equus restaurant. High tea is served Tuesday through Saturday from 3 to 4:30 p.m.

One of Tarrytown's best-known residents was Washington Irving, author of *Rip Van Winkle, The Legend of Sleepy Hollow,* and *Diedrich Knickerbocker's History of New York.* Irving described his home, **Sunnyside,** as "a little old-fashioned stone mansion, all made up of gable ends, and as full of angles and corners as an old cocked hat."

Irving lived at Sunnyside from 1836 to 1843 and again from 1846 until his death in 1859. Here he entertained such distinguished visitors as Oliver Wendell Holmes, William Makepeace Thackeray, and Louis Napoleon III. On view here is the writing desk where Irving penned *Astoria,* his account of the

They Trod Shod

In the summer of 1938, to celebrate the 250th anniversary of the settling of New Rochelle, a group of children made a pilgrimage to New York City. They were commemorating the long trek the region's first settlers, the Huguenots, had to make to attend church. According to tradition, these early churchgoers made the trek barefooted. But the children put on their shoes after the first block.

Pacific Northwest, as well as *The Crayon Miscellany, Wolfert's Roost,* and *The Life of George Washington.* In his leisure hours, Irving laid out Sunnyside's splendid flower gardens, arborways, and orchards, which still flower and bear fruit to this day.

Located at 89 West Sunnyside Lane (1 mile south of the Tappan Zee Bridge on Route 9) in Tarrytown, Sunnyside (914-591-8763; www.hudsonvalley.org) is open daily 11 a.m. to 6 p.m. except Tuesdays and major holidays from April through October, and weekends 10 a.m. to 4 p.m. from November through December.

One of the most popular times to visit Sunnyside is during **Legends Weekend** in October (914-631-8200; www.hudsonvalley.org). Dramatic readings of *The Legend of Sleepy Hollow* take place at both Sunnyside and Philipsburg Manor, along with a host of family activities based on Irving's tale—magic shows, ghost stories, woodland walks, ghostly "apparitions," and even an appearance by the headless horseman himself.

The town of North Tarrytown, home to two impressive old churches, was so closely identified with Irving's tale that it officially changed its name to Sleepy Hollow. The **Old Dutch Church of Sleepy Hollow** on Route 9 (845-631-1123), built in 1685, is still heated by a woodstove, and hence opens seasonally; Sunday services are held at 10:15 a.m. from the third week in June through the first week in September. Tours are given Saturday and Sunday from 2 to 4 p.m. from Memorial Day through October; Monday, Wednesday, and Thursday from 1 to 4 p.m. from Memorial Day through Labor Day; or by appointment.

Adjacent to the Old Dutch Church, the creator of the headless horseman rests in peace in the **Burying Ground** (www.olddutchburyingground.org) alongside the likes of Andrew Carnegie and William Rockefeller. Free guided tours are given daily at 2 p.m. Memorial Day through October.

The tiny **Union Church of Pocantico Hills** on Route 448 (914-631-2069; www.ucph.org) has a magnificent collection of stained-glass windows by Henri Matisse and Marc Chagall, which were commissioned by the Rockefeller family. It's open daily except Tuesday from April through October, weekdays 11 a.m. to 5 p.m., Saturday 10 a.m. to 5 p.m., and Sunday 2 to 5 p.m.; and from November through December,

lovelynyack

Across the water from Tarrytown lies the village of Nyack, a regional tourist attraction. The town is brimming with fine dining, boutiques, arts, film, live music, and theater. The hub of summer concerts and live entertainment can be found at *Riverspace on Main Street.* Visit www.nyack.org for more information.

weekdays (except Tuesday) 11 a.m. to 4 p.m., Saturday 10 a.m. to 4 p.m., and Sunday 2 to 4 p.m. Admission is $5. Church activities may preempt visiting hours.

The menu at the lovely ***Crabtree's Kittle House Restaurant and Country Inn*** changes daily, but the food, ambience, and service remain consistently superb. Guests can choose a cold salad or hot appetizer, with offerings such as ricotta gnudi with a nicoise olive crumble, sweet tomatoes, and petit basil. Entrees might include olive-oil poached codfish on lacinato kale with toasted garlic and a bottarga emulsion; or Hudson Valley Moulard duck magret with vanilla parsnip, sour cherries, and Trumpet Royale mushrooms. For many, dessert is the high point of a meal in this 1790 mansion, with fanciful confections such as a Valhrona chocolate cremeaux tart with raspberry dust and pistachio ice cream. *Wine Spectator* magazine has awarded the restaurant its "Grand Award of Excellence" every year since 1994 for having one of the most outstanding restaurant wine lists in the world—more than 60,000 bottles and 6,000 selections.

Crabtree's Kittle House Restaurant and Country Inn, 11 Kittle Rd., Route 117, Chappaqua (914-666-8044; www.kittlehouse.com), has twelve guest rooms with private bath that rent for $184 per night, double occupancy. Lunch is served weekdays, dinner nightly, and brunch on Sunday from noon to 2:30 p.m. Reservations are highly recommended, especially on weekends. There's live jazz in the Tap Room Friday and Saturday evenings.

Sing Sing Prison in Ossining isn't known for its food and hospitality, rather for making getting sent "up the river" part of the vernacular of tough-guy talk. Built in 1826 by convict labor, Sing Sing became famous when "Father" Pat O'Brien walked "gangster" Jimmy Cagney "the last mile" to its electric chair in *Angels with Dirty Faces.*

Today a replica of the chair, along with confiscated weapons and other artifacts, is part of an in-depth audiovisual exhibit at the ***Ossining Heritage Area Park Visitors Center*** (the Joseph G. Caputo Community Center) at 95 Broadway, Ossining (914-941-3189; www.nysparks.state.ny .us/heritage-sites). Open every day except Sunday from 10 a.m. to 4 p.m. Admission is free.

While it's off the beaten path, the Croton Dam is not easily overlooked— it's the second-largest hand-hewn structure in the world. Built in 1892, the dam is 297 feet high and 2,168 feet long; it's estimated that it contains as much stone as Egypt's Great Pyramid. The reservoir behind the dam supplies about 400 million gallons of water to New York City each day. The dam is part of ***Croton Point Park*** and the trailhead for the 26-mile-long Old Croton Aqueduct Trail, which ends at 173rd Street in Manhattan.

From Sing Sing to Ossining

Ossining was once called Sing Sing and the aging marble buildings scattered throughout the town were built by the labor of convicts. While Ossining may boast hip and trendy boutiques and restaurants, it's still well known as the home of Sing Sing Prison, still in operation today. The Joseph G. Caputo Community Center at 95 Broadway offers life-size exhibits of the prison and the Old Croton Aqueduct. An electric chair sits on exhibit, a replica of an original that electrocuted 614 people to death. Two Sing Sing cells are also on display that guests can wander into. You'll also find literature, photos, and information on the prisoners who quarried the marble in town. A bit of trivia: for years the Yankees visited Sing Sing to play with the inmates, and it's reported that Babe Ruth hit his longest home run on the prison field. Free admission; call (914) 762-8150 for more information.

Croton Point Park, Route 129, Croton-on-Hudson (914-862-5290; www .westchestergov.com), is open 8 a.m. to dusk. There is an $8 fee per car from Memorial Day to Labor Day.

Peekskill is home to more than 100 artists who work in a variety of mixed and traditional media. Many of them host **Open Artist Studio Tours** the first weekend in June, and there are two one-hour guided art tours on Saturday and Sunday, leaving from the gazebo (free). For more information and an updated list of events, contact Peekskill Arts Council at (914) 734-1292 or peekskillartscouncil.org. If you're visiting between mid-June and October, stop at the **Peekskill Farmers' Market** on Bank Street. For information contact the Peekskill Business Improvement District at (914) 737-2780 or downtown peekskill.com.

The **Hudson Valley Center for Contemporary Art** opens its doors for exhibitions and programs to bring attention to contemporary art and how it is used in social issues. It also offers artist-in-residence programs and educational outreach to the public through special programs. Recently, the center led the Public Tile Project to celebrate the Dutch heritage of the area. The center worked with 2,000 school students to design their own tiles to form a trail from the Peekskill Train Station to the center. The center is open on weekends from noon to 6 p.m. and by appointment; tours available upon request. Admission costs $5 for adults, $4 for seniors over 65, and students (with valid ID) and children $2. Call (914)788-0100 or visit 1701 Main St. You can find a schedule of events and exhibits at www.hvcca.org.

Year-round in Peekskill, enjoy the flavor of local art at the local favorite **Peekskill Coffee House** (101 South Division St.; 914-739-1287; http:// peekskillcoffee.tumblr.com). The shop features an "artist of the moment," and serves up hot coffee and snacks during live musical performances. After a cappuccino, head over to **Bruised Apple Books** (923 Central Ave.; 914-734-7000; www.bruisedapplebooks.com) for used, out-of-print, and rare books along with CDs and movies. Unique to the area, they also offer maps and outdoor guides on the Hudson Valley region among 50,000 titles.

Another important figure of the early Republic, political rather than literary, made his country home to the northeast at Katonah. This was John Jay, whom George Washington appointed to be the first chief justice of the United States and who, with Alexander Hamilton and James Madison, was an author of the *Federalist Papers*. Jay retired to the farmhouse now known as the John Jay Homestead in 1801, after nearly three decades of public service, and lived there until his death in 1829.

His son William and his grandson John Jay II lived at the old family homestead, as did John II's son Col. William Jay II, a Civil War officer of the Union Army. The last Jay to live at the Katonah estate was Eleanor Jay Iselin, the colonel's daughter. After her death in 1953, the property was purchased by Westchester County and turned over to the State of New York as a state historic site.

Having survived so long in the Jay family, the John Jay Homestead is still well stocked with furnishings and associated items that date back to the days when the great patriot lived here. Sixty acres of John Jay's original 900-acre farm are part of the state historic site.

The **John Jay Homestead State Historic Site,** 400 Route 22, Katonah (914-232-5651; www.johnjayhomestead.org) is open April through October, with tours on the hour, Tuesday through Saturday 10 a.m. to 5 p.m. and Sunday 11 a.m. to 5 p.m.; November through March, Wednesday through Saturday 10 a.m. to 4 p.m. and Sunday 11 a.m. to 4 p.m. There is a fee of $7 for adults and $5 for seniors; children under 12 are free. The grounds are open from dawn to dusk year-round.

Rosen House at Caramoor is yet another of New York's impressive estates. It was built by Walter and Lucie Dodge Rosen, who filled it with personal treasures and created the home that eventually became an integral location to the International Music Festival. Like the wealthy robber barons, the Rosens purchased entire rooms from Europe's palaces and churches and had them reconstructed in their own Spanish-style villa—resulting in an arts and antiques collection that is, to say the least, eclectic. In 1945 they bequeathed the estate as a center for music and art in memory of their son. During the 1950s the festival was expanded and outdoor concerts were presented in the Spanish courtyard. As the festival's reputation grew, Lucie Rosen constructed a larger space, the Venetian Theater, which opened in 1958.

Twenty of the house's magnificent rooms are open to the public; docent tours last about an hour. In the opulent music room, there are chamber concerts throughout the year. On Thursday and Friday afternoons from 1:30 to 4 p.m., tea is served on the family's original china in the Summer Dining Room.

At Rosen House at Caramoor, 149 Girdle Ridge Rd., Katonah (914-232-5035; www.caramoor.org), guided tours are offered May through December, Wednesday through Sunday from 1:15 to 4 p.m. (Last tour at 3 p.m.) Admission is $10 for adults, free for children 16 and under.

In 1907 financier J. P. Morgan built a stone-and-brick Tudor mansion on a hillside overlooking the Hudson River Valley for his friend and minister, William S. Rainsford.

The mansion was privately owned until 1973, when it was restored and reborn as a French restaurant called **Le Château.** Today, with its dogwood-lined approach, patio and gardens, richly paneled rooms, and elegantly set tables, the restaurant serves classic French food presented in grand style.

Among the house specialties at Le Château are French onion soup; snails with garlic butter; roasted breast and braised leg of duck with honey; and chateaubriand for two. Elegant desserts include a chocolate and Grand Marnier soufflé and crème brûlée. A three-course prix fixe dinner is offered Monday to Thursday for $43, and for $46 on Friday and Saturday. Sunday brunch ($34) includes a dessert buffet.

Almost Better than His Pulitzer

When people talk about the romance of the rails, they seldom have commuter trains in mind. But New York's Metro-North, which hauls thousands of suburbanites in and out of Grand Central Station each day, has taken on a bit more panache ever since it began naming individual cars after prominent people associated with its territory along the Hudson Valley.

None of these cars is more freighted with poignant associations for Westchester commuters than the John Cheever. Cheever, a longtime resident of Ossining, was the great chronicler of postwar suburban life. His heroes and heroines poured into Grand Central from places like Shady Hill and Bullet Park, imaginary in name only, and rode back each night to seek love and redemption among their rhododendrons.

If you're walking along the Hudson at twilight and see the *John Cheever* roll by, raise a phantom glass (very dry, with an olive) to those phantom commuters and to the man who made their longings universal.

Le Château, Route 35 at the junction of Route 123, South Salem (914-533-6631; www.lechateauny.com), serves dinner nightly except Monday and a seasonal Sunday brunch. Reservations and jackets are required.

During a late-night walk in Tallahassee, Florida, in 1991, acclaimed French pianist Hélène Grimaud had a life-changing moment. She claimed she connected with a she-wolf, probably part dog and part wolf. In her memoir, *Wild Harmonies: A Life of Music and Wolves,* Mlle. Grimaud described how the animal slid under her outstretched hand of its own volition. The touch made her feel a spark shoot through her body and she became aware of a "primeval force" calling to her.

It was then that Grimaud conceived her mission: to change the image of wolves as villainous creatures and to educate the public that wolves are essential "biodiversity engineers" that preserve the balance among animal and plant species.

In 1999, with her then-companion, J. Henry Fair, Grimaud opened the **Wolf Conservation Center** in South Salem, a twenty-nine-acre facility that houses seventeen wolves. If you read any interviews with her, you'll see how confused many of her fans seem to be while trying to wrap their heads around balancing a music career with wolves. But Grimaud seems to think they go hand in hand. The pianist feels if you conquer your fear of wolves, you'll open yourself up to unknown worlds, including classical music. Some of the wolves are "socialized," which means they are on view to the public. Others are protected from human contact so that they can eventually be returned to the wild.

The Wolf Conservation Center, P.O. Box 421, South Salem (914-763-2373; www.nywolf.org), offers visits by appointment, arranged online. Click on the "News" link to see what programs are available and to register.

Muscoot Farms is an agricultural holdout in the rapidly developing Westchester landscape. Dating to the early 1900s, the 777-acre working farm has a twenty-three-room main house, barns and outbuildings, antique equipment, a large demonstration vegetable garden (harvested produce is donated to the local food bank), and lots of animals. Weekends are crowded with locals and tourists; in addition to hayrides (offered Sunday from May to October), agricultural programs cover topics such as sheepshearing and harvesting. There's also a full roster of seasonal festivals. The farm, on Route 100 in Katonah (914-864-7282; muscootfarm.org), is open daily 10 a.m. to 4 p.m. Closed Thanksgiving Day, Christmas Day, and New Year's Day.

With the help of an elephant and farmer turned circus showman, the town of **Somers** became the "Cradle of the American Circus." Old Bet (formerly known as Betty) was an African elephant showcased in Boston in 1804 and caught Somers local Hachaliah Bailey's eye. Four years later he saw her again and eagerly bought her in a cattle market. Her new owner began to charge neighbors for a look, and he became like a one-man circus with a trained dog, horse, pigs, and, of course, his girl, Old Bet. She became regarded as "the mother of America's carnival business." Bailey took his act on the road and on July 24, 1868, a farmer in Maine shot her out of anger that poor people would spend their money to see her. Visit www.somershistoricalsoc.org/museum .html for more information. The Somers' museum is located on the third floor of the **Elephant Hotel** (now home to The Somers Historical Society) on 335 US 202. You'll know you've arrived when you see a wooden elephant affixed to the top of a granite shaft. Erected in 1827, it seems to fit in quite nicely with the red, brick Federal Period building. Open on Thursday from 2 p.m. and by appointment by calling (914) 277-4977.

Central Valley

Named for a prominent nineteenth-century family, the town of Brewster in southern Putnam County is home to the **Southeast Museum.** The museum is an archive of the diverse enterprises that have taken root here over the years, including mining, railroading, circuses, and even the manufacture of condensed milk.

The first Europeans settlers arrived in Brewster around 1725, and for more than one hundred years, they farmed and set up modest cottage industries. In the mid-nineteenth century, Brewster's economic horizons expanded with the arrival of the Harlem Railroad, which became part of Commodore Vanderbilt's vast New York Central system, as well as the Putnam Line Railroad, a division of the New York and New Haven Line.

In years gone by Brewster was also the winter quarters for a number of small circuses, many of which were later consolidated by P. T. Barnum, who hailed from nearby Bridgeport, Connecticut. The colorful array of early American circus memorabilia and other collections is housed in the 1896 **Old Town Hall of Southeast** at 67 Main St., Brewster (845-279-7500; www.southeast museum.org). Hours are 10 a.m. to 4 p.m., Tuesday through Saturday, April through December. Donations are requested.

Visitors to the **Chuang Yen Monastery** in Carmel, home of the Buddhist Association of the United States, are greeted by 10,000 statues of the Buddha arrayed on the lotus terrace. Enter the cavernous Tang Dynasty-style Great Buddha Hall to view the largest Buddha statue in the Western hemisphere, a 37-foot-high statue designed by Professor C. G. Chen. Chen also painted the 8-foot-high, 104-foot-long murals depicting scenes from the "Pure Land," or Amitabha Buddha, that cover the walls.

The Chuang Yen Monastery, at 2020 Route 301, Carmel (845-225-1819; www.baus.org), welcomes visitors who wish to tour the buildings and grounds or to stay, study, and meditate.

The nonprofit Dia Art Foundation was founded in 1974 by Philippa de Menil and Heinger Friedrich, both collectors of works by important artists of the 1960s and 1970s. Located on 31 acres on the banks of the Hudson River, the museum occupies a historic printing facility that was built in 1929 by the National Biscuit Company (Nabisco). It houses works by such major artists as Andy Warhol, Cy Twombly, Bruce Nauman, Walter de Maria, and Richard Serra.

Dia:Beacon, Riggio Galleries, 3 Beekman St., Beacon (845-440-0100; www.diaart.org), is open 11 a.m. to 6 p.m. Thursday through Monday during the summer, and 11 a.m. to 4 p.m. Friday through Monday in winter. Guided tours are given every Saturday at 1 p.m. The museum is closed on Thanksgiving, Christmas Eve, Christmas, New Year's Eve, and New Year's Day. The cafe and bookshop open at 10:30 a.m. year-round. Admission is $10 for adults, $7 for seniors and students, and children under 12 are free.

Not all of the Hudson Valley landowners were well-to-do. Most were burghers of a far more modest stamp, as was the case of the family life preserved at the *Van Wyck Homestead Museum,* a National Historic Site, east of the river in Fishkill. The house was begun in 1732 by Cornelius Van Wyck, who had purchased his nearly 1,000 acres of land from an earlier 85,000-acre Dutchess County estate, and was completed in the 1750s with the construction of the West Wing. For all the land its owners possessed, the homestead is nevertheless a modest affair, a typical Dutch country farmhouse.

Like so many other farmhouses, the Van Wyck Homestead might have been forgotten by history had it not played a part in the American Revolution. Located as it was along the strategic route between New York City and the Champlain Valley, the house was requisitioned by the Continental Army to serve as headquarters for General Israel Putnam. Fishkill served as an important supply depot for General Washington's northern forces from 1776 to 1783. Military trials were held at the house; one such event was reputedly the source used by James Fenimore Cooper for an incident in his novel *The Spy*.

Another factor leading to the homestead's preservation was its having reverted to the Van Wyck family after the revolution ended. Descendants of its builder lived there for more than 150 years. Today it is operated by the Fishkill Historical Society as a museum of colonial life in the Hudson Valley. The house features a working colonial kitchen fireplace with a beehive oven, which is used during special events. An interesting sidelight is the exhibit of

Revolutionary War artifacts unearthed in the vicinity during archaeological digs sponsored by the society.

The Van Wyck Homestead Museum, 504 Route 9 (near the intersection of Routes 9 and 84), Fishkill (845-896-9560; www.hudsonrivervalley.com), is open June through October on Saturday and Sunday from 1 to 4 p.m. and by appointment. Admission is free, donations are suggested. Special events include September and holiday craft fairs, a June midsummer festival, and a St. Nicholas Day holiday tour.

Lewis Country Farms, a sixteen-acre farm with restored 1861 barns (complete with silo, original post-and-beam ceiling supports, and fieldstone walls), is an all-season kids' stop and shopping mecca.

As you would expect in a region known for fine seasonal produce as well as wine, the Hudson Valley has many farms and farm markets. Visit www .dutchestourism.com/farm.asp for a list, along with information on farm-related events and activities.

In 1847 Samuel F. B. Morse, inventor of the telegraph and Morse code, purchased one hundred acres of land and a seventeen-year-old Georgian house. With the help of his friend, architect Alexander Jackson Davis, he transformed the original structure into a Tuscan-style villa. Today, *Locust Grove, Samuel Morse Historic Site,* a unique combination of 150 acres of nature preserve, historic gardens, landscaped lawns, vistas, and architecture, is one of the most handsome of the Hudson River estates. In 1963 it became the first in the valley to be designated a National Historic Landmark.

Original family furnishings are exhibited in period room settings and include rare Duncan Phyfe and Chippendale pieces. Paintings include works by Morse himself as well as by artists such as George Inness. There's also a rare bound collection of *Birds of America* by J. J. Audubon. A replica of "the invention of the century" is on exhibit in the Morse Room.

Locust Grove Estate, 2683 South Rd. (Route 9), Poughkeepsie (845-454-4500; http://lgny.org), is open daily May through Thanksgiving and weekends in April and December from 10 a.m. to 5 p.m. (last guided tour begins at 3:15 p.m.). Admission is $10 for adults, $6 for those between the ages of 3 and 18. There is no fee to walk the grounds, which are open from 8 a.m. to dusk.

In the late 1800s, Poughkeepsie wanted to corner the market as a mercantile giant and looked to build a large bridge across the Hudson. The *Poughkeepsie-Highland Railroad Bridge* opened in 1889 at 6,700 feet long and 212 feet high, but was quickly overshadowed by the media frenzy surrounding the opening of the Brooklyn Bridge (which was not as high or as long). The bridge is regarded as a leader in the Industrial Revolution and one of the first links connecting Eastern New York with New England. During its peak, some 50 trains crossed its tracks each day. Over the years, more highways and infrastructure were built and bridge maintenance was neglected. A fire nearly destroyed the tracks in 1974, as water couldn't be pumped up high enough to quench the blaze.

Now dubbed the **Walkway Over the Hudson,** the longest and highest walkway bridge in the world opened to the public on October 3, 2009. The renovations and hard work coincided with the 400th anniversary of Henry Hudson's exploration of the river. Views over the Hudson Valley are as expansive as they are breathtaking, and visitors can't help but feel they're seeing it through the awed eyes of their ancestors from the 19th century. The **Hudson State Historic Park** and walkway are open daily from 7 a.m. to sunset. Access the walkway from Parker Avenue in Poughkeepsie and Havilland Road in Highland. Visit www.walkway.org or call (845) 454-9649 for more information.

The Culinary Institute of America (CIA) was founded in 1946 as a trade school to train returning World War II veterans in the culinary arts; it has morphed into one of the most renowned culinary schools in the world. Among its distinguished graduates are *Gourmet* magazine executive chef and TV personality Sara Moulton, chef-restaurateur Charlie Palmer, and *Iron Chef*'s Cat Cora.

Since America launched its love affair with the Food Network, the CIA has become a veritable hub of culinary activity, attracting not only serious students and food professionals, but also enthusiastic "foodies" who sign up for the school's one-day courses and cooking "boot camps." With forty-one state-of-the-art kitchens and bakeshops, the CIA is a food-lover's Eden.

The CIA has also played a major role in making the Hudson Valley a culinary destination, serving as the setting for popular food and wine events and turning out students who have gone on to work in the region's restaurants. In addition, the five student-staffed restaurants on the CIA's 150-acre campus attract tens of thousands of food-lovers each year, all eager to sample the "homework" turned out by the culinary stars of the future. They take great pride in preparing nutritionally balanced meals from regional farms or local food producers.

St. Andrew's Cafe, open Monday through Friday for lunch and dinner, serves a selection of dishes featuring fresh seasonal ingredients with an Asian touch. The **Ristorante Caterina de' Medici,** open Monday through Friday for lunch and dinner, is located in the Colavita Center for Italian Food and Wine and showcases the indigenous foods of Italy's various regions. The casual **Al Forno Room,** located within the Ristorante Caterina de' Medici, serves pizza, salad, and antipasti. The **Escoffier Restaurant,** open Tuesday

Follow the Food (and Wine)

The annual *Taste of the Hudson Wine and Epicurean Arts Festival* at the Culinary Institute of America in Hyde Park takes place in November and is one of the major food and wine events in the region. It features dozens of restaurants and food suppliers from the Hudson Valley and celebrates everything culinary. For more information, call (845) 431-8707 or visit www.tastehv.org.

Also in November is the annual *Hudson Valley Restaurant Week* (actually ten days), a culinary fest featuring bargain-priced prix-fixe lunches and dinners at restaurants throughout the region. For more information, visit www.HudsonValley RestaurantWeek.com.

through Saturday, features classic French cuisine, but with a lighter contemporary touch. Come in country-club or business casual and leave the jeans and sneakers at home.

The *American Bounty Restaurant,* open Tuesday through Saturday for lunch and dinner, serves regional American dishes as well as a daily special from the Julia Child Rotisserie kitchen with a focus on regional specialties and local ingredients from the Hudson River Valley.

Top off all that delicious local flavor at the *Apple Pie Bakery Cafe* for a selection of sandwiches, pastries, and breads, also available for takeout. Open Monday through Friday from 7:30 a.m. to 6:30 p.m. Reservations are necessary for the formal restaurants but not for the Al Forno Room or the cafe. Call (845) 471-6608 Monday through Friday 8:30 a.m. to 5 p.m. for all reservations.

Foodies and professionals alike gather at the CIA's *Conrad N. Hilton Library,* a $7.5-million facility that houses 74,000 volumes, a video viewing center, and a video theater. The library is open Monday through Thursday 7:30 a.m. to 11 p.m., Friday 7:30 a.m. to 5 p.m., Saturday 10 a.m. to 5 p.m., and Sunday noon to 11 p.m.

The Culinary Institute of America is on Route 9, 1946 Campus Dr., Hyde Park (845-452-9600; www.ciachef.edu).

Whenever Eleanor Roosevelt took time out from the many causes she championed before, during, and after her husband's presidency, she retreated to *Val-Kill,* a small, fieldstone cottage that FDR built for her in 1925 by a stream on the grounds of the Roosevelt family estate. The cottage became the permanent home for two of their close friends, New York Democratic Committee co-workers Nancy Cook and Marion Dickerman, and whenever Eleanor returned home, she would opt to stay here rather than in the nearby family mansion presided over by Franklin's autocratic mother, Sara Delano Roosevelt.

In 1926 the women, along with Caroline O'Day, built a second, larger building to house Val-Kill Industries, intended to teach farm workers how to manufacture goods, thus keeping them from migrating to large cities in search of work. Until the business closed in 1936—a victim of the Great Depression— the workers manufactured replicas of Early American furniture, weavings, and pewter pieces. At this point, Mrs. Roosevelt converted the building into apartments for herself and her secretary Malvina "Tommy" Thompson, and added several guest rooms. She renamed the building Val-Kill Cottage and wrote to her daughter: "My house seems nicer than ever and I could be happy in it alone! That's the last test of one's surroundings." Among the visitors to Val-Kill were John F. Kennedy, Adlai Stevenson, Nikita Khrushchev, and Jawaharlal Nehru.

After Mrs. Roosevelt died in 1962, several developers tried to take over her home, but they were thwarted when a group of concerned citizens organized to preserve the site. In 1977 President Jimmy Carter signed a bill creating the **Eleanor Roosevelt National Historic Site.** Today visitors can tour the cottages and grounds.

Eleanor Roosevelt National Historic Site, on Route 9G, 4097 Albany Post Rd., Hyde Park (800-337-8474; www.nps.gov/elro), is open May through October, daily 9 a.m. to 5 p.m.; and from November through April, Thursday to Monday 9 a.m. to 5 p.m. Admission is $8 for adults; children under 15, free.

Heading north past Hyde Park, we're back in mansion territory. Homes such as Philipse Manor Hall were built by men whose fortunes were founded in vast landholdings, but palaces such as **Staatsburg,** formerly Mills Mansion State Historic Site, represent the glory days of industrial and financial captains—the so-called Gilded Age of the late nineteenth century. The idea behind this sort of house building was to live not like a country squire but like a Renaissance doge.

Ogden Mills's neoclassical mansion was finished in 1896, but its story begins more than a hundred years earlier. In 1792 the property on which it stands was purchased by Morgan Lewis, great-grandfather of Mills's wife, Ruth Livingston Mills. Lewis, an officer in the revolution and the third post independence governor of New York State, built two houses here. The first burned in 1832, at which time it was replaced by an up-to-date Greek Revival structure. This was the home that stood on the property when it was inherited by Ruth Livingston Mills in 1890.

But Ogden Mills had something far grander in mind for his wife's legacy. He hired a firm with a solid reputation in mansion building to enlarge the home and embellish its interiors—a popular firm among wealthy clients, one that went by the name of McKim, Mead, and White.

The architects added two spacious wings and decked out both the new and the old portions of the exterior with balustrades and pilasters more reminiscent of Blenheim Palace than anything previously seen in the Hudson Valley. The interior was (and is) French, in Louis XV and XVI period styles—lots of carving and gilding on furniture and wall and ceiling surfaces, along with oak paneling and monumental tapestries.

The last of the clan to live here was Ogden L. Mills, at one time U.S. secretary of the treasury, who died in 1937. One of his surviving sisters donated the home to the State of New York, which opened it to the public as a state historic site.

Staatsburg, off Route 9, Staatsburg (845-889-8851; www.staatsburgh.org), is open from mid-April through October, Wednesday through Saturday 10 a.m. to 5 p.m. and Sunday 11 a.m. to 5 p.m. It reopens after Thanksgiving through December. Admission is $5 for adults, $4 for seniors and students; children under 12 free.

To reserve your own room at a mansion, try the **Belvedere Mansion,** a grand Greek Revival hilltop estate overlooking the Hudson River. Guests choose from one of the beautifully appointed "cottage" rooms—each with its own entrance and private bath—in a separate building facing the mansion, or one of the smaller "cozies." A full country breakfast is served fireside in the winter and, in warmer months, alfresco in a pavilion gazebo overlooking a fountain and pond. A candlelit dinner in the elegant restaurant might include delicacies such as an appetizer of gâteau of wild mushrooms and chèvre with a truffle vinaigrette and entrees such as braised lamb shank with saffron risotto, artichokes, and mint.

Belvedere Mansion, 10 Olde Route 9 in Staatsburg (845-889-8000; www .belvederemansion.com), is open year-round, except Christmas Eve and Christmas Day. Rates range from $95 to $105 for the "cozies" to $275 in the mansion. Rooms in the Carriage House range from $150 to $195; in the Hunt Lodge, suites are available including one with a fireplace, for $250 to $450; the Zen Lodge is $140 to $200. A bridal suite called the Hunt Master Suite is also available, as well as a three-bedroom suite in the mansion for $300 to $350. Guests have use of the tennis court and outdoor pool.

Troutbeck, on the banks of the trout-filled Webatuck River in Amenia, is an English-style country estate that functions as a corporate conference center during the week and as a country inn on weekends. The 422-acre retreat, with its slate-roofed mansion with leaded windows, is a perfect place for a romantic weekend. There are nine fireplace bedrooms, many rooms with canopy beds, an oak-paneled library, gardens—even a pool and tennis courts. And, of course, gourmet dining.

The former home of poet-naturalist Myron B. Benton, Troutbeck was a gathering place for celebrities during the early decades of the twentieth century. Ernest Hemingway, Sinclair Lewis, and Teddy Roosevelt are said to have been houseguests of the Springarn family, who owned the house from 1902 to 1978.

The restaurant, open to the public for lunch and dinner Wednesday through Saturday and Sunday brunch, has an excellent kitchen and features dinner entrees such as smoked Maine lobster and oven-braised Black Angus veal shanks. The dessert menu, with "everything that you always wanted to try," includes goodies such as Georgia peach and ginger-cream strudel.

bassoprofundo

The year 2003 saw a New York State record for striped bass caught in freshwater, when a 55-pounder was taken on the Hudson River. The record saltwater striper, taken off Montauk Point on Long Island, tipped the scales at 76 pounds.

Troutbeck, 515 Leedsville Rd., Amenia (845-373-9681 or 800-978-7688; www.troutbeck.com), is open year-round. Weekend rates include two nights' lodging and meals, and range from $650 to $1,050 a couple.

The Wetmore family, which owns **Cascade Mountain Winery and Restaurant,** says of its product: "Regional wine is a way of tasting our seasons past. Last summer's sunshine, the snows of winter, rain, and frost; it's all there in a glass." You can sample the Hudson Valley's seasons past at the vineyard, which offers tours and tastings weekends year-round from 11 a.m. to 5 p.m. The coveted restaurant is available for private parties only.

Cascade Mountain Winery and Restaurant is on Cascade Mountain Road in Amenia (845-373-9021; www.cascademt.com).

Although its location is off the beaten path, the **Old Drovers Inn** is very much on the main track for those of us who love gourmet dining and superb accommodations. Winner of some of the industry's most prestigious awards, including AAA's Four Diamond Award and an award of excellence for its wine

Have a Grape Day

As one of the nation's oldest wine-making regions, the Hudson Valley boasts dozens of wineries; a number offer tours and tastings. **The Dutchess Wine Trail** (www.dutchesswinetrail.com), for example, includes the **Clinton Vineyards in Clinton Corners** (845-266-5372; www.clintonvineyards.com) and the **Millbrook Vineyards and Winery** (845-758-6335; www.millbrookwines.com).

list and cellar from *Wine Spectator,* the inn, a Relais and Chateau property, was also named one of the five Gourmet Retreats of the Year in Andrew Harper's *Hideaway Report.*

At **Innisfree Garden,** Eastern design concepts blend with American techniques to create a "cup garden," with origins in Chinese paintings dating back a thousand years.

The cup garden draws attention to something rare or beautiful, segregating it so that it can be enjoyed without distraction. It can be anything—from a single rock covered with lichens and sedums to a meadow. Each forms a three-dimensional picture. Innisfree Garden is a series of cup gardens—streams, waterfalls, plants—each its own picture and each a visual treat.

Innisfree Garden, Tyrrel Road, Millbrook (845-677-8000; www.innisfree garden.org), is open May 7 to October 20, Wednesday through Friday 10 a.m. to 4 p.m. and weekends and legal holidays 11 a.m. to 5 p.m. It is closed Monday and Tuesday except legal holidays. Admission is $4 for those 6 years and older on weekdays and $5 on weekends and holidays. A picnic area is open to visitors.

The **Old Rhinebeck Aerodrome,** 3 miles upriver from the town of Rhinebeck, is more than just a museum—many of the pre-1930s planes exhibited here actually take to the air each weekend.

The three main buildings at the aerodrome house a collection of aircraft, automobiles, and other vehicles from the period 1900–37 and are open throughout the week. On Saturday and Sunday, though, you can combine a tour of the exhibits on the ground with attendance at an air show featuring both original aircraft and accurate reproductions. Saturdays are reserved for flights of planes from the Pioneer (pre–World War I) and Lindbergh eras. On Sundays the show is a period-piece melodrama in which intrepid Allied fliers do battle with the "Black Baron." Where else can you watch a live dogfight?

All that's left at this point is to go up there yourself, and you can do just that. The aerodrome has on hand a 1929 New Standard D-25—which carries four passengers wearing helmets and goggles—for open-cockpit flights of fifteen minutes' duration. The cost is $65 per person, and rides are available on weekends, before and after the show.

Old Rhinebeck Aerodrome, 9 Norton Rd., Rhinebeck (845-752-3200; www .oldrhinebeck.org), is open varying hours and its schedule of events regularly changes. Check the Web site for ongoing shows.

America's oldest continuously operated hotel, the **Beekman Arms,** opened for business as the Traphagen Inn in 1766. A meeting place for American Revolutionary War generals, the Beekman was also the site of Franklin

Delano Roosevelt's election eve rallies from the beginning of his career right through his presidency. Visitors can choose from one of thirteen rooms in the main inn, the motel, or in the forty-four room ***Delamater Inn*** (845-786-7080), a block away, built in 1844 and one of the few early examples of American Gothic residences still in existence. The inn's accommodations include seven guest houses, several with fireplaces, clustered around a courtyard.

The Beekman Arms and Delamater Inn, Route 9, Rhinebeck (845-876-7077; www.beekmandelamaterinn.com), are open year-round. Rates range from $120 to $190 in the Arms, $100 to $140 in the contemporary motel, and $120 to $195 in the Delamater House. Guests can expect a general price range of $120to $300, depending on building, style, size of room, season, weekday, weekend or holiday. All rooms are non-smoking and have private bath, TV, phone, and a complimentary decanter of sherry and continental breakfast. A two-night minimum stay is required weekends from May through October and holiday weekends. Lunch, dinner, and Sunday brunch are served in the restaurant, and there is a cozy tap room.

John and Jan Gilmor create a variety of mouth-blown and hand-pressed stemware, tableware, decorative vessels, and ornaments from glass that John formulates from scratch, working with his wife to develop unique colors and finishes. Their pieces are featured in international and presidential collections. At ***Gilmor Glassworks,*** 2 Main St., at the corner of Routes 22 and 44 in Millerton (518-789-6700; www.gilmorglass.com), visitors are invited to watch the artists while they work at the glass furnaces but are urged to call ahead to find out when the "hot process" can be observed. First-quality and irregular pieces are on sale. Gallery hours are 10:30 a.m. to 5 p.m. on Monday through Saturday, and Sunday 11 a.m. to 4 p.m. Call ahead, Gilmore Glassworks frequently hosts late hours, or unexpectedly closes for ongoing renovations.

Kaatsbaan is "dedicated to the growth, advancement, and preservation of professional dance." Facilities at the 153-acre site overlooking the Hudson River include a 160-seat performance theater and three dance studios.

Kaatsbaan International Dance Center is located at 120 Broadway, Tivoli. Visit www.Kaatsbaan.org or call (845) 757-5106 for a list of events.

There was a time when every schoolchild could recite, by heart, that the *Clermont* was the first successful steamboat, built by Robert Fulton and tested on the Hudson River. Less commonly known, however, is that the boat formally registered by its owners as *The North River Steamboat of Clermont* took its name from the estate of Robert R. Livingston, chancellor of New York and a backer of Fulton's experiments. ***Clermont,*** one of the great family seats of the valley, overlooks the Hudson River near Germantown.

The story of Clermont begins with the royal charter granted to Robert Livingston in 1686, which made the Scottish-born trader Lord of the Manor of Livingston, a 162,000-acre tract that would evolve into the entire southern third of modern-day Columbia County. When Livingston died in 1728, he broke with the English custom of strict adherence to primogeniture by giving 13,000 acres of his land to his third son. This was Clermont, the Lower Manor, on which Robert of Clermont, as he was known, established his home in 1728.

Two more Robert Livingstons figure in the tale after this point: Robert of Clermont's son, a New York judge, and his son, a member of the Second Continental Congress who filled the now-obsolete office of state chancellor. It was the chancellor's mother, Margaret Beekman Livingston, who rebuilt the house after it was burned in 1777 by the British (parts of the original walls are incorporated into the present structure).

The Livingston family lived at Clermont until 1962, making various enlargements and modifications to their home over time. In that year the house, its furnishings, and the 500 remaining acres of the Clermont estate became the property of the State of New York.

The mansion at Clermont State Historic Site (also a National Historic Landmark) has been restored to its circa 1930 appearance; however, the collections are primarily half eighteenth- and half nineteenth-century French and early American. Tours of Clermont include the first and second floors. An orientation exhibit and a short film are given at the visitor center. There are formal gardens, woodsy hiking trails, and spacious landscapes (perfect for picnics) on bluffs overlooking the Hudson.

Clermont, 1 Clermont Ave., off Route 9G, Germantown (518-537-4240; www.friendsofclermont.org), is open Tuesday through Sunday and on Monday holidays from 11 a.m. to 5 p.m. (last tour at 4 p.m.). From November through March, hours are 11 a.m. to 4 p.m. (last tour at 3:30 p.m.), weekends only. The grounds are open and free daily year-round from 8:30 a.m. to sunset. The Visitor Center is open from April through October, Tuesday through Sunday and Monday holidays 10:30 a.m. to 5 p.m. and November through March, weekends 11 a.m. to 4 p.m. The Heritage Music Festival is held in mid-July. Admission to the mansion is $5 for adults, $4 for seniors, $1 for children 5 to 12, and children under 5 are free.

Want to paddle a sea kayak around the Statue of Liberty? How about past Sing Sing Prison or up through the northern Hudson Highlands past Bannerman's Castle on Pollepel Island? *Atlantic Kayak Tours,* the largest sea kayaking business in the tri-state area, offers these tours and many more throughout the waters of Connecticut, New Jersey, and the Empire State, and you don't need any experience to join up. Call (845) 246-2187 or visit atlantickayaktours .com for updated tours and information.

Known for his mammoth landscapes and his theatrical presentations, Hudson River School master Frederic Edwin Church built a Persian Gothic castle, *Olana,* commanding a magnificent view of the river south of the town of Hudson.

Olana draws heavily upon Islamic and Byzantine motifs. Persian arches abound, as do Oriental carpets, brasswork, and inlaid furniture. The overall aesthetic is typically Victorian, with no space left empty that could possibly be filled with things. What makes Olana atypical, of course, is the quality of the things.

Although Church employed as a consultant Calvert Vaux, who had collaborated with Frederick Law Olmsted on the design of New York's Central Park, the artist was the architect of his own house. When scholars describe Olana as a major work of art by Church, they are not speaking figuratively; the paints for the interior were mixed on his own palette.

The grounds at Olana State Historic Site, Route 9G, Hudson, are open from 8 a.m. to sunset daily throughout the year with tours in the home from 11 a.m. to 4 p.m. on Friday and Saturday, and on Sunday from noon to 4 p.m. with the last tour starting promptly at 3 p.m. from November through March. If you're visiting April through October, tours run from 10 a.m. to 5 p.m. with the last tour at 4 p.m. Admission is $9 adults, $8 seniors and students with ID, and children 12 and under are free. The Evelyn and Maurice Sharp Gallery tours are $6 adults, $5 seniors and students, or a combined tour pass of $12 adults, $10 seniors and students. On weekends and Monday holidays through Halloween, there is a $5 entry fee per vehicle from 10 a.m. to 5 p.m. The fee can be credited toward a house tour if tickets are available.

Nearly seventy antiques shops fill five historic walking blocks on Warren Street in Hudson. Furniture, clocks, porcelains, rugs, ephemera—the antiques district is a collector's dream. Most shops are open Thursday through Tuesday. For information call the *Hudson Antique Dealers Association* at (518) 828-1999 or check their Web site at www.hudsonantiques.net. For a complete list of shops, contact Columbia County Tourism Department at (800) 724-1846 or www.bestcountryroads.com.

On July 13, 1865, Barnum's American Museum, located at the corner of Ann Street and Broadway in Manhattan and filled with the "wonders of the world," caught fire. Volunteer fire companies, some in newly introduced steam engines, rushed to the rescue and managed to save, among other things, "Old Glory," the flag that was flying from a mast on the roof.

Today Old Glory is one of just 2,500 fire-related articles on display at the **FASNY Museum of Firefighting,** which documents nearly 300 years of firefighting history and houses one of the country's largest collections of fire-fighting apparatuses and memorabilia. Of the sixty-eight firefighting engines on display, the majority are nineteenth-century hand pumpers, ladder trucks, and hose carts, including a 1725 Newsham, the first successful working engine used in New York.

The museum is next door to the Volunteer Firemen's Home, a health care facility for volunteer firefighters who continue to volunteer, this time as museum guides.

The FASNY Museum of Firefighting, 117 Harry Howard Ave., Hudson (518-828-7695 or 800-479-7695; www.fasnyfiremuseum.com), is open 10 a.m. to 5 p.m. daily except major holidays. Admission is $5 for adults, $2 for children 5 and older, children under 4, free; family rate, $10.

Get off the beaten path to Route 23 out of Hillsdale to Craryville, hang a left onto West End Road and then right onto Rodman Road (or just follow the signs)—to **Rodgers Book Barn.** The secondhand shop is considered by many bibliophiles to be one of the best in the country. The two-story barn is packed from floor to ceiling with some 50,000 books. The collection is eclectic with inexpensive '50s potboilers, tomes on European and American history, gardening books, and rare out-of-print editions in dozens of categories. The shop's owner, Maureen Rodgers, encourages browsing to the point of inviting patrons to bring along a lunch to enjoy in the grape arbor next to the herb garden.

Rodgers Book Barn, 467 Rodman Rd., Hillsdale (518-325-3610), is open November through March, Friday to Monday 11 a.m. to 5 p.m.; April through October, Thursday to Monday 11 a.m. to 5 p.m.

The **Crandell Theatre** first opened its doors on Christmas Day 1926. Today, Columbia County's oldest and largest movie theater, a Spanish-style building of brick and stucco, remains proudly independent in a world of megaplexes. Get there early, grab a bag of freshly popped popcorn, and head for the balcony. You'll get a true blast from the past along with a first-run movie for only $5 a ticket for adults and $4 for children. The theater is on Main Street in Chatham (518-392-3331). Visit http://crandelltheatre.com for more information.

East of Albany

The **Shaker Museum and Library** in Old Chatham is housed in a collection of buildings located just 12 miles from Mount Lebanon, New York, where the Shakers established one of their first U.S. communities.

The Shakers, formally known as the United Society of Believers in Christ's Second Appearing, were a sect founded in Britain and transplanted to America just prior to the revolution. A quietist, monastic order dedicated to equality between the sexes, sharing community property, and the practice of celibacy, the sect peaked in the middle nineteenth century with about 6,000 members. Today there are fewer than a dozen Shakers living in a community at Sabbathday Lake, Maine.

Ironically, it is the secular aspects of Shaker life that are most often recalled today. The members of the communities were obsessive in designing simple and pure crafts and furniture for daily life. "Shaker furniture" has become a generic term for the elegantly uncluttered designs they employed. In their pursuit of the perfect form dictated by function, they even invented now ubiquitous objects such as the flat broom.

The Shaker Museum amassed a collection of more than 18,000 objects, half of which are on display. The main building contains an orientation gallery that surveys Shaker history and provides highlights of the rest of the collection. The museum's library contains one of the two most extensive collections of Shaker material in the world. The cafe serves snacks and beverages.

The Shaker Museum and Library is at 88 Shaker Museum Rd. (off County Route 13), Old Chatham (518-794-9100; www.shakermuseumandlibrary.org). Check the Web site for upcoming events and programs.

In 1624 Dutchmen sailed up the Hudson River and established a fur-trading station called Fort Orange at present-day Albany. Within twenty-five years it was a thriving community. Across the river is the town of Rensselaer, named for the family who held the "patroonship," or feudal proprietorship, of the vast area on the east bank. **Crailo,** built in the early eighteenth century by the first Patroon's grandson, recalls a time when the Dutch were still the predominant cultural presence in the area.

ringaround thecollar

According to local lore Mrs. Hannah Lord Montague of Troy spawned a new industry when, in 1825, she cut the soiled collars off her husband's otherwise clean shirts so she would only have to wash the dirty parts.

Crailo changed with time and tastes. A Georgian-style east wing, added in 1762, reflected the increasing influence of the English in the area; Federal touches were added later in the century. Since 1933 the house has served as a museum of the Dutch in the upper Hudson Valley. Exhibits include seventeenth- and eighteenth-century prints and archaeological artifacts, many from the Fort Orange excavation of 1970–71.

Born in the USA

During the War of 1812, Troy brickmaker Samuel Wilson opened a slaughterhouse and sold meat to a government contractor named Elbert Anderson. All of his beef and pork were stamped us-ea, and soldiers made up a story that the us, which stood for United States, actually stood for "Uncle Sam" Wilson, and thus Uncle Sam was born. A monument to his memory stands at the head of 101st Street in Troy.

Crailo State Historic Site, 9½ Riverside Ave., Rensselaer (518-463-8738; www.nysparks.state.ny.us/historic-sites), is open mid-April through late October, Wednesday through Sunday from 11 a.m. to 4 p.m. Crailo is also open on Tuesday in July and August. From November through March, visits are by appointment only. Monday through Friday 11 a.m. to 4 p.m. Tours are given on the hour and half-hour; the last tour is at 4 p.m. It is also open Memorial Day, Independence Day, and Labor Day. Admission is $5 for adults, $4 for senior citizens, free for children ages 12 and under. Group tours with preregistration, $4 per person.

Ever wondered about the history of big guns? Or who currently makes them? See a complete overview of America's artillery history and learn more about the Watervliet Arsenal at the *Watervliet Arsenal Museum.* Pore over 400-year-old one-of-a-kind guns, artillery weapons, 155 mm howitzers, gun carriages, 60mm lightweights, Civil War weapons, and 16-inch WWII battleship guns. Just as unique as its collection is its home in the Iron Building that was erected under the leadership of arsenal commander Major Mordecaii. Listed on the National Register of Historical Landmarks, the entire 30,000-square-foot building is made from an impressive collection of cast and wrought iron trusses, cast iron plates, and sheet steel roofing. The arsenal was originally founded in 1813 to support the efforts of the War of 1812 and a museum opened to showcase guns through history. You can also see weapons and information dating back to the 1600s. The arsenal is still active, and is currently the only producer of large guns and makes all tank guns that are in use today.

The Watervliet Arsenal Museum is located at 1 Buffington St. in Watervliet (about 7 miles from Albany) and is open from Sunday through Thursday from 10 a.m. to 3 p.m. It is free to the public. The museum is located on defense grounds, so visitors will need to show identification. Call (518) 266-5805 or visit www.wva.army.mil for more information or to arrange a special tour or research opportunities.

Hoosic Valley

The Battle of Bunker Hill is a military misnomer of the revolution. It wasn't actually fought on Bunker Hill (it took place on Breed's Hill, also in Charlestown, Massachusetts). Similar is the story of the 1777 Battle of Bennington, an American victory that laid the groundwork for the defeat and surrender of General Burgoyne at Saratoga that October. The battle, in which American militiamen defended their ammunition and supplies from an attacking party made up of British troops, Tory sympathizers, mercenaries, and Indians, took place not in Bennington, Vermont, but in Walloomsac, New York. True, the stores that the British were after were stashed in the Vermont town, but the actual fighting took place on New York soil.

The State of New York currently maintains the site of the battle as an official state historic site. It's on a towering hilltop in eastern Rensselaer County's Grafton Lakes State Park, and is studded with bronze and granite markers that captivate readers with details of the troops on the American militia's triumphal day. The spot is located on the north side of Route 67 and is open May 1 through Labor Day, daily 10 a.m. to 7 p.m.; Labor Day to Veterans Day, weekends only 10 a.m. to 7 p.m. Visitors can check road conditions by calling **Bennington Battlefield State Historic Site** at (518) 279-1902 or get general information at (518) 686-7109 or www.nysparks.state .ny.us/historic-sites. The Visitor Center is open from Memorial Day to Columbus Day, Wednesday, Friday, and Saturday from 1 to 4 p.m. On a clear day you can enjoy fine views of the Green Mountain foothills, prominent among which is Bennington's obelisk monument. Drive over to visit the monument and give the Vermonters their due—but really, doesn't "Battle of Walloomsac" have a nice ring to it?

Will Moses, a great-grandson of the renowned primitive painter Grandma Moses, is a folk artist whose minutely detailed paintings reflect the charm and beauty of the tiny rural community where he lives. Lithographs, printed by master lithographers from original oil paintings done by Will, are exhibited and sold, along with offset prints, at **Mt. Nebo Gallery,** 60 Grandma Moses Rd., Eagle Bridge (518-686-4334 or 800-328-6326; www.willmoses.com). The gallery is open Monday through Friday 9 a.m. to 4 p.m., Saturday 10 a.m. to 5 p.m., and Sunday noon to 5 p.m.

Our next stop on this ramble up the east shore of the Hudson deviates from the history of the Shakers and taps into the monastic spirit. Cambridge, the home of the **New Skete Communities,** houses a group of monks, nuns, and laypeople organized around a life of prayer, contemplation, and physical work. Founded in 1966 within the Byzantine Rite of the Roman Catholic

Church, the New Skete Communities have been a part of the Orthodox Church in America since 1979.

Visitors to New Skete are welcome at the community's two houses of worship. The small Temple of the Transfiguration of Christ, open at all times, contains a number of icons painted by the monks and nuns, while the larger Church of Christ the Wisdom of God—open to visitors only during services—has, imbedded in its marble floor, original pieces of mosaic that were brought from the A.D. 576 Church of Saint Sophia (Holy Wisdom) in Constantinople. Worship services are usually twice daily; with one service on Saturday.

As in many monastic communities, the monks and the nuns of New Skete help support themselves through a wide variety of pursuits. An important part of their life is the breeding of German shepherds and the boarding and training of all breeds of dogs. The monks have even written two successful books, *How to Be Your Dog's Best Friend* and *The Art of Raising a Puppy*. At their gift shop they sell their own cheeses, smoked meats, fruitcakes, the famous New Skete cheesecakes, dog beds, religious cards made by the nuns, and original painted icons.

The Communities of New Skete are in Cambridge. The convent is accessible from the village of Cambridge via East Main Street on Ash Grove Road, and the monastery is farther out of town on New Skete Lane. For information

REGIONAL TOURIST INFORMATION— EAST OF THE HUDSON

Columbia County Tourism
(800) 724-1846 and (518) 828-3375
www.columbiacountyny.com

Dutchess County Tourism
3 Neptune Rd.
Poughkeepsie
(800) 445-3131
www.dutchesstourism.com

Hudson Valley Tourism
(845) 463-4000
www.travelhudsonvalley.org

Poughkeepsie Area Chamber of Commerce
One Civic Center Plaza
Poughkeepsie
(845) 454-1700
www.pokchamb.org

Putnam County Tourism
(800) 470-4854 and (845) 225-0381
www.visitputnam.org

Rensselaer County Tourism
1600 Seventh Ave.
Troy
(518) 270-2959
www.rensco.com

visit www.newskete.com or call the monks at (518) 677-3928 or the nuns at (518) 677-3810. The bakery is currently open from 10 a.m. to 4 p.m. with varying Cheesecake Bakery Tour hours.

Places to Stay East of the Hudson

HOPEWELL JUNCTION

Le Chambord
2737 Route 52,
Hopewell Junction
(845) 221-1941
www.lechambord.com

HYDE PARK

Journey Inn Bed and Breakfast
One Sherwood Place
(845) 229-8972
www.journeyinn.com

MILLERTON

Simmons' Way Village Inn and Restaurant
33 Main St. (Route 44)
(518) 789-6235
www.simmonsway.com

PEEKSKILL

Peekskill Inn
634 Main St.
(800) 526-9466 or
(914) 739-1500
www.peekskillinn.com

POUGHKEEPSIE

Alumnae House, The Inn at Vassar College
161 College Ave.
(800) 546-7282 or
(845) 437-5445
www.aavc.vassar.edu/
house/index.html

Pougkeepsie Grand Hotel
40 Civic Center Plaza
(845) 485-5300

RHINEBECK

Bittersweet Bed and Breakfast
470 Wurtemburg Rd.
(845) 876-7777
www.bittersweetbedand
breakfast.com

Gables at Rhinebeck
6358 Mill St.
(845) 876-7577

The Looking Glass Bed and Breakfast
28–30 Chestnut St.
(845) 876-8986
www.thelookingglassbandb
.com

Whistlewood Farm Bed & Breakfast
52 Pells Rd.
(845) 876-6838
www.whistlewood.com

TARRYTOWN

Tarrytown House Estate and Conference Center
49 East Sunnyside Lane
(800) 553-8118
www.tarrytownhouseestate
.com

TIVOLI

Madalin Hotel
53 Broadway
(845) 757-2100
www.madalinhotel.com

TROY

Olde Judge Mansion
3300 Sixth Ave.
(518) 274-5698
www.oldejudgemansion
.com

WHITE PLAINS

Renaissance Westchester Hotel
80 West Red Oak Lane
(914) 694-5400
www.marriott.com

Bardavon 1869 Opera House
35 Market St.
Poughkeepsie
(845) 473-2072
www.bardavon.org

Boscobel
1601 Route 9D, Garrison
(845) 265-3638
www.boscobel.org

The Children's Museum of Science and Technology
250 Jordan Rd.
(518) 235-2120
www.cmost.org

FDR's Home and Library (Springwood)
4097 Albany-Post Rd. (Route 9)
Hyde Park
(800) FDR-VISIT
www.nps.gov/hofr/

Frances Lehman Loeb Art Center Vassar College
124 Raymond Ave.
Poughkeepsie
(845) 437-5632
www.fllac.vassar.edu

Kykuit (Rockefeller Estate)
150 White Plains Rd.
Sleepy Hollow
(914) 631-8200
www.hudsonvalley.org

Lebanon Valley Dragway
1746 Route 20
West Lebanon
(518) 794-7130
www.dragway.com

Madam Brett Homestead
50 Van Nydeck Ave.
Beacon
(845) 831-6533

Mary Flagler Cary Arboretum
Route 44A
Millbrook
(845) 677-5359

Montgomery Place
River Road
Annandale-on-Hudson
(845) 758-5461

Philipsburg Manor
Croton-on-Hudson
(914) 631-8200
www.hudsonvalley.org

Taconic State Park
Route 344 off Route 22
near Copake Falls
(518) 329-3993
nysparks.state.ny.us

Van Cortlandt Manor
Croton-on-Hudson
(914) 631-8200
www.hudsonvalley.org

Vanderbilt Mansion National Historic Site
Route 9
Hyde Park
(845) 229-7770
www.nps.gov/vama

Wilderstein
64 Morton Rd.
Rhinebeck
(845) 876-4818
www.wilderstein.org

Places to Eat East of the Hudson

AMENIA

Cascade Mountain Winery & Restaurant
Flint Hill Road
(845) 373-9021

BEACON

Sukhothai Restaurant
516 Main St.
(866) 838-6973
www.sukhothainy.net

GARRISON

The Bird and Bottle Inn
1123 Old Albany Post Rd.
(off Route 9D)
(845) 424-2333
www.thebirdandbottleinn
.com

Valley Restaurant at the Garrison
2015 Route 9
(845) 424-3604
www.thegarrison.com

HASTINGS-ON-THE-HUDSON

Buffet de la Gare
155 Southside Ave.
(914) 478-1671

HOPEWELL JUNCTION

Le Chambord
2737 Route 52
(845) 221-1941
www.lechambord.com

KATONAH

Blue Dolphin Ristorante
175 Katonah Ave.
(914) 232-4791
www.thebluedolphinny.com

OSSINING

Brasserie Swiss
118 Croton Ave.
(914) 931-0319
www.brasserieswiss.com

POCANTICO HILLS

Blue Hill at Stone Barns
630 Bedford Rd.
(914) 366-9600
www.bluehillstonebarns
.com

POUGHKEEPSIE

Cosimo's
120 Delafield St.
(845) 485-7229
www.cosimosrestaurant
group.com

RHINEBECK

Sabroso
22 Garden St.
(845) 876-8688
www.sabrosorestaurant
.com

TARRYTOWN

Equus
The Castle on the Hudson
400 Benedict Ave.
(914) 631-3646
www.castleattarrytown
.com

Lago di Como
27 Main St.
(914) 631-7227
www.lagodicomorestaurant
.com

Santa Fe Restaurant
5 Main St.
(914) 332-4452
www.santaferestaurant
.com

THE ADIRONDACKS

To many Manhattanites, upstate New York can mean anything north of Westchester, but to really appreciate the grandeur of the Empire State, city dwellers must motor past Albany and its suburbs to reach the Adirondack Mountains. The Adirondacks count forty-two peaks that soar over 4,000 feet, including Mt. Marcy, near Lake Placid, the state's highest elevation at 5,344 feet above sea level.

Although readily accessible from I-87, much of the Adirondacks remain fringed with wildlife and vegetation, thanks to the Adirondack Park, which encompasses some six million acres of state and private land east of Lake Champlain, including Lake George and northern Saratoga County.

It was certainly the area's incredible natural beauty—rugged mountains, clear lakes and streams, tall pines—that attracted many of the fortunes of the Gilded Age to the Adirondacks. They summered here on great "camps," estates that sprawled over thousands of acres, setting a pattern for generations of children, who bunked in somewhat less luxurious circumstances. But these society swells were not the first to discover the Adirondacks: visitors will discover museums and sites that document the rich history of the land and its people,

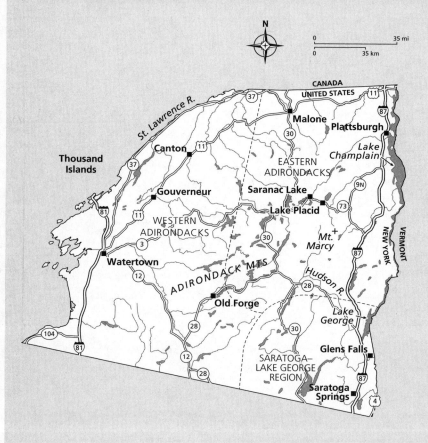

N

0   35 mi
0   35 km

CANADA
UNITED STATES

37

11

87

Malone

Plattsburgh

30

Canton

11

Lake
Champlain

Thousand
Islands

37

EASTERN
ADIRONDACKS

Gouverneur

Saranac Lake

9N

81

11

Lake Placid

73

WESTERN
ADIRONDACKS

30

Mt.
Marcy

3

NEW YORK

VERMONT

Watertown

12

ADIRONDACK MTS

87

Hudson R.

28

Old Forge

28

Lake
George

30

12

Glens Falls

104

81

28

SARATOGA–
LAKE GEORGE
REGION

87

Saratoga
Springs

4

St. Lawrence R.

from the Indian nations to the settlers who carved towns out of the woods, building cabins and boats, and, yes, even the comfortable outdoor chairs that take their name from this region.

(Note: The overall place-to-place direction followed in this chapter is counterclockwise—south to north to west.)

Saratoga–Lake George Region

To horse-racing fans, Saratoga Springs is simply "The Spa," an annual exodus from New York City, when the August race meeting at Saratoga Racetrack forces touts out into the fresh air. Many hotel rooms are booked from the year before, everywhere from the stately old Adelphi Hotel to the national chains to the many B&Bs housed in lovely old Victorian houses. But there's so much more to Saratoga than racing—there is a rich history to discover as well as the mineral springs, and concerts and shows at the Saratoga Performing Arts Center (www.spac.org), summer home to the Philadelphia Orchestra and the New York City Opera and Ballet.

When puzzling over an exacta gets too taxing, relax and "take the cure" at the *Lincoln Baths* or the *Roosevelt Baths,* both built in the 1930s and modeled after the grand spas of Europe. They offer a full menu of facials, massages, and other treatments to complement the traditional effervescent mineral water bath, a uniquely relaxing experience.

The baths are a short stroll from the *Gideon Putnam Resort and Spa,* the grand Georgian Revival–style edifice at the center of the 2,300-acre Saratoga Spa State Park. The resort is a gracious setting for every sort of leisure activity—tennis, golf, swimming, horseback riding, jogging, and, in winter, ice-skating and cross-country skiing. The renovated Gideon Putnam has returned to its roots, when the flamboyant interior designer Dorothy Draper envisioned bold colors and patterns for its grand lobby and gracious restaurants. Rates at

AUTHOR'S FAVORITES—ADIRONDACKS

Adirondack Museum	Moose River Recreation Area
Fort Ticonderoga	National Museum of Racing and Hall of Fame
Frederic Remington Art Museum	
Hattie's	Thousand Islands Inn

the Gideon Putnam vary according to season, with rooms running from $109 up to $555, with many value-added golf and spa packages offered outside of racing season. Call (800) 732-1560 or go to www.gideonputnam.com for more on the hotel and the baths.

Tradition reveals the Indians of the Saratoga region visited High Rock Spring as early as 1300 to gain strength from the "Medicine Spring of the Great Spirit." Four hundred seventy years later, in 1771, Sir William Johnson, suffering from a wound received in the Battle of Lake George, was carried on a litter by Mohawk Indians from Johnstown to High Rock Spring. After a short stay his health improved noticeably, and the reputation of the spring quickly spouted.

John Arnold may have been the first person to recognize the commercial value of the mineral waters at Saratoga Springs. In 1774 he purchased a crude log cabin built on a bluff overlooking High Rock Spring, improved it, and opened an inn. Thirteen years later, Revolutionary War hero Alexander Bryan purchased the inn, the only Saratoga hotel until 1801, when Gideon Putnam built the Grand Union Hotel. Now *The Olde Bryan Inn,* the inn has been a lodge, tavern, restaurant, and private dwelling. Today you can enjoy prime rib, Gorgonzola New York sirloin, homestyle turkey dinner, or just a pint.

The Olde Bryan Inn, 123 Maple Ave., Saratoga Springs (518-587-2990; www.oldbryaninn.com), is open Sunday through Thursday 11 a.m. until 10 p.m., and Friday and Saturday 11 a.m. to 11 p.m. The tavern is open daily until midnight.

Lincoln and Roosevelt are not the only tubs in town anymore; *The Crystal Spa* day spa at 120 South Broadway, adjacent to the Grand Union Motel, offers a full array of facials, massages, and body treatments. It also boasts mineral baths in water pumped from the Rosemary Spring. Patrons can also drink the spring water right from a fountain housed beneath a restored Victorian gazebo. Call (518) 584-2556 or go to www.thecrystalspa.net for the latest treatments and prices.

A Gas Explosion

The discovery of a process to extract carbonic gas (used to make the new carbonated beverages) from Saratoga Springs's waters in 1890 was almost the resort's death knell. Over the next few decades, many of its wells were being pumped bone dry. In 1910, to protect its natural resources, the state purchased 163 springs and 1,000 acres of land surrounding them, and constructed baths, a research institute, a Hall of Springs, and the Gideon Putnam hotel.

Between 1823 and 1889 mineral waters from approximately thirty springs in Saratoga County were bottled and distributed around the world, and an industry was born. The *National Bottle Museum,* housed in a 1901 former hardware store in Ballston Spa's historic district, documents the rise and decline of that industry. Through exhibits of antique bottles and glassmaking tools, videos, and artifacts, it tells the story of a time past, when young men were indentured to the owners of glass factories and apprenticed for fifteen years to become glassblowers in the glasshouses that made bottles and jars by hand. It re-creates an industry and a way of life that have vanished from the American scene.

The National Bottle Museum, 76 Milton Ave., Ballston Spa (518-885-7589; www.nationalbottlemuseum.org), is open daily from June 1 to September 30, 10 a.m. to 4 p.m.; October 1 to May 31, open Monday through Friday 10 a.m. to 4 p.m. and closed weekends. Recommended donation is $2 for adults. Devotees of glassworks can call ahead to sign up for one of the four-hour, weekend or evening glassblowing courses given by guest artisans in the museum's flameworking shops. A resident instructor currently teaches on Tuesday evening and on Saturday to master working glass in a torch.

For those born too late to see Secretariat or Seabiscuit in the flesh, the history and traditions of the sport are thoroughly chronicled at the *National Museum of Racing and Hall of Fame,* directly across from the Saratoga Race Course. Patrons enter the museum through an actual starting gate, complete with life-size representations of a horse, jockey, and starter. Some of the highlights: paintings of outstanding horses, the saddle and boots used by jockey Johnny Loftus on Man o' War, a Hall of Fame, and the actual skeleton of a thoroughbred. *Race America,* filmed at racetracks and stud farms across the country, is shown in the theater. Video booths lining the walls provide films of some of racing's greats.

The National Museum of Racing and Hall of Fame, 191 Union Ave., Saratoga Springs (518-584-0400; www.racingmuseum.org), is open year-round. daily from 10 a.m. to 4 p.m. Monday through Saturday, noon to 4 p.m. on Sunday; during the Saratoga racing season, 9 a.m. to 5 p.m. For winter hours, call or check the Web site. Admission is $7 for adults and $5 for senior citizens, students, and children 6 to 18.

Folks in Saratoga Springs have been flocking to *Hattie's* for Southern fried chicken and biscuits since 1938, and we're assured by the present owner, Jasper Alexander, that Hattie's New Orleans recipes haven't changed. "We've kept her most popular dishes, like fried chicken and pan-fried pork chops, and added some Creole specialties," explains Jasper. Everything from slow-cooked barbecued spare ribs, Hoppin' John (black-eyed peas with chopped onion, salt

ANNUAL EVENTS IN THE ADIRONDACKS

JANUARY

Lake George Polar Plunge
Lake George
(800) 705-0059
www.lakegeorgewintercarnival.com

World Cup Freestyle
Lake Placid
(518) 523-1655
www.orda.org

FEBRUARY

Empire State Winter Games
Lake Placid
(518) 523-1655
www.orda.org

Winter Carnival
Saranac Lake
(518) 891-1990
www.saranaclake.com

APRIL

St. Clement's Saratoga Horse Show
Saratoga Springs
(518) 587-2623
www.saintclementshorseshow.com

MAY

The Adirondack Paddle Fest
Inlet
(315) 357-6672
www.mountainmanoutdoors.com/
AdirondackPaddlefest

Maple Festival
Croghan
(518) 523-9258

JUNE

Americade Motorcycle Rally
Lake George
(518) 798-7888
www.tourexp.com

and pepper, butter, and pork), blackened catfish, Creole jambalaya to gumbo is authentically prepared and moderately priced.

Hattie's, 45 Phila St., Saratoga Springs (518-584-4790; www.hattiesrestaurant .com), is open daily from 5 to 10 p.m.; enjoy courtyard dining in the summer.

The *Petrified Sea Gardens* consists of the exposed remains of a sea reef that thrived here beneath the Cambrian Sea 500 million years ago. Known since 1825 and properly identified in 1883, the "gardens" are the fossilized remains of cabbage-like plants related to modern algae. The reef they formed would have teemed with trilobites, brachiopods, and rudimentary snails, the fossils of some of which are visible among the plant fossils at this site. When the primordial seas receded, the vegetation was exposed, fossilized beneath layers of sediment, and eventually exposed again by the shearing action of the glaciers.

Lake Placid Film Festival
Various locations around Lake Placid
(518) 523-3456
www.lakeplacidfilmfestival.com

LARAC Arts Festival
Glens Falls
(518) 798-1141
www.larac.org/festivals.html

JULY

Hats Off to Saratoga
Saratoga Springs
(518) 584-3255
www.saratoga.org

Long Lake Regatta
Long Lake
(518) 624-3077
www.longlake-ny.com

AUGUST

Travers Festival Week
Saratoga Springs
(518) 584-3255
www.saratoga.com

SEPTEMBER

Adirondack Balloon Festival
Glens Falls
(800) 365-1050
www.adirondackballoonfest.org

OCTOBER

Adirondack Art and Craft Festival
Saratoga Springs
(802) 425-3399
www.craftproducers.com

World's Largest Garage Sale
Warrensburg
(518) 623-2161
www.warrensburggaragesale.com

DECEMBER

First Night
Saranac Lake
www.firstnightsaranaclake.org

Visitors walk among the ancient plants at the Petrified Sea Gardens and search for gray, layered nodules resembling broken, protruding sections of petrified cabbage. Among the vegetation is the "Iroquois Pine," one of the largest in the Adirondacks and estimated to be 300 years old. There are hands-on activities for children in the nature center.

Petrified Sea Gardens, 42 Petrified Sea Gardens Rd. (off Route 29), Saratoga Springs (518-584-7102; www.petrifiedseagardens.org), is open May (starting Mother's Day weekend) Saturday, Sunday, and Memorial Day 11 a.m. to 5 p.m.; June, Thursday through Monday 11 a.m. to 5 p.m.; July and August, daily 11 a.m. to 5 p.m.; September to mid-October, Thursday through Monday 4 a.m. to 5 p.m.; and late October to early November, weekends 11 a.m. to 5 p.m. Admission is $3.75 for adults, $2.75 for senior citizens, $3 for college students with I.D., and $2 for children 6 to 16. Call for group rates.

South Glenn Falls—Cooper's Cave

South Glenn Falls in Saratoga County may look like a sleepy upstate town on the way to somewhere else. But literary buffs and romantics can "step into a novel" and explore Cooper's Cave, the inspiration of *Last of the Mohicans* by James Fenimore Cooper. The Mohicans called the Hudson River *Muhheakunnuk,* or "river that flows two ways" as a nod to the tidal flow that forces salt into the water, causing it to temporarily stand still and then reverse its direction. Cooper found the river setting and ominous cave the ideal setting for his famed novel. Access the viewing platform adjacent to the cave and look down to the cave tucked away under Cooper's Cave Bridge connecting South Glens Falls to City of Glens Falls to see if you can evoke the romantic setting of the novel. View from Memorial Day until Halloween from 9 a.m. to 8 p.m.; free admission. Call (518) 793-1455 or visit www.sgfny.com for more information.

One of the first major victories for the colonial forces over the British, The Battle of Saratoga encouraged France to enter the war on the American side. The battle took place in October 1777 on the shores of the Hudson River, near present-day Stillwater, and the battleground is preserved in the 3,200-acre **Saratoga National Historical Park,** where visitors can also tour the colonial Philip Schuyler house on summer weekends. There is a weekly charge of per car to access the park's 10-mile tour road (call for current prices). The Saratoga National Historical Park Visitor Center, 648 Route 32, Stillwater, is open daily except Thanksgiving and Christmas. Call (518) 664-9821, ext. 224, or visit www.nps.gov/sara for more information.

In June 1885, President Ulysses S. Grant was suffering from throat cancer and longing for fresh air and a healthier climate. He and his family moved from New York City to Saratoga County into a summer cottage on top of Mt. McGregor, 8 miles from Saratoga Springs. At the cottage he continued work on his memoirs and, two weeks after completing them, died on July 23, 1885.

The house at **Grant Cottage State Historic Site** is preserved as Grant left it, from the bed where he died to the floral pieces sent from around the country. It is operated by the Friends of the Ulysses S. Grant Cottage, in cooperation with the New York State Office of Parks, Recreation, and Historic Preservation.

Grant Cottage State Historic Site, Mt. McGregor Road, Wilton (mailing address: P.O. Box 2294, Wilton 12831; 518–587-8277; www.grantcottage.org), is open Memorial Day through Labor Day, Wednesday through Sunday 10 a.m. to 4 p.m.; through Columbus Day weekends only from 10 a.m. to 4 p.m. Groups need advance reservations and the site can make special arrangements to open for groups in spring and fall, even when not open to the public. Admission is $4 for adults, $3 for senior citizens and students, and $2 for children 6 to 12.

At the age of 19, Marcella (Kochanska) Sembrich made her operatic debut in Athens, Greece, singing in a number of the great opera houses in Europe before joining New York's Metropolitan Opera Company for its first season in 1883. She returned to Europe until 1898 and rejoined the Metropolitan Opera until 1909, when her farewell prompted the most sumptuous gala in the Met's history. She was also founder of the vocal departments of the Juilliard School in New York and the Curtis Institute in Philadelphia and was a preeminent teacher of singing for twenty-five years. She often brought students to a studio near her summer home in Bolton Landing on Lake George. The **Sembrich Opera Museum,** in Mme. Sembrich's converted studio, displays operatic memorabilia she collected from her debut to her death in 1935.

Summer events include studio talks, a lakeside lecture series, a master class in voice, and occasional recitals or chamber concerts.

achipbyany othername

One day "Aunt Kate" Weeks, a cook at a hotel on Saratoga Lake, tried to make perfectly crisp french fried potatoes. Instead she created "Saratoga Chips," now known as potato chips.

The Sembrich Opera Museum, 4800 Lake Shore Dr., Route 9N, Bolton Landing (518-644-2431; www.thesembrich.org), is open daily June 15 through September 15, 10 a.m. to 12:30 p.m. and 2 to 5:30 p.m. Admission is free; donations are suggested.

The **House of Frankenstein Wax Museum** in Lake George is part wax museum and part haunted house. The museum claims "the creatures roaming the halls of this house are not living . . . yet they are not dead. For as you shall see for yourself, they move and talk and sometimes they even scream!" Visitors are greeted with recorded screams and barreling dummies throughout the journey of over fifty exhibits. You can even throw the switch at an electrocution if you're feeling adventurous. Check out the "Amazing Room of Rats" while you're there in between running from Dracula and the Wolfman. You can choose to just tour the wax museum, haunted house, or do a combo tour. Smaller kids who are prone to frights should skip this offbeat attraction.

The House of Frankenstein Wax Museum is located at 213 Canada St. and is open from April 2 to Halloween; hours vary depending on the month and day, but it is often open as late as 11 p.m. Tickets run $8.99 for adults, $7.99

for students 13 to 17 years old, $4.99 for children 6 to 12, and adult combo tickets for $13.99 for one tour of Dr. Morbid's Haunted House and one tour of Frankenstein Wax Museum. Visit www.frankensteinwaxmuseum.com or call (518) 668-3377 for a calendar of hours and events.

Eastern Adirondacks

Fort Ticonderoga stands on a promontory jutting into the southern end of Lake Champlain. It was built by the French in 1755 when the colonial administration in Quebec needed a southern defense in its struggle against Great Britain for control of Canada. Called Fort Carillon, it was built from earth and timbers in the classic French fortress design. It was later upgraded to stone, with four pointed bastions presenting an interlocking field of fire against attackers.

In 1758 the Marquis de Montcalm repelled a massive attack by the British, but a year later Lord Jeffrey Amherst captured the fort and renamed it "Ticonderoga." Seventeen years later, and three weeks after the Battles of Lexington and Concord, Ethan Allen and Benedict Arnold captured "Fort Ti" from the British "in the name of the Great Jehovah and the Continental Congress," giving the Americans their first victory of the revolution.

Last garrisoned in 1777, Fort Ti might be little more than a roadside marker had it not been for the efforts of the Pell family to protect the site since 1820 and the commitment of Stephen and Sarah Pell to restore it beginning in 1908. Today, guides in eighteenth-century clothing roam the meticulously reconstructed grounds and a host of events including live artillery demonstrations and fife and drum musters help bring the fort to life.

Visitors can stride along the ramparts, view the earthworks built during both the French and Indian Wars and the American Revolution, examine the barracks, and visit the museum housing North America's largest collection of eighteenth-century artillery as well as paintings, furniture, and military memorabilia. Just outside the fort is the battlefield where, in 1758, Montcalm devastated the 42nd Highland ("Black Watch") Regiment.

Tours of the 600-acre garrison grounds, offered daily, include the "King's Garden," a 1920s-era formal flower garden, and demonstration vegetable gardens including a Native American garden and children's garden, and the fort. Family programs called Fife and Drum Corps are hosted during July and August. Throughout the season there are numerous special events, including a Grand Encampment of the French and Indian War in late June, a Scottish Festival in mid-June, and a Revolutionary War Encampment in September. Call for information.

Fort Ticonderoga, 100 Fort Rd., Route 74 East, Ticonderoga (518-585-2821; www.fortticonderoga.org), is open from May 20 through October 20, daily 9:30 a.m. to 5 p.m. Admission is $15 for adults, $13.50 for seniors, $6 for children ages 7 to 12, and free for children under 7. The Log House is open for breakfast, lunch, and snacks.

As a sidelight to a Fort Ticonderoga visit, drive to the summit of nearby **Mt. Defiance** for a panoramic view of the Champlain Valley. Hop aboard the M/V *Carillon* to visit **Mt. Independence,** site of a Revolutionary War fort, across Lake Champlain in Vermont.

Located west of Ticonderoga and nestled in the Adirondacks, lies **Garnet Hill Lodge,** a remote resort on 600 acres of land that was built by members of the Barton family in 1933 when they came to the area to mine garnet. The architecture of the main lodge is rustic Adirondack-style, but

nobarking

Adirondack is an Anglicism of the Iroquois word for the Algonquin Indians, whom they called "Ha-De-Ron-Dah" or "bark-eaters" for their habit of eating certain types of tree bark.

some of the rooms, complete with whirlpool baths and hot tubs, are anything but rustic. The resort offers a host of activities, including tubing, mountain biking, and a special course on fly-fishing. The lodge, at 13th Lake Rd. in North River (800-497-4207; www.garnet-hill.com), is open year-round.

Visitors can tour the **Barton Mines** and look for gemstones in the open pits at Garnet Mine Tours on Barton Mines Road. The mines are open daily from late June through early October, 9:30 a.m. to 5 p.m. Monday through Saturday; 11 a.m. to 5 p.m. Sunday; and on weekends through Columbus Day. A fee is charged for a lecture. Visitors must be escorted in the mines. Call (518) 251-2706 or go to www.garnetminetours.com for information.

Try the Brandied French toast with sautéed apples at **Goose Pond Inn** (800-806-2601 or 518-251-3434. www.goosepondinn.com), a charming, antiques-filled, turn-of-the-century bed-and-breakfast just a mile from Gore Mountain Ski Center. The inn, open year-round, is on Main Street in North Creek. Rates range from $85 to $125 for a mid-week double to $115 to $160 on weekends and holidays.

North of Ticonderoga, Lake Champlain remains narrow enough for a single military installation to have commanded both shores and governed the passage of ship traffic in the eighteenth century. This was the purpose of the fortifications that now lie in ruins at **Crown Point State Historic Site** (www.nysparks.state.ny.us/historic-sites).

Crown Point housed the French Fort St. Frederic in the late 1600s. It served as the staging area for French raids on English settlements in New England and the Hudson Valley. The fort was designed as a stone citadel within outer walls and defended by fifty cannons, swivel-mounted guns, and a garrison of 80 to 120 soldiers.

After it was abandoned by the French in 1759, General Jeffrey Amherst seized the fort for the British, and ordered it enlarged. In 1775 American militiamen captured the fort from the British and used it as headquarters for the navy under Benedict Arnold until 1776.

In 1910 the private owners conveyed the property to the state in an effort to preserve the ruins. Today, the walls, foundations, and partial structures survive and in 1975 the area officially became a state historic site. The following year the new visitor center and museum were opened. Highlights of the museum exhibits include artifacts uncovered at the site during extensive archaeological digs.

The visitor center at *Crown Point State Historic Site,* at the Lake Champlain Bridge, 4 miles east of Routes 9N and 22, Crown Point (518-597-4666), is open May through October, Wednesday through Monday 9 a.m. to 5 p.m. Grounds are open until Columbus Day from 9 a.m. to dusk. There is a $5 admission fee for each car on weekends and holidays; an admission fee is charged for the museum at all times. Group visits by advance reservation.

Tiny Essex lies in the foothills of the Adirondacks on the shore of Lake Champlain and is one of the state's loveliest villages. Founded in the eighteenth century and one of the earliest European settlements on the lake, it is listed on the National Register of Historic Places. Streets lined with homes and public buildings reflect a multitude of styles including Federal, Greek Revival, Italianate, and French Second Empire. Stumble upon the 1853 Greek Revival twenty-room mansion with 18-inch-thick cut stone walls called *Greystone.* It took four years to complete and has been restored by its present owners.

There are a handful of lodging options in town, including the *Essex Inn* (518-963-8821; www.theessexinn.com). It is one of the oldest structures in town and has been in almost continuous operation since it was built in 1810. Extensively renovated in 1986, the inn has nine guest rooms (seven with private bath) and rates of $95 to $160 on up include a full breakfast. There are several restaurants in town, including one at the inn, which serves meals alfresco when the weather permits.

If you want to take a short boat ride, the *Essex-Charlotte Ferry* (802-864-9804; ferries.com/south-schedule.asp) crosses the lake in just twenty minutes to Charlotte, Vermont. If you're on foot, there's not much to see on the other side, but you can hop off and catch a return ferry in a half hour. The ferry does not operate when there is ice on the lake.

For general information contact the Lake Placid/Essex County Convention and Visitors Bureau, Lake Placid, Olympic Center, 49 Parkside Dr., Lake Placid, NY 12946; (518) 523-2445 or (800) 447-5224; or www.lakeplacid.com.

Head to the *Adirondack Museum* at *Blue Mountain Lake* for a chronicle of the Adirondack experience throughout the years. Located on a ridge overlooking Blue Mountain Lake, the museum rambles through twenty-two separate exhibit buildings on a thirty-acre compound and has been called the finest regional museum in the United States.

The museum focused on the locals and their relationship to their environment, mountain setting, and settlement over the past two centuries. As befits an institution that began in an old hotel, the museum tells the story of how the Adirondacks were discovered by vacationists in the nineteenth century, especially after the 1892 completion of the railroad to nearby Raquette Lake.

See examples of nineteenth-century hotel and cabin rooms, restored turn-of-the-century cottage houses, and a large collection of rustic "Adirondack furniture" enjoying a revival among interior designers. Financier August Belmont's private railroad car *Oriental* is also on display and serves as a reminder of the days when grand conveyances brought the very wealthy to spend their leisure time at Adirondack mansions and clubs.

The workaday world of the Adirondacks is recalled in mining, logging, and boatbuilding exhibits. The museum also exhibits a collection of handmade canoes and guideboats, including some of the lightweight masterpieces of nineteenth-century canoe-builder J. H. Rushton. The lovely sloop *Water Witch* hangs in the renovated gatehouse.

Special attention is given to what has been written and painted using Adirondack subjects. The museum's picture galleries display the work of artists from the Hudson River School and later periods.

The Adirondack Museum, Routes 28N and 30, Blue Mountain Lake (518-352-7311; www.adkmuseum.org), is open daily from Memorial Day weekend through Columbus Day, 10 a.m. to 5 p.m. Admission is $16 for adults ages 13 and older; $15 age 62 and over and students and military personnel; $8 ages 6 to 12; children 5 and under free. Allow three to five hours for your visit.

Camp Santanoni in Newcomb is one of the most spectacular, yet least known, of the thirty-five Gilded Age Adirondack "Great Camps" surviving today and is part of a 12,900-acre estate within the Adirondack Forest Preserve. Robert and Anna Pruyn of Albany commissioned architect Robert H. Robertson to design their Japanese-inspired, six-building log complex on the shores of Newcomb Lake. The main lodge buildings, completed in 1893, required 1,500 spruce trees for their construction. The buildings' common roof covers 16,000 square feet and is composed of fifty-eight distinct planes to resemble a bird in flight.

The more than forty-five buildings were saved from demolition and placed on the National Register of Historic Places following their 1972 acquisition by the state and are under the care of an organization called Adirondack Architectural Heritage, which has undertaken a massive program of stabilization and restoration.

Santanoni is unusual even among remote Great Camps. Its main buildings are inaccessible except by nonmotorized travel. From the rambling six-bedroom structure incorporating a stone gateway arch, visitors must continue for nearly 5 miles to reach the lake and main lodge. This requires hiking, mountain biking, or cross-country skiing to traverse the generally flat terrain. In summer you can rest for the night before beginning the trip back, or go on to Moose Pond, which is nestled even deeper within the preserve. There are eight designated primitive campsites around Newcomb Lake.

Interns posted at the gate lodge and main lodge during the summer months provide interpretive information on the property, and a program of three guided tours is offered. For tour schedules and general information on Camp Santanoni, contact Adirondack Architectural Heritage, 1790 Main St., Civic Center, Keeseville 12944 (518-834-9328; www.aarch.org).

Siamese Ponds Wilderness Region in western Warren County is a wilderness areaencompassing hundreds of miles of state-maintained trails and tote roads winding over hills and mountains, past streams, ponds, and lakes. Rockhounds will love exploring the passageways and valleys through a wide variety of rock formations. They were carved by glaciers of the Ice Age and by erosion caused by aeons of tumbling rocks carried along mountain streams, and hikers have found numerous exposed veins of minerals and semiprecious stones.

Siamese Ponds Wilderness Region has entrance points from Stony Creek, Thurman, Wevertown, Johnsburg, North Creek, and North River. Information is available in *Adirondack Trails: Central Region* guide, published by the Adirondack Mountain Club (518-668-4447; www.adk.org).

With its thirty-one-acre campus, resident naturalists, and live exhibits, the **Wild Center** has been described as a base camp for the Adirondacks. Here you can visit theaters showing high-definition films, explore hands-on nature exhibits, and encounter hundreds of live animals that live in the woods and waters: rare native trout, river otters, and even turtles the size of walnuts.

Three trails wind through the Wild Center, leading to boardwalks over Blue Pond, to raised overlooks at the oxbow marsh on the Raquette River.

The museum's Waterside Cafe serves a mix of locally produced fare and beverages from 10 a.m. to 6 p.m. daily. The Wild Center is located at 45 Museum Dr., Tupper Lake (518-359-7800; www.wildcenter.org). Visit daily from Labor Day through October from 10 a.m. to 5 p.m.; November 1 through Memorial Day on Friday through Sunday from 10 a.m. to 5 p.m. The center is open during Christmas week, and Presidents week as well as Monday holidays. Closed the entire month of April. From Memorial Day to Columbus Day, the museum is open daily from 10 a.m. to 6 p.m. An adult ticket is $15; a youth ticket (ages 4 to 14) is $9; a senior ticket is $13.

Raquette Lake's **Great Camp Sagamore** is a prototypical Adirondack Great Camp. The National Historic Site with twenty-seven buildings was erected in 1897 by William West Durant, who later sold it in 1901 to Alfred Vanderbilt as a wilderness retreat. After Vanderbilt died on the *Lusitania* in 1915, his widow continued to entertain family and friends as "the hostess of the gaming crowd" for the next thirty-nine years.

Visitors to Sagamore can take a two-hour guided tour and, with reservations, stay overnight in one of the double-occupancy rooms (twin beds, bathroom down the hall). Buffet meals are served in the dining hall overlooking the lake. There are also 20 miles of hiking trails, canoeing, and a semi-outdoor bowling alley. Request a program catalog to learn about special events.

Great Camp Sagamore, Sagamore Road, P.O. Box 40, Raquette Lake 13436 (315-354-5311), has guided daily tours from Memorial Day to the third weekend in June on Saturday and Sunday at 1:30 p.m. The third weekend in June through Labor Day, it is open daily at 10 a.m. and 1:30 p.m. From Labor Day to Columbus Day, it is open daily at 1:30 p.m. Admission runs $14 per adult and $7 per child. The proprietors remind potential guests that "Sagamore is not a hotel, motel, or resort. It is, instead, a complete experience in living a 'bit of history' in an incomparable setting." Guests must be part of a program to stay at the grounds and per-person rates include accommodations, meals, hiking trails, canoes, tennis courts, and all facilities. Fees vary depending on the program, but ranges from $270 to $499 per person for a minimum two-night stay. For further information on accommodations, check the Web site at www.sagamore.org.

More than 435 species of plants and trees, 18 varieties of orchids, and 28 varieties of ferns thrive in the Adirondacks' largest block of remote public land. The 50,000-acre **Moose River Recreation Area** is also home to the Arctic Skipper, carnivorous Harvester, and other rare butterfly species. Catch a glimpse of them traversing over 40 plus miles of roads and 27 miles of trails. Camping is provided at 140 primitive sites.

Nearby find the 500-foot boardwalk that permits visitors to traverse a rare open bog mat at **Ferd's Bog,** just off Uncas Road in Inlet. Among the numerous unusual plants growing here are several species of rare orchids, including the white-fringed, rose Patagonia, and grass pink. Also watch for bug-eating pitcher plants.

Both of these areas are administered by New York State's Department of Environmental Conservation. For information call (315) 354-4611 or visit www .dec.ny.gov.

The Artworks, an artists' cooperative on Main Street in downtown Old Forge, features art and craftwork by Adirondack artists. Media include pottery, stained glass, jewelry, fine arts, basketry, folk art, fabric art, and photography. The shop is open year-round. After Labor Day, hours are Sunday through Thursday, 10 a.m. to 5 p.m.; Friday and Saturday 10 a.m. to 8 p.m. For additional seasonal hours call (315) 369-2007.

Old Forge Hardware, "The Adirondacks' Most General Store," describes itself as "A Living Museum of Functional and Aesthetic Necessities: Everything from Abacuses to Zoom Binoculars" and has served the area since 1900. Old Forge Hardware, 104 Fulton St., Old Forge (315-369-6100; www.oldforgehard ware.com), is open daily year-round except Easter, Thanksgiving, Christmas, and New Year's. Hours vary with the season, so call ahead.

Explore one of the world's largest ice arena complexes at the **Olympic Center Sports Complex** in downtown Lake Placid. The venue for the 1932 and 1980 Winter Olympic Games was home to the unlikely victory in 1980 of the young U.S. hockey squad over the U.S.S.R.'s powerhouse Red Army team, dubbed "Miracle on Ice." The complex has four indoor rinks, a museum, cafeteria, and gift shop. Skate from late June through early September on weekdays for just $6 indoor, $7 outdoor (skate rental is $3). There are ice shows most Saturday nights throughout the summer months.

Rocket 45 mph down the only dedicated bobsled run in America on a wheeled sled. The sleds are piloted by professional drivers and brakemen at the **Verizon Sports Complex.** Sled from late June through mid-October, Wednesday through Sunday from 10 a.m. to 12:30 p.m. and 1:30 to 4 p.m. The fee is $65 for the bobsled ($75 in winter), $50 for the skeleton, and $45 for the luge; the ride is subject to weather and bobsled run conditions. Call (518) 523-4436 for information.

Other activities at the complex include biathlon target shooting (late June through Labor Day), Wednesday through Sunday 10 a.m. to 4 p.m. with a charge of $33 ($15 for the range only); and mountain biking on Mt. Van Hoevenberg (rentals available). From early July through late August, freestyle aerial skiing demonstrations (the skiers end up in the pool) are held on

Wednesday at the MacKenzie-Intervale Ski Olympic Jumping complex, and, on Saturday, Nordic ski jumping is held at the 90-meter jump in summer and at both the 90- and 120-meter hills in winter.

Visitors can take a ride up the chairlift gondola at Whiteface Mountain, visit the Skydeck observation area at the Olympic Jumping Complex, skate on the Olympic Speed Skating Oval, and explore the Olympic Sports Complex. Look for discounts on the Lake Placid Bobsled Experience, Olympic Center Tour, Be a Biathlete, Miracle Moments photo merchandise and other programs by purchasing a Kodak Summer Olympic Sites Passport for just $29 a person.

For information on all of the activities and special events, call the Olympic Center Main Office, Lake Placid, at (518) 523-1655 or (800) 462-6236, or visit whitefacelakeplacid.com.

According to the old spiritual, John Brown's body lies a-moulderin' in the grave. You can see for yourself at the *John Brown Farm State Historic Site* in North Elba, near Lake Placid. Brown was a militant abolitionist who led the 1859 raid on the U.S. arsenal at Harper's Ferry, Virginia, in hopes of arming black slaves to revolt against their masters. The plan failed, and Brown was executed and buried here, along with two of his sons and several of his followers, who were killed at Harper's Ferry.

Brown moved to this area in 1849 and tried to establish an agricultural community called Timbucto for free blacks. His quest for freedom failed, and Brown joined his sons in Kansas during the volatile 1850s, when the struggle to decide whether the territory would be admitted to the Union as a slave state or a free state earned it the nickname "Bloody Kansas." Brown, of course, made a name for himself in Kansas, taking part in the clash at Osawatomie.

The farmhouse at the John Brown Farm State Historic Site, 115 John Brown Rd., Lake Placid (518-523-3900; www.nysparks.state.ny.us/historic-sites), is open from May 1 to October 31, daily (except Tuesday) 10 a.m. to 5 p.m. The grounds are open all year during daylight hours. Admission for house tours is $2 for adults, $1 for seniors, and children 12 and under, free.

At the *Adirondack Guideboats Woodward Boat Shop,* Chris Woodward builds Adirondack guide boats using the same techniques that one of the boat's original builders, Willard Hanmer used back in the 1930s. And he's still making them in the same building. The boats are used for hunting and reflect an indigenous style of the region between Saranac Lake and Old Forge. Chris also makes and sells paddles, seats, and oars and sells boat accessories. The shop, at 3 Hanmer Ave., Saranac Lake (518-891-3961), is generally open on weekdays 9 a.m. to 5 p.m. or by appointment. Call ahead to make sure he'll be there.

In 1887 Robert Louis Stevenson set sail from Bournemouth, England, for a small farmhouse in Saranac Lake, the village he dubbed "the Little Switzerland in the Adirondacks." He lived here with his family and wrote *The Master of Ballantrae* and *The Wrong Box,* skated at nearby Moody Pond, and enjoyed life in the mountains. He wrote to a friend of his life here: "We are high up in the Adirondack Mountains living in a guide's cottage in the most primitive fashion. The maid does the cooking (we have little beyond venison and bread to cook) and the boy comes every morning to carry water from a distant spring for drinking purposes. It is already very cold but we have calked the doors and windows as one calks a boat, and have laid in a store of extraordinary garments made by the Canadian Indians."

Today the cottage is preserved in its original state and holds the country's largest collection of Stevenson's personal mementos. You can see his Scottish smoking jacket, with a sprig of heather in the breast pocket, original letters, and his yachting cap. There's a plaque here by sculptor Gutzon Borglum, donated by the artist who regarded the writer as "the great sculptor of words."

The **Robert Louis Stevenson Memorial Cottage & Museum,** Stevenson Lane, Saranac Lake (518-891–1462; www.robertlouisstevensonmemorialcottage

Elves Wanted

Many places call themselves **Santa's Workshop,** but how many are actually located in the North Pole by way of New York. This forerunner of modern theme parks opened in 1949 as the inspiration of Lake Placid businessman Julian Reiss and designer/artist Arto Monaco. The result of this collaboration spawned a fantasy village populated by storybook characters where children ride the Candy Cane Express or the Christmas Carousel, visit with Santa and Mrs. Claus, and mail out cards postmarked "North Pole, NY" and "Santa's Workshop."

Santa's Workshop is in the High Peaks area of Adirondacks Park on the Whiteface Mountain Memorial Highway (Route 431), 1½ miles northwest of the intersection with Route 86 in the town of Wilmington (800-806-0215 or 518-946-2211; www.north poleny.com). General admission is $19.95 for adults, $17.95 for seniors and children 2 to 16. The park is open from late June to early September, Tuesday to Saturday, and from early September through late December, generally on Saturday and Sunday. Hours vary; in early December, the park is open Sunday evenings; as the holidays approach, it's open Monday through Friday evenings as well. Call ahead or check the Web site to avoid disappointment.

From mid-November through mid-December, two-night family packages are offered; they include lodging (at various nearby properties), breakfasts and dinners, entertainment, and admission to Santa's Workshop.

.org), is open July through Columbus Day, Tuesday to Sunday 9:30 a.m. to noon and 1 to 4:30 p.m. The rest of the year it is opened by appointment. Admission is free; donations are welcome.

Almost six million acres of the **Adirondack State Park** includes some of the state's finest out-of-the-way attractions and offers some of its best opportunities to leave civilization behind. The park is a unique mixture of public and private lands. Approximately 130,000 year-round residents live in 105 towns and villages, but 43 percent of the total acreage is state owned, constitutionally protected "forever wild" land.

Stop at one of the two Adirondack Park Agency's Visitor Interpretive Centers (adkvic.org): **Paul Smiths VIC,** 802 State Route 30, Paul Smiths (518-327-3000); or **Newcomb VIC,** 5922 State Route 28N, Newcomb (518-582-2000). Both are open daily year-round from 9 a.m. to 5 p.m. except Thanksgiving and Christmas. Admission is free. If you're interested in camping at one of the 500 campsites spread over forty-eight islands on three of the Adirondack's most scenic lakes, request the brochure "Camping in the New York State Forest Preserve."

The Adirondacks and much of New York State were once the territory of the Iroquois Confederacy. Perhaps the most politically sophisticated of all the tribal groupings of North American Indians, the Iroquois comprised five distinct tribes of the Mohawks, Senecas, Onondagas, Oneidas, and Cayugas. They were later joined by the Tuscaroras to form the "six nations" of the confederation. The history and contemporary circumstances of the Iroquois are documented in the **Six Nations Indian Museum,** a "living museum" that presents its material from a Native American point of view.

The museum opened in 1954 and was built by the Faddens, members of the Mohawk Nation, and is still operated and staffed by members of that family. The museum's design reflects the architecture of the traditional Haudenosaunee (Six Iroquois National Confederacy) bark house. The longhouse is a metaphor for the Confederacy, symbolically stretching from east to west across ancestral territory.

howit'sdone

Park administrators from throughout the world have come to New York State to study the management of Adirondack State Park.

The museum, brimming with artifacts, is a reminder that for centuries before Europeans arrived, the Iroquois were building a society. Throughout the season Native Americans visit to talk about their histories, cultures, and their people's contributions to contemporary society.

The Six Nations Indian Museum, Roakdale Road (County Route 30), Onchiota (518-891-2299; www.tuscaroras.com), is open daily except Monday

But What about Bridesmaids?

In earlier times, the mothers of Iroquois maidens arranged the marriages of their daughters. A girl would acknowledge her mother's choice by placing a basket of bread at the prospective bridegroom's door. If he and his mother accepted, they would send a basket of food back to the girl and her family. If the offer was turned down, the girl's offering would remain untouched.

from July 1 through Labor Day, 10 a.m. to 5 p.m. and by appointment from May to June and September to October. Admission is $2 for adults and $1 for children.

The Delords moved into their new home just three years before the War of 1812 came to Plattsburgh with a southward thrust by British forces along Lake Champlain. But the enemy was repelled later that month by the Delords' friend Commodore Thomas Macdonough in the Battle of Plattsburgh.

Unlike most of the provincial bourgeois family homes during the nineteenth century, the **Kent-Delord House** survived remarkably intact. Today it offers an opportunity to see how an upper-middle-class family lived from the days just after the revolution through the Victorian age and see a distinguished collection of American portrait art, including the work of John Singleton Copley, George Freeman, and Henry Inman.

The Kent-Delord House Museum, 17 Cumberland Ave., Plattsburgh (518-561-1035; www.kentdelordhouse.org), is open March and April by appointment; May through December, Tuesday through Saturday from noon to 4 p.m.; the last tour begins at 3:15 p.m. Admission is $5 for adults, $3 for students, and $2 for children under 12.

Yarborough Square showcases the works of about 200 artists and craftspeople from the United States and Canada. A large collection of pottery, stoneware, porcelain, raku, metal sculptures, handcrafted jewelry, recycled glass, wrought-iron pieces, and candles are on display. The gallery also represents several painters and numerous craftspeople. It's at 672 Bear Swamp Rd., Peru, (518) 643-7057, and is open daily from 10 a.m. to 6 p.m.

The **Alice T. Miner Museum** was created in 1824 by Mrs. Miner, a pioneer in the colonial revival movement and wife of railroad industrialist and philanthropist William H. Miner. She worked until her death for the next twenty-six years to assemble the collection in the fifteen-room museum. The exhibit includes period pieces of miniature furniture once toted about by traveling salesmen. Look for a large collection of china, porcelain, and glass; War of 1812 muskets; and other objects of early Americana.

The Alice T. Miner Museum, 9618 Main St., Route 9, Chazy (518-846-7336; www.minermuseum.org), is open Tuesday through Saturday 10 a.m. to 4 p.m., with guided tours at 10 a.m., noon, and 2 p.m.; closed December 23 through March; open in April by appointment only. Admission is $3 for adults, $2 for seniors, and $1 for students. School groups are free.

Western Adirondacks, Saint Lawrence Valley, and Thousand Islands

The *Akwesasne Cultural Center* is dedicated to preserving the past, present, and future of the Akwesasne Mohawk people, whose history in the area dates back thousands of years. The museum houses more than 3,000 artifacts and an extensive collection of black-ash splint basketry. It also offers classes in the traditional art forms of basketry, quillwork, and water drums. The library also houses one of the largest Native American collections in northern New York and includes information on indigenous people throughout North America.

Akwesasne Cultural Center, 321 State Route 37, Hogansburg (518-358-2461; www.akwesasneculturalcenter.org), is open Monday through Thursday 8:30 a.m. to 4 p.m., Friday 8:30 a.m. to 3:30 p.m. Call for guided tours. Suggested museum contribution is $2 for adults, $1 for children ages 5 to 16, and children under 5, free.

Horace Greeley famously said, "Go west, young man," and young Frederic Remington followed. Born in 1861 in Ogdensburg, on the St. Lawrence Seaway, Remington quit Yale at the age of nineteen and headed for the wide open spaces. He spent five years traveling, taking in the vistas and the cowboys and the horses that would inspire his paintings and sculpture. By 1885 he was already making his name as an illustrator and artist. When Remington died after an operation in 1909, he was at the peak of his popularity. His widow returned to Ogdensburg and bequeathed the artist's collection of paintings and sculpture to the Ogdensburg Public Library. The collection now forms the *Frederic Remington Art Museum,* housed in the 1810 house where Mrs. Remington lived until her death.

The collection includes bronzes, oil paintings, and hundreds of pen-and-ink sketches by Remington, as well as pictures he collected by his contemporaries, including Charles Dana Gibson and Childe Hassam.

The Frederic Remington Art Museum, 303 Washington St., Ogdensburg (315-393-2425; www.fredericremington.org), is open from May 1 through October 31, Monday through Saturday 10 a.m. to 5 p.m. and Sunday 1 to 5 p.m.; from November 1 to April 30, hours are Wednesday through Saturday

11 a.m. to 5 p.m. and Sunday 1 to 5 p.m. Closed major holidays. Admission is $9 for adults, $8 for senior citizens and students 16 and older, and free for children 15 and under.

Hotel magnate George C. Boldt, who owned the Waldorf-Astoria in New York and the Bellevue-Stratford Hotel in Philadelphia, bought *Heart Island* at the turn of the century from a man named Hart. But that's not what inspired its name. The hotelier physically reshaped the island into the configuration of a heart as a token of devotion to his wife, Louise. He envisioned the entire project to be a monumental expression of his love. And to think most of us would settle for a dozen red roses.

Construction of a six-story castle and numerous outbuildings began in 1900. Boldt hired masons, woodcarvers, landscapers, and other craftspeople from all over the world to execute details ranging from terra-cotta wall inlays and roof tiles to a huge, opalescent glass dome. He planned and erected a smaller castle as a temporary residence and eventual playhouse, and built an underground tunnel for bringing supplies from the docks to the main house. There were bowling alleys, a sauna, and an indoor swimming pool.

Louise Boldt died suddenly in 1904. George Boldt, heartbroken, wired his construction supervisors to stop all work. The walls and roof of the castle were essentially finished, but crated fixtures such as mantels and statuary were left where they stood, and the bustling island fell silent. Boldt never again set foot in his empty castle, on which he had spent $2.5 million.

Boldt died in 1916, and two years later the island and its structures were purchased by Edward J. Noble, the inventor of Life Savers candy. Noble and his heirs ran the deteriorating castle as a tourist attraction until 1977, when it was given to the Thousand Islands Bridge Authority, which has invested millions of dollars in rehabilitation efforts to preserve the historic structure.

Boldt Castle, Heart Island, Alexandria Bay (315-482-2520 or 800-8-ISLAND; www.boldtcastle.com), is accessible via water taxi from the upper and lower docks on James Street in Alexandria Bay, as well as to tour-boat patrons

Lock and Load?

Fifty years ago, the village of Mannsville, 21 miles south of Watertown, was the site of an orphan asylum run by the Klu Klux Klan for some thirty orphaned children of its clan members. The Klan Haven Home occupied an oversized frame house set on 300 acres, where boys trained in agriculture and the girls learned what was then called "domestic science." Presumably, the children also learned a special "Klan" brand of social sciences. It has long since ceased to operate.

departing from both the American and the Canadian shores. The castle is open from May 8 to October 3, Saturday and Sunday 10 a.m. to 6:30 p.m.; July and August, daily 10 a.m. to 7:30 p.m. Occasionally special events have different hours, call ahead. Admission is $7 for adults and $4.50 for children ages 6 to 12. Groups of twenty or more, senior citizens, and military personnel receive a discount. The Yacht House is open from May 15 to October 3 from 10 a.m. to 6:30 p.m. with $4 admission for adults, and $2 children 6 to 12.

The remaining thirty rooms of Hart's original home were erected on Wellesley Island and became the Thousand Islands Country Club, a place for ladies to sit sipping afternoon tea while the men played a round of golf. In later years a newer clubhouse was built across the street, and the Hart House was renamed the Golf Course House.

what's in the water?

The St. Lawrence River is renowned for game fishing. Among the most common: large- and smallmouth bass, Northern pike, yellow perch, and walleye.

In 1994 Rev. Dudley Danielson and his wife, Kathy, bought the now rundown thirty-room club house and have painstakingly converted it into the elegant **Hart House Inn.** Many of the dwelling's original features have been retained and renovated, including a massive pink granite fireplace in the lobby entrance. Each of the five beautifully decorated guest suites has a canopied bed, Italian ceramic tile whirlpool bath, views of the St. Lawrence, and fireplaces. Three rooms and suites in the older wing (open May through October) have private baths; the classic two-room Sunset Suite is perfect for a family of five, with library fireplace, two bedrooms, and deck with a great river view. A multi-course candlelit breakfast is served on the wraparound porch overlooking the golf course (in the winter, it's served in the dining room with a fireplace).

Kathy is the granddaughter of a Hungarian innkeeper and takes great pride in her cooking. Reverend Danielson officiates at many weddings in his Grace Chapel; it also serves as a retreat for quiet contemplation.

The Hart House, 21979 Club Rd., Wellesley Island, 13640 (315-482-LOVE or 888-481-LOVE; www.harthouseinn.com), is open year-round. Rates range from $155 for a classic room midweek to $325 for the stunning Kashmir Garden suite. In winter, two-night packages feature an elegant fireside dinner.

Embrace the sleek mahogany runabouts and graceful skiffs that plied the waters of the Thousand Islands and other Gilded Age resorts at the **Antique Boat Museum** in Clayton. The museum is a freshwater boat-lover's dream, housing some 200 historic small crafts of slender, mirror-finished launches, antique canoes, distinctive St. Lawrence River skiffs, and handmade guideboats.

The Antique Boat Museum takes no sides in the eternal conflict between sailing purists and "stinkpotters," being broad enough in its philosophy to house a fine collection of antique outboard and inboard engines. This includes the oldest outboard known to exist. The one distinction rigidly adhered to pertains to construction material: all of the boats exhibited here are made of wood.

The Antique Boat Museum, 750 Mary St., Clayton 13624 (315-686-4104; www.abm.org), is open from mid-May through mid-October, daily from 9 a.m. to 5 p.m. Admission is $12 for adults, $11 for seniors and AAA members, $10 for college students, $6 for children ages 6 to 17; military personnel and children under 6 free. Special family rates run $30.

When the ***Thousand Islands Inn*** opened in 1897, it was one of more than two dozen hotels serving visitors to the region. Today it is the last of the great hostelries that still offers guests all the amenities of a full-service establishment.

In addition to its distinction as a survivor, the inn has yet another claim to fame: Thousand Island salad dressing was first served to the dining public here in the early 1900s. The tasty dressing was created by Sophia LaLonde for her husband, a guide, to serve to fishing parties as part of their shore dinners. One of his clients, a New York City stage actress named May Irwin, loved the dressing and gave it the name Thousand Island. She also gave the recipe to George C. Boldt, owner of Boldt Castle and New York's Waldorf-Astoria Hotel. He ordered his maître d', Oscar Tschirky, to put it on the hotel menu. But the Thousand Islands Inn had already made it into the record book: LaLonde had also given the recipe to Ella Bertrand, whose family owned the inn, then called the Herald Hotel.

Most of the rooms have a view of the St. Lawrence River and have been restored to re-create the flavor of the late 1800s, but with all modern conveniences. The inn's restaurant is a recipient of the Golden Fork Award of the Gourmet Diners Society of North America. It serves three meals daily.

The Thousand Islands Inn is at 335 Riverside Dr., Clayton (315-686-3030 or 800-544-4241; www.1000-islands.com/inn). Room rates range from $75 to $150. The inn is open from mid-May through mid-September.

Sail to a foreign land with ***Horne's Ferry,*** the only international auto/passenger ferry on the St. Lawrence River, crossing over to Wolfe Island, Ontario, Canada, in just fifteen minutes. The ferry makes hourly crossings from 8 a.m. to 7 p.m. daily from early May through late October. Rates are $13 each way for a car and driver, and $2 for additional passengers or pedestrians. For information write to ferry@kos.net, call (315) 783-0638, or visit www.hornesferry.com.

The only place in the northeastern United States to see prairie smoke, a flower whose feathery plumes expand as it goes to seed, is in ***Chaumont***

Barrens. The unique "alvar" landscape is characterized by a mosaic of austere, windswept vegetation.

Alvar sites lie scattered along an arc from here, through Ontario, to northern Michigan. Scientists hypothesize that the landscapes, distinguished by a linear pattern of vegetation, were formed during the retreat of the last glacier approximately 10,000 years ago. They believe a huge ice dam burst and a torrent swept away all surface debris and dissolved limestone bedrock along cracks and fissures.

The rare combination of extreme conditions at **Chaumont** have created a 2-mile landscape of exposed outcrops, fissures, moss gardens, patches of woods, shrub savannas, and open grasslands.

Chaumont Barrens Preserve, on Van Alstyne Road, Chaumont, is a property of the Nature Conservancy and is open daily from early May through early fall during daylight hours. For information call (585) 546-8030 or visit www .nature.org.

We take for granted the international cooperation exemplified by the St. Lawrence Seaway. Their peaceful coexistence allows pleasure craft to sail unimpeded along the boundary waters of the St. Lawrence River and Lake Ontario. Nearly a century ago, the U.S. Navy kept an active installation at **Sackets Harbor Battlefield,** on Lake Ontario's Black River Bay, in case of a possibility of war with Canada. And during the War of 1812, this small lakeport saw combat between battling American and British forces.

At the time the war began, Sackets Harbor was the site of a busy shipyard and supply depot. Americans launched their attack upon Toronto here in 1813, and a month later the tables were turned when the depleted American garrison at the harbor was beleaguered by a British attack upon the shipyard. The defenders repulsed the attack but lost most of their supplies to fire in the course of the struggle.

Today's visitor to Sackets Harbor can still see many of the facilities of the old naval base, including officers' homes and sites associated with the 1813 battle.

Ski NY

When the first coat of fresh powder falls, so many skiers think about heading for the Green Mountains of Vermont. But there are more than thirty renowned ski resorts to pick from in New York, including the 4,867-foot Whiteface Mountain and the site of two Olympic downhills. This Adirondack State Park peak boasts the greatest vertical drop in the East, a thirteen-acre terrain park, and a 450-foot super half-pipe. Get weather updates and other information on New York ski stations at www.skiandrideny.com.

Sackets Harbor Battlefield State Historic Site, 504 West Main St., Sackets Harbor (315-646-3634; www.sacketsharborbattlefield.org), is open from Memorial Day to Columbus Day and the first two weekends in December from Thursday to Monday 10 a.m. to 5 p.m. and Sunday 1 to 5 p.m. Admission is $3 for adults, $2 for seniors and students, free for children under 12.

Before setting out on the state's only National Scenic Byway, the 454-mile Seaway Trail, stop at the Seaway Trail Discovery Center, housed in a three-story, 1817 limestone, Federal-style former hotel overlooking the lake. The New York State Office of Parks, Recreation and Preservation opened the facility to provide a "windshield" overview of the trail and its unique characteristics. Nine rooms of exhibits highlight the area's natural history, recreation, agriculture, people, architecture, and maritime history.

The *Seaway Trail Discovery Center,* Ray and West Main Streets, Sackets Harbor (800-SEAWAY-T; www.seawaytrail.com/discoverycenter.asp), is open year-round: daily May through October from 10 a.m. to 5 p.m.; November through April, Tuesday through Saturday from 10 a.m. to 5 p.m. Admission is $4 for adults, $3 for AAA members and seniors, and $2 for children.

The *American Maple Museum and Hall of Fame* is dedicated to preserving the history and evolution of the North American maple syrup industry with three floors of antique sugaring equipment, logging tools, and artifacts. There are replicas of a sugarhouse and a lumber camp kitchen, and a Hall of Fame. The museum hosts three all-you-can-eat pancake breakfast fundraisers a year—in February, May, and September.. There is also an ice cream social around July 1, with entertainment and maple treats and a Maple Weekend in mid-March. In December, satisfy your sweet tooth with "Christmas in Croghan," with hot chocolate and maple cream on crackers. Call for dates.

The American Maple Museum and Hall of Fame, Main Street, Route 812, Croghan (315-346-1107; www.lcida.org/maplemuseum.html), is open Friday, Saturday, and Monday, 11 a.m. to 4 p.m. from Memorial Day to June 30; daily except Sunday, 11 a.m. to 4 p.m. from July 1 to early September. Admission is $4 for adults; $1 for children 5 to 14; $10 per family (two adults with two or more children for a max of 10 people total).

The *North American Fiddler's Hall of Fame & Museum* preserves, perpetuates, and promotes the art of fiddling and the dances pertaining to the art. Dedicated to "each and every fiddler who ever made hearts light and happy with his lilting music," the museum displays artifacts and collects tapes of fiddlers. Since its inception in 1976, it has inducted a new member (or members) into its Hall of Fame each year. The museum, across from Cedar Pines Restaurant, Motel, and Campground in Osceola, is open part-time on Sunday from 1 to 5 p.m. from Memorial Day through the first Sunday in October (except for the third weekend in September), during major events, and by appointment. Appointments are strongly encouraged, as hours can vary. For information call (315) 599-7009 or visit www.nysotfa.com.

In the latter part of the nineteenth century, Joseph and John Moser emigrated from Alsace-Lorraine to Kirschnerville. They cleared a plot of land, built a dwelling, purchased farm animals, and brought the rest of their family from overseas. The Mosers were Mennonites, and three generations lived and worshiped here until the 1980s, when the farm was purchased by a group who wanted it to be preserved as a living history of the life and faith of the area's settlers.

Today the **Mennonite Heritage Farm,** under the auspices of the Adirondack Mennonite Heritage Association, tells of the life of the early Amish-Mennonite settlers. A Worship Room showcases the original benches used for meetings held in homes on a rotational basis until 1912, when the Croghan Mennonite Church was built. There are also a number of outbuildings, including a granary with a display of early tools and equipment.

On the first Saturday of July, the farm holds a special, day-long Zwanzigstein Fest featuring traditional Mennonite foods and crafts, a petting zoo, bread and butter and ice-cream making demonstrations, and horse-pulled wagon rides. The highlight of the day is the mini-auction of quilts, "comforts," and antiques.

The Mennonite Heritage Farm, Erie Canal Road, Croghan (315-346-1122; off-season, 315-853-6879 or 315-376-8502; www.sites.google.com/sites/amhahs), is open varying hours during July and August, or by appointment. Admission is charged only for the fest, but donations are gratefully accepted at any time.

The man who built **Constable Hall** was presented with a rather generous birthright of four million acres of Adirondack wilderness. His father, William Constable Sr., purchased the property with two other New York City capitalist real-estate speculators and ultimately became the principal owner and chief developer. He sold large tracts to European and American land companies and families from New England and launched the settlement of the north country. In 1819 William Constable Jr. built a Georgian mansion patterned on

needforcheese

Lowville is the world's largest cream cheese manufacturing plant at Kraft Foods and is host to the annual **Cream Cheese Festival.** Guests are entertained by Cream Cheese Bigo, Cream Cheese Toss, Cream Cheese Mural painting, and a milk-the-cow contest. The World's Biggest Cream Cheese Cake is also on hand to feed the masses. Visit www.creamcheese festival.com for more information.

a family-owned estate in Ireland, and five generations of the Constable family lived there until 1947, when the house became a museum. The original deed is just one of the family mementos displayed at the home, which still has many of its original furnishings.

Constable Hall, Constableville (315-397-2323; constablehall.org), is open daily except Monday from the end of May through September. Hours are Wednesday through Saturday 10 a.m. to 4 p.m., and Sunday 1 to 4 p.m. Admission is $5 for adults and $3 for children.

There are barely a dozen lighthouses in North America where visitors can stay overnight, including **Selkirk Lighthouse.** It was built in 1838 on Lake Ontario at the mouth of the Salmon River and is listed on the National Register of Historic Places. The lighthouse is heated, has four bedrooms (two single and four double beds), a kitchen, living room, bathroom, and color cable TV with HBO. The lighthouse can be rented from April through early December and sleeps up to ten people; rates are from $155 (Sunday to Thursday) to $195 (Friday and Saturday). The lighthouse is part of a five-acre compound that includes a charter fishing fleet, cabins, boat rentals, and a launch ramp.

For information contact Salmon River Lighthouse Marina, 6 Lake Rd. extension, Pulaski 13142; (315) 298-6688; www.cashtonscreations.homestead.com.

Just north of Utica in the foothills of the Adirondacks, you'll find **Steuben Memorial State Historic Site.** Frederick von Steuben was a Prussian officer who emigrated to the United States in 1777 at the age of 47 to help drill the soldiers of the Continental Army. His first assignment was a challenging one. He was sent to the American winter encampment at Valley Forge, where morale was flagging and discipline was practically nonexistent in the face of elemental hardship such as hunger and bitter cold.

Von Steuben got his troops marching in file, practicing classic military drill, and fighting effectively with the eighteenth-century frontline weapon of choice, the bayonet. The German émigré even found time to write a masterful treatise on military training, *Regulations for the Order and Discipline of the Troops of the United States*.

Having served as inspector general of the Continental Army until the end of the war, von Steuben was richly rewarded by the nation of which he had lately become a citizen. Among his other rewards was a New York State grant of 16,000 acres of land. Allowed to pick his own site, he chose the area partially occupied today by the Steuben Memorial State Historic Site and built a simple two-room log house.

In 1936 the state erected a replica of von Steuben's house on a site located within the fifty acres it had recently purchased as his memorial. The drillmaster is buried beneath an imposing monument not far from here, despite his wish that he lie in an unmarked grave. The cabin is open to visitors, and historical interpretations reflecting the military life of the Revolutionary War soldier are held at the memorial. Staff members are available to discuss the baron's life.

The Steuben Memorial State Historic Site, Starr Hill Road, Remsen (315-768-7224; www.nysparks.state.ny.us/historic-sites), is open from mid-May to Labor Day, Wednesday through Saturday and Monday holidays 10 a.m. to 5 p.m., Sunday 1 to 5 p.m. Guided tours are available; call ahead. Admission is free; special events charge a nominal fee.

Places to Stay in the Adirondacks

ALEXANDRIA BAY

The Edgewood Resort
22467 Edgewood Rd.
(315) 482-9923
www.theedgewoodresort
.com

GLENS FALLS

Glens Falls Inn
25 Sherman Ave.
(646) 824-8379
www.glensfallsinn.com

KEENE

Bark Eater Inn
124 Alstead Hill Lane
(866) 603-3245
www.barkeater.com

LAKE LUZERNE

The Lamplight Inn
231 Lake Ave.
(800) 262-4668
www.lamplightinn.com

LAKE PLACID

Golden Arrow Lakeside Resort
150 Main St.
(800) 582-5540 or
(518) 523-3353
www.golden-arrow.com

High Peaks Resort
2384 Saranac Ave.
Lake Placid
(800) 755-5598 or
(518) 523-4411
www.highpeaksresort.com

NORTH CREEK

Copperfield Inn
307 Main St.
(877) 235-1466
www.copperfieldinn.com

ROCK CITY FALLS

The Mansion
801 Route 29
(518) 885-1607 or
(888) 996-9977
www.themansionsaratoga
.com

SARANAC LAKE

Hotel Saranac of Paul Smiths College
100 Main St.
(800) 937-0211 or
(518) 891-2200
www.hotelsaranac.com

SARATOGA SPRINGS

Adelphi Hotel
346 Broadway
(518) 587-4688
www.adelphihotel.com

Batcheller Mansion Inn
20 Circular St.
(800) 616-7012 or
(518) 584-7012
www.batchellermansioninn
.com

WARRENSBURG

Merrill Magee House
3 Hudson St.
(518) 623-2449
www.merrillmageehouse
.com

Seasons Bed and Breakfast
3822 Main St.
Warrensburg
(518) 623-3832
www.Seasons-bandb.com

WELLESLEY ISLAND

Hart House Inn Bed and Breakfast
21979 Club Rd.
Wellesley Island
(888) 481-LOVE (5683)
www.harthouseinn.com

Adirondacks Regional Information
(800) 487-6867 or (518) 846-8016
www.adk.com

Lake George Regional Chamber of Commerce
P.O. Box 272
Lake George
(518) 668-5755 or (800) 705-0059
www.lakegeorgechamber.com

Lake Placid/Essex County Visitors Center
49 Parkside Dr.
Lake Placid
(800) 44-PLACID or (518) 523-2445
www.lakeplacid.com

The 1,000 Islands Welcome Center
43373 Collins Landing
Alexandria Bay
(800) 847-5263 or (315) 482-2520
www.visit1000islands.com

Plattsburgh–North Country–Lake Champlain Regional Visitors Center
7061 Route 9
Plattsburgh
(518) 563-1000
www.northcountrychamber.com

Saranac Lake Chamber of Commerce
39 Main St.
Saranac Lake
(800) 347-1992
www.saranaclake.com

Saratoga Convention and Tourism Bureau
60 Railroad Place
Saratoga Springs
(518) 584-1531
www.discoversaratoga.com

Saratoga County Chamber of Commerce
28 Clinton St.
Saratoga Springs
(518) 584-3255
www.saratoga.org

Town of Webb Visitor Center
P.O. Box 68
3140 State Route 28
Old Forge 13420
(315) 369-6983
www.oldforgeny.com

Urban Heritage Area Visitors Center
297 Broadway
Saratoga Springs
(518) 587-3241
www.saratoga.org

Warren County Tourism Municipal Center
1340 State Route 9
Lake George
800-95-VISIT
www.visitlakegeorge.com

Whiteface Mountain Regional Visitors Bureau
P.O. Box 277
Whiteface Mountain 12997
(518) 946-2255 or (888) WHITEFACE
www.whitefaceregion.com

Places to Eat in the Adirondacks

ALEXANDRIA BAY

Captain Thomson's
45 James St.
(315) 482-9961 or
800-ALEX BAY
www.captthomsons.com

LAKE LUZERNE

Waterhouse Restaurant
85 Lake Ave.
(518) 696-3115

LAKE PLACID

Averil Conwell Dining Room
5 Mirror Lake Dr.
(518) 523-2544

Great Adirondack Steak and Seafood Company
34 Main St.
(518) 523-1629
www.greatadirondack
steakandseafood.com

MAYFIELD

Lanzi's on the Lake
Route 30
(518) 661-7711

Olde Bryan Inn
123 Maple Ave.
(518) 587-2990
www.oldebryaninn.com

WHITEHALL

Finch and Chubb
82 North Williams St.
(518) 499-2049
www.visitwhitehall.com

OTHER ATTRACTIONS WORTH SEEING IN THE ADIRONDACKS

Akwesasne Mohawk Casino
873 State Route 37
Hogansburg
(518) 358-2222 or (877) 99-CASINO
www.mohawkcasino.com

Almanzo Wilder Farm
Stacy Road Burke
(518) 483-1207
www.almanzowilderfarm.com

Ausable Chasm
Route 9
Ausable Chasm
(866) RV-CHASM
www.ausablechasm.com

Enchanted Forest/Water Safari
3183 Route 38
Old Forge
(315) 369-6145
www.watersafari.com

Gore Mountain
Peaceful Valley Road
North Creek
(518) 251-2411 or (800) 342-1234
www.goremountain.com

High Falls Gorge
Route 86, Wilmington Notch
Wilmington
(518) 946-2278
www.highfallsgorge.com

Natural Stone Bridge and Caves
535 Stone Bridge Rd.
Pottersville
(518) 494-2283
www.stonebridgeandcaves.com

Plattsburgh State Art Museum
SUNY, 101 Broad St.
Plattsburgh
(518) 564-2474
organizations.plattsburgh.edu/museum/

THE MOHAWK VALLEY

The Mohawk Valley has long been an integral artery between the East Coast and the Great Lakes, and countless Americans have passed through here via Indian trails, the Erie Canal, Commodore Vanderbilt's "Water Level Route" of the New York Central railroad, and today's New York State Thruway. Here Jesuit missionaries met their end at the hands of the Iroquois, James Fenimore Cooper's Deerslayer stalked, and homesteaders struck out for the Midwest along a water-filled ditch, in barges pulled by draft animals. Surely, this is one of the most storied corridors of the republic.

Along the way, people settled towns and made guns in Ilion, pots and pans in Rome, and gloves in Gloversville. But much of this gently rolling country is still left to agriculture.

This chapter begins in Albany and heads west to Syracuse, loosely following the route of the Mohawk River as well as the New York State Thruway.

Capital Region

The capital of the Empire State, **Albany** encompasses all the trappings of a government seat with posh homes and

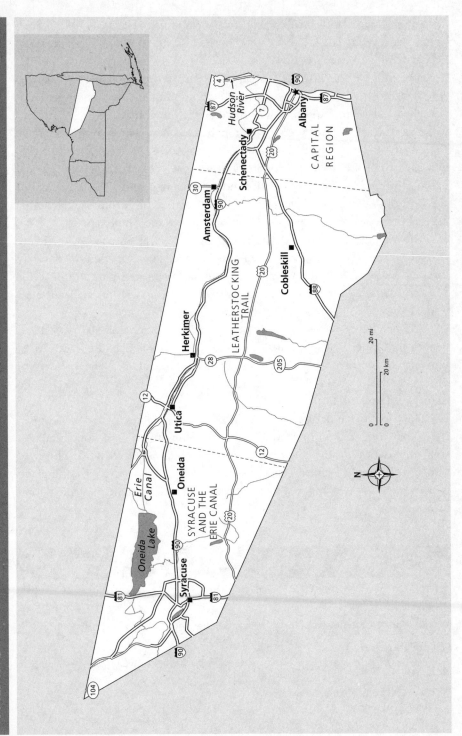

LEATHERSTOCKING TRAIL

SYRACUSE AND THE ERIE CANAL

Hudson River

Erie Canal

Oneida Lake

CAPITAL REGION

Albany

Schenectady

Amsterdam

Cobleskill

Herkimer

Utica

Oneida

Syracuse

20 mi

20 km

N

restaurants, traffic, and ornate architecture including the State Capitol building, partly designed by H. H. Richardson. There's also the four monolithic, marble-clad state office towers so closely associated with the grandiose visions of the late governor Nelson Rockefeller. But visit the *Albany Institute of History and Art* to discover the art, history, and culture of Albany and the upper Hudson River Valley from the seventeenth century to the present.

The Hudson River School is well represented here with works by painters Cole, Durand, and Cropsey and a collection of early Hudson Valley furniture and silver. But the institute exhibits fine examples of an even older regional genre, portraits of the seventeenth- and eighteenth-century Dutch settlers of the Hudson Valley. These pictures echo the Dutch genre paintings that left us a detailed record of the comforts of burgher life in the Netherlands.

The Albany Institute of History and Art, 125 Washington Ave., Albany (518-463-4478; www.nysparks.state.ny.us/historic-sites), is open Wednesday through Saturday 10 a.m. to 5 p.m. and Sunday noon to 5 p.m. Admission is $10 for adults, $8 for senior citizens and students, and $6 for children ages 6 to 12.

The Schuylers were among the earliest of the Dutch colonial period settlers of the upper Hudson Valley involved in trading, agriculture, land development, and local politics. The most renowned member of the family was Philip Schuyler (1733–1804), whose manorial home is today preserved as the *Schuyler Mansion State Historic Site.*

Philip Schuyler designed the elegant mansion himself in the Georgian style, with rose-colored brick walls, graceful fenestration, and double-hipped roof (the awkward hexagonal brick entry vestibule is an 1818 addition). He furnished it largely with purchases he made during a 1761–62 trip to England and today it houses an excellent collection of colonial and Federal period furnishings.

AUTHOR'S FAVORITES—MOHAWK VALLEY

Children's Museum	Remington Arms Museum
Fort Klock Historic Restoration	Schoharie Crossing State Historic Site
Iroquois Indian Museum	
Mid-Lakes Navigation Company, Ltd.	Walter Elwood Museum
The Petrified Creatures Museum of Natural History	

Top Dog

On top of the Arnoff Moving and Storage Company, you can see the world's largest RCA Nipper dog standing proudly. The building was once the tallest in Albany and Nipper was perched wearing an aircraft beacon on his right ear to warn incoming aircraft. Nipper has been hanging out on the same roof since 1954, when it was the RTA Corporation building on Broadway. In February, Nipper glows in a hue of red lights as a nod to an American Heart Association promotion. To see him, drive south on I-787 to Clinton Avenue exit, turn right and head north on Broadway and look for Nipper on your right just past Miss Albany Diner.

After Schuyler died in 1804, this architectural gem was sold and used as an orphanage before being acquired by the state in 1912.

The Schuyler Mansion State Historic Site, 32 Catherine St., Albany (518-434-0834; www.nysparks.state.ny.us/historic-sites), is open mid-May through October, Wednesday through Sunday 11 a.m. to 5 p.m., last tour 4 p.m.; November through mid-May by appointment. Also open on Memorial Day, Independence Day, and Labor Day. Admission is $4 for adults, $3 for senior citizens and students, children 12 and under, free.

In 1774 Mother Ann Lee, founder of the Shakers, left England with a small band of followers and came to New York City. A few years later the group established the country's first *Shaker settlement* in a town named Watervliet (now part of the town of *Colonie*).

Today the *Shaker Heritage Society* maintains a memorial to this historic settlement. Among the points of interest are a garden with some one hundred varieties of herbs (one of the early Shakers' major trade crops), the Ann Lee Pond nature preserve, and the Shaker Cemetery, where Lee and many of her followers are buried. The museum and gift shop are located in the 1848 Shaker Meeting House, on the grounds of the Ann Lee Home.

The Shaker Heritage Society, Albany Shaker Road, Albany (518-456-7890; www.shakerheritage.org), is open February to October Tuesday through Saturday 9:30 a.m. to 4 p.m.; November and December Monday through Saturday 10 a.m. to 4 p.m.; closed during January. Guided tours are $3 per person, children under 12 are free. Admission is free, but donations are accepted.

Philip Schuyler dreamed of developing a canal and lock system in New York state. It wasn't untilthree decades after his death that canal building really hit its stride in the United States, turning formerly sleepy villages into canal boomtowns involved in the lucrative trade between New York City and points

ANNUAL EVENTS IN THE MOHAWK VALLEY

FEBRUARY

Annual Colonial Dinner
Schenectady
(518) 374-0263
www.schist.org

APRIL

Proctor's Annual Laughter Arts Festival
Schenectady
(518) 382-3884
www.proctors.org

MAY

Tulip Festival
Albany
(518) 434-2032
www.albanyevents.org

JUNE

A Taste of Syracuse
Downtown Syracuse
www.downtownsyracuse.com

Annual Hall of Fame Game
Cooperstown
(888) HALL-OF-FAME
www.baseballhalloffame.org

Old Songs Festival of Traditional Music
Altamont
(518) 765-2815
www.oldsongs.org

JULY

Baseball Hall of Fame Induction
Cooperstown
(888) HALL-OF-FAME
www.baseballhalloffame.org

Empire State Games
Albany
(518) 474-8889
www.empirestategames.org

Glimmerglass Opera
Cooperstown
(607) 547-2255
www.glimmerglass.org

New York State Rhythm and Blues Festival
Syracuse
www.nysbluesfest.com

Syracuse Arts and Crafts Festival
Syracuse
(315) 422-8284
www.syracuseartsandcraftsfestival.com

AUGUST

The Great New York State Fair
Syracuse
(800) 475-FAIR or (315) 487-7711
www.nysfair.org

OCTOBER

Halloween at Howe Caverns
Howes Cave
(518) 296-8900
www.howecaverns.com

Lafayette Apple Festival
Cicero
www.lafayetteapplefest.org

NOVEMBER

Christmas Parade
Schenectady
(518) 372-5656

DECEMBER

First Night
Albany
(518) 434-2032

Holiday Festival of Trees
Syracuse
(315) 474-6064
www.albanyinstitute.org

west. Among the towns is *Waterford,* located near Cohoes just upriver from Albany.

Founded by the Dutch as Halfmoon Point in the early 1620s at the confluence of the Mohawk and Hudson rivers, Waterford was incorporated under its present name in 1794 and is today the oldest incorporated village in the United States. In 1799 it became the head of sloop navigation on the Hudson, but its glory days of commerce came in the 1820s, when the new Champlain and Erie canals made the town an important waystation on a statewide transportation system.

Waterford prospered as a small manufacturing center during the nineteenth century, but it wasn't long before the railroads superseded the canal system. The legacy of this era is the village's lovely residential architecture, much of it in the regionally significant "Waterford" style characterized by Federal details and Dutch-inspired single-step gables. Such architectural distinctions have earned the village center inclusion on the National Register of Historic Places. The historic district is the subject of tours given during "Canalfest" the second Saturday of May each year. It features boat rides, hayrides, a boat show, a craft fair, food, and entertainment.

shortandsteamy

The country's first railroad, with an 11-mile track, ran between Albany and Schenectady.

From April through October in the village center at Erie Canal Lock 2, a series of outdoor exhibits details the history of the 1823 canal and the present-day barge canal.

Waterford attractions outside the village center include the *Champlain Canal,* this section of which was dug in 1823 and is still filled with water; the *Waterford Flight,* a series of five locks on the still-operating New York State Barge Canal, whose 169-foot total rise is the highest in the world; a state park at Lock 6; and *Peebles Island State Park. Waterford Historical Museum and Cultural Center,* 2 Museum Lane (off Saratoga Avenue), Waterford (518-238-0809; www.waterfordmuseum.com), is open from May 15 through October 1, Wednesday through Friday from 11 a.m. to 2 p.m., Saturday from 10 a.m. to 4 p.m., and Sunday from 2 to 4 p.m.; October 2 through October 24, Saturday and Sunday 2 to 4 p.m.; closed holiday weekends. Hours vary each year; check the Web site or call for details. Admission is free.

Leatherstocking Trail

The *Walter Elwood Museum* of the Mohawk Valley, located in a former school, offers an overview of the area's diverse history as well as an eclectic

Leatherstocking Legacy

The leather leggings worn by Yankees who settled in this area gave birth to the region's nickname, the Leatherstocking Trail. James Fenimore Cooper immortalized the name in his *Leatherstocking Tales,* which recounted the adventures of wilderness scout Natty Bumppo. Cooper is buried in the family plot in Cooperstown's Christ Church cemetery.

collection of historical and natural objects. Among its 20,000 artifacts, the fossilized footprint of a Tyrannosaurus rex, the earliest television set (on permanent loan from the Edison Museum in Menlo Park, New Jersey), and an exhibit depicting life in the Victorian era complete with a life-size home with four furnished rooms.

One of the few museums in the country owned by a public school, it is named for a local teacher who opened a museum and bird sanctuary in 1940 so students could study nature and wildlife.

The Walter Elwood Museum of the Mohawk Valley, 366 West Main St., Route 5, Amsterdam (518-843-5151; walterelwoodmuseum.org), is open Monday through Friday from 9 a.m. to 4 p.m., evenings and weekends by appointment. Admission runs $4 adults, $2 seniors, and children 12 and under free.

The Erie Canal and the feats of engineering that its building entailed are the focus of *Schoharie Crossing State Historic Site,* farther up the Mohawk, at Fort Hunter. Seven canal-related structures dating from three periods of the waterway's construction or expansion are preserved here and provided with interpretive displays that explain their use. The visitor center has an exhibit on the Erie Canal and information on the site and surrounding area. *Putnam's Canal Store,* at Yankee Hill Lock 28 on Queen Anne's Road (2.2 miles east of the visitor center), was built during the 1850s and served as a store along the enlarged Erie Canal for many years. It now houses an exhibit on Erie Canal stores.

Along the old canal towpath are views of modern-day barge traffic on the Mohawk River, the depth of which in this area allows it to be used as a link in the New York State barge canal system.

Schoharie Crossing State Historic Site, 129 Schoharie St., Fort Hunter (518-829-7516; www.nysparks.state.ny.us/historic-sites), is open May through October 31 and Memorial Day, Independence Day, and Labor Day, Wednesday through Saturday 10 a.m. to 5 p.m. and Sunday 1 to 5 p.m. The grounds are open all year during daylight hours. Admission is $3 per person.

Buried in the depths of Cobleskill lies a network of **Secret Caverns.** Most of the caverns were formed during the last ice age when waterfalls poured off melting glaciers and burrowed glacial potholes into the ground. As the potholes scattered across crevices in bedrock, the acidity from the melting water wore down the rock and left behind a maze of hidden caverns.

More recently, in 1928, a rural farmer named Leon Lawton lost two cows on the property. They were seen trying to escape the heat and found a cool breeze in the woods. The cows, Lucky and Floyd, were drawn to the cool relief and nosed their way into the Secret Caverns before plummeting to the cavern floor 85 feet deep. A local civil engineer, Roger Mallery, heard about the discovery and organized five local teenagers with a spelunking hobby. After climbing down 85 feet on a rope, they had to crawl on their stomachs for 200 feet in 42 degree water and mud to get to a standing area. This is where they discovered the 100-foot underground waterfall. Mallery promptly bought the land and in 1929 opened the caves to the public for 40 cents a trip. Back then the 40 cent admission fee got you 100 feet of rope, a helmet, a flashlight, and a bag lunch before being sent out on your four-hour, unguided tour. Stairways and walkways eventually followed before cement steps were constructed.

Today guests travel down the stairs into a cavern of Coeymans and Manlius limestone. You can see where the rock physically began transitioning from the period of lower Devonian Age to upper Silurian Age. Look for the line of changing rock, dubbed "the line of cleavage." Fossils are tucked into the walls of the cavern; keep an eye out for them during your descent or ask your guide to point one out. Look up to see golden calcite "icicles" called stalactites.

Tours depart from Secret Caverns' Lodge about every 15 to 20 minutes from 9 a.m. to 6:30 p.m. in April and May and again from September through November from 10 a.m. to 4:30 p.m. Tours last approximately 30 minutes. Adult admission (16 and older) is $16, children 6 to 15 are $8, and children 5 and under are free. Strollers are not permitted and "frontpacks" are permitted with extreme caution. Wear comfortable shoes and a sweatshirt, the caves are around 50 degrees even on a hot summer day. Appointments are strongly encouraged by calling (518) 296-8558. Visit www.secretcaverns.com for more information.

Long before there were canals or barges in this part of New York State, the waters of the Mohawk and its tributaries carried the canoes of the Iroquois. The Mohawk Valley was the heart of the empire of the Five Nations, one of which was the Mohawk. In present-day Auriesville stood the palisaded village of Mohawk longhouses called Ossernenon in the seventeenth century. In 1642, a raiding party of Indians returned with three French and twenty Huron captives in custody. Among the French were a Jesuit priest, Isaac Jogues, and his lay assistant, René Goupil.

Goupil was tomahawked to death when his attempt to teach a child the sign of the cross was interpreted as the casting of an evil spell. Jogues was rescued by the Dutch during a Mohawk trading foray to Fort Orange, and he returned to Europe and eventually Quebec. But he volunteered to go back to Ossernenon in May 1646, as part of a group attempting to ratify a peace treaty with the Mohawks, and was captured near the village by a faction of the tribe favoring a continuation of hostilities. Both he and a lay companion, Jean Lalande, were killed by tomahawk-wielding braves in October of that year. Canonized by the Roman Catholic Church in 1930 along with five Jesuit missionaries martyred in Canada, Jogues, Goupil, and Lalande are honored at the **National Shrine of the North American Martyrs** in Auriesville.

The shrine, which occupies the hilltop site of the original Mohawk village of Ossernenon amid 600 verdant acres, is maintained by the New York Province of the Society of Jesus, the same Jesuit order to which Isaac Jogues belonged. Founded in 1885, the shrine welcomes 40,000 to 50,000 visitors each year during a season lasting from the first Sunday in May to the last Sunday in October. Mass is celebrated in the vast "Coliseum," the central altar of which is built to suggest the palisades of a Mohawk village; there are also a Martyrs' Museum, rustic chapels, and a retreat house.

For information on the schedule of observances at the National Shrine of the North American Martyrs, 136 Shrine Rd., Auriesville, call (518) 853-3033 or visit www.martyrshrine.org. Hours change during the year, call ahead for an updated calendar.

fittingfamous fingers

Daniel Storto (www.danielstorto gloves.com) is the last of a breed—he's the only custom glove maker left in Gloversville. Settling in the one-time glove capital of America in 2002, Storto set up shop to carry on his business of handcrafting gloves for clients such as Whoopi Goldberg, Diane Keaton, and Madonna.

The **National Shrine of Blessed Kateri Tekakwitha,** off Route 5, Fonda (518-853-3646; www.katerishrine .com), is open daily from 9 a.m. to 6 p.m. Admission is free.

Just north of Fonda and nearby Johnstown lies **Gloversville,** home of the **Fulton County Historical Society & Museum.** Gloversville was originally called Kingsborough, but the townspeople adopted the present name in 1828 in homage to the linchpin of the local economy in those days—tanning and glove making. The glove industry provides the Fulton County Museum with its most interesting exhibits, housed in the Glove and Leather Room. Visitors can peruse the state's only glove-manufacturing display, a complete small glove factory of the last century, donated to the museum and reassembled in its original working format.

There is also a Weaving Room, where craftspeople demonstrate the technique of turning raw flax into the finished product; an Old Country Kitchen; a nineteenth-century Lady's Room, complete with costumes and cosmetics; a Country Store; an old-time Candy Store; an Early Farm display; and a Country Schoolroom. Be sure not to miss the Indian Artifact exhibit on the first floor.

The Fulton County Historical Society & Museum, 237 Kingsboro Ave., Gloversville (518-725-2203; fultoncountymuseum.com), is open May, June, and September, Tuesday through Saturday noon to 4 p.m. and Sunday 10 a.m. to 4 p.m.; July and August, Tuesday through Saturday 10 a.m. to 4 p.m. Admission is free; however, donations are appreciated.

Fate plays a capricious hand in deciding which industries a town will be noted for. Gloversville got gloves; *Canajoharie,* our next stop along the Mohawk, got chewing gum. Town native Bartlett Arkell was president of the Beech-Nut Packing Company in the 1920s. Because of Arkell and his success in business, Canajoharie also came into possession of the finest independent art gallery of any municipality its size in the United States: the *Canajoharie Library and Arkell Museum at Canajoharie.*

Arkell's beneficence to his hometown began with his donation of a new library in 1924. Two years later he donated the funds to build an art gallery wing on the library, and over the next few years he gave the community the magnificent collection of paintings that forms the bulk of the gallery's present holdings. Subsequent additions were made in 1964 and 1989.

This institution has evolved into more than just an art gallery with a library attached, but an art gallery with a small town attached. The roster of American painters exhibited here is astounding and completely out of scale with what you would expect at a thruway exit between Albany and Utica. The Hudson River School is represented by Albert Bierstadt (*El Capitan*), John Kensett, and Thomas Doughty. There is a Gilbert Stuart portrait of George Washington. The Winslow Homer collection is the third largest in the United States. The eighteenth century is represented by John Singleton Copley; the nineteenth, by such luminaries as Thomas Eakins, George Inness (*Rainbow*), and James McNeill Whistler (*On the Thames*). Among twentieth-century painters are Charles Burchfield, Reginald Marsh, N. C. Wyeth and his son Andrew (*February 2nd*), Edward Hopper, Thomas Hart Benton, and even Grandma Moses. There is also a Frederic Remington bronze, *Bronco Buster.* Add a collection of eighty Korean and Japanese ceramics, the gift of the late Colonel John Fox, and you have all the more reason—as if more were needed—to regard Canajoharie as a destination in itself rather than a stop along the way.

Admission to the Canajoharie Library and Arkell Museum at Canajoharie, 2 Erie Blvd., Canajoharie (518-673-2314; www.clag.org, arkellmuseum.org), is $7 for adults, $5 for students and seniors, children 11 and under, free. Hours vary throughout the year; call ahead for details.

Life was tough in the Mohawk Valley in 1750, when Johannes Klock built the farmhouse-fortress preserved today as the *Fort Klock Historic Restoration.* Located above the river at St. Johnsville, Fort Klock is a reminder that defensible stout-walled outposts were not unique to the "Wild West" of the late 1800s; in 1750 the Mohawk Valley was the Wild West.

Like his neighbors scattered along the river, Johannes Klock engaged in fur trading and farming. Canoes and bateaux could be tied up in the cove just below the house, yet the building itself stood on high enough ground and at a sufficient distance from the river to make it easily defensible should the waters of the Mohawk bring foes rather than friendly traders. The stone walls of Fort Klock are almost 2 feet thick and are dotted with "loopholes" that enabled inhabitants to fire muskets from protected positions within.

Fort Klock and its outbuildings, including a restored Dutch barn, are now restored and protected as a registered National Historic Landmark. They tell a substantial part of the story of the Mohawk Valley in the eighteenth century during a time when the hardships of homesteading were made even more difficult by the constant threat of the musket, the tomahawk, and the torch. The homesteaders may have gotten their wish that such threats are today nonexistent, however, probably did not anticipate the severity of their replacements.

Fort Klock Historic Restoration, Route 5, St. Johnsville (518-568-7779; www.fortklockrestoration.org), is open from Memorial Day through mid-October, Tuesday through Sunday 9 a.m. to 5 p.m. Admission is $3 for adults, $1 for children over 5.

The *Iroquois Indian Museum* details the history of the Iroquois Confederacy, but it also specializes in researching the pre-Revolutionary Schoharie Mohawk who lived here. The museum's discovery of a 9,600-year-old Mohawk site is an important part of its archaeological exhibits.

The museum traces the history of the Mohawk and other nations of the Confederacy. The main building at the museum resembles an Iroquois longhouse, and visitors explore the museum in a counterclockwise direction, in the same way that longhouse dancers move.

Two log homes at the edge of the museum's forty-five-acre nature park were moved from Canada's largest Iroquois community, the Six Nations

Reserve. A Children's Iroquois Museum on the ground floor utilizes a hands-on approach to help interpret the adult museum for children.

The Iroquois Indian Museum, 324 Caverns Rd., Howes Cave (518-296-8949; www.iroquoismuseum.org), is open daily from July 1 through Labor Day weekend, Monday through Saturday 10 a.m. to 5 p.m. and Sunday noon to 5 p.m.; April, May, June, and Labor Day through December, open Tuesday through Saturday 10 a.m. to 5 p.m. and Sunday noon to 5 p.m. It is closed January through March, December 24 and 25, Easter, and Thanksgiving. Admission is $8 for adults, $6.50 for senior citizens and students ages 13 to 17, and $5 for children ages 5 to 12.

Anyone craving milk shakes and ice-cream sundaes served up at an authentic, old-fashioned soda fountain head to the ***Historic Throop Drug-store.*** It is the oldest store in Schoharie County, and dates back to the 1800s.

The pharmacy is owned by David and Sarah Goodrich. David, a registered pharmacist, is also a history buff. The couple meticulously restored the pharmacy to look much as Throop's did in the 1920s and 1930s, with antique druggists' bottles, old issues of *Life* magazine, and old-time ice-cream parlor chairs, where you can savor freshly baked Danish, homemade soups, or your favorite frozen confection.

Historic Throop Drugstore, Main Street, Schoharie, (518) 295-7300, is open Monday through Friday 8:30 a.m. to 5:30 p.m.; Saturday the pharmacy is open from 9 a.m. to noon, and the soda fountain is open to "whenever"; closed Sunday.

Renovating a building takes painstaking effort; restoring an entire section of a town is a formidable undertaking. The erstwhile resort community of ***Sharon Springs,*** whose waters were said to equal those of Germany's Baden-Baden in therapeutic value, thrived in the mid- to late-1800s when people came seeking cures for everything from "malarial difficulties" to "biliary derangements."

Don't miss the self-guided Historic Main Street Tour. Twenty plaques lining both sides of the historic district depict the village's golden era with stories, architectural facts, diary excerpts from the 1860s, and hundreds of photos from the nineteenth century.

Although in far fewer numbers, people still come to Sharon Springs for the waters. They drink the sulfurous brew at the octagonal beaux-arts White Sulphur Temple and have a facial splash in Blue Stone Spring, once used extensively as a "lotion for inflammatory conditions of the eye." In July and August, bathers can also soak in the original tubs of the Imperial Baths. Each summer, the Sharon Springs Citizens Council of the Arts hosts a free Wednesday evening music and theater series in Chalybeate Park. During the summer, from 2 to 4 p.m. daily, the Sharon Historical Society opens its museum in a restored 1860 schoolhouse on Main Street. Be sure to sign the guest wall at the fourteen-room Cobbler & Company (518-284-2067) on Main Street, a combination museum/gift shop, which sells everything from English china to penny candy.

For information on Sharon Springs, visit www.sharonsprings.com.

Just out of town, *Clausen Farms* (Route 20, P.O. Box 395, Sharon Springs 13459, 518-284-2527; www.reu.com/clausen), an eighty-acre Victorian estate and llama farm, has four guest rooms in the main house, which dates to the late 1700s (open year-round) and seven in the Casino, a Victorian gentleman's guesthouse completed in 1892 (open April through October). The inn has great views of the Mohawk Valley, an 1892 swimming pool with a fountain, a 1911 bowling alley with original pins and balls, and cross-country skiing. Call for current rates.

To sports fans, Cooperstown is practically synonymous with baseball. Devotees and fanatics come from all over the country to visit the National Baseball Hall of Fame and Museum, but many miss the three-story *National Baseball Hall of Fame Library* located in a separate building connected to the museum. It's a treasure trove of baseball with a collection of more than 2.5 million items including clippings, photographs, books, videos, movies, recordings—practically everything ever uttered or written about baseball. Established in 1939, the library is used by researchers but is open to visitors, who are invited to browse at their leisure. During your visit include the fifty-six-seat Bullpen Theater, where visitors can view the best in baseball highlight films and footage of the game's greatest plays.

The National Baseball Hall of Fame Library, 25 Main St., Cooperstown (607-547-0330 or 607-547-7200; www.baseballhalloffame.org), is open daily 9 a.m. to 5 p.m., with half-hour tours throughout the day, during summer months. From Memorial Day Weekend through Labor Day, the museum stays open until 9 p.m. Museum visitors can enter the library at no additional charge over the entry fee of $16.50 for adults, $11 for seniors, $6 for children, free for active and retired military and children under 6; discounts for AAA members.

But there's so much more to Cooperstown than baseball. It's the quintessence of small-town America, founded in 1786 on the southern shore of Otsego Lake by William Cooper, father of author James Fenimore Cooper. Stand on the veranda of the historic *Otesaga Resort Hotel* at sunset (perhaps with a beverage), looking out over the eighteenth green to the incredible expanse of clear, blue water reflecting an impressionist's palette of colors. You'll see why Cooper called it "Glimmerglass" in his *Leatherstocking Tales*.

Built in 1909 by the Clark family, discreet patriarchs of Cooperstown, the Otesaga is at once a part of and apart from Main Street's small-town charms, just a short walk from its front gates. This landmark Georgian Revival edifice, with its mammoth white-columned entry contrasting with the redbrick structure, offers guests a complete destination. In addition to lodgings they'll get fine dining, a cozy pub, and excellent recreation in the form of a vintage 1909 Emmett Devereux layout, the Leatherstocking Golf Course that has been rated among the top public courses in the East.

At the Otesaga Resort Hotel, 60 Lake St., Cooperstown (800-348-6222; www.otesaga.com), rates vary seasonally, starting at $330 a night for a standard double room, with suites going up to $650 a night. Ask about the many golf and holiday packages.

Just down the street from the Otesaga, the ***Fenimore Art Museum*** serves as a showcase for the New York State Historical Association, featuring changing exhibits of works largely from the eighteenth through early twentieth centuries, with an emphasis on paintings, early photographs, textiles, and other items relating to the American experience. Among the works are Hudson River School paintings by such luminaries as Thomas Cole and Asher B. Durand, folk art, and period furniture and paintings associated with Mr. Cooper.

The museum's $10-million, 18,000-square-foot American Indian Wing exhibits the Eugene and Clare Thaw Collection of American Indian Art, more than 700 masterpieces spanning 2,400 years that highlight the artistry of North America's indigenous peoples. The Great Hall features a selection of large-scale objects from regions throughout North America.

The museum, overlooking the lake, boasts a formal terrace garden and restaurant with outdoor seating that overlooks the tranquil lake.

Right across the street is the twenty-three-acre ***Farmers' Museum,*** a cluster of historic buildings where the trades, skills, and agricultural practices of nineteenth-century rural New York State come to life. The museum's 1845 Village Crossroads is made up of ten early-nineteenth-century buildings all built within 100 miles of Cooperstown and moved here as life-size working exhibits. Among the buildings are a tavern, blacksmith's shop, one-room schoolhouse, and print shop. All are furnished in period-style, and the museum interpreters perform the tasks appropriate to each building. Penny candy is sold at Todd's General Store. Lippitt Farmstead, a nineteenth-century house, barn, and outbuilding complex, presents farming practices of the day. The Herder's Cottage serves a light menu.

Be sure to include a visit to the historical ***Seneca Log House,*** at one time the home of a traditional Seneca family. At the site the daily life of a Seneca family in the 1840s is replicated as closely as possible. A docent demonstrates crafts of the period, including basketmaking, beadwork, and the making of tourist-related objects, and special seasonal events are held here throughout the year.

Among the special events are an old-time Fourth of July, the September Harvest Festival, and a Candlelight Evening at Christmastime that features hot wassail and holiday activities. The Farmers' Museum, 5775 State Highway 80 (Lake Road), Cooperstown (888-547-1450; www.farmersmuseum.org), is open April through May and mid-October through the end of the month, Tuesday through Sunday 10 a.m. to 4 p.m.; admission is $9 for adults, $8 for seniors, $4 for children ages 7 to 12. The museum is open daily from 10 a.m. to 5 p.m. from late May through mid October; admission is $11 for adults, $9.50 for seniors, $5 children ages 7 to 12.

Fenimore Art Museum, 5798 State Highway 80 (Lake Road; 888-547-1450; www.fenimoreartmuseum.org), is open April through late May, and mid-October through December, Tuesday through Sunday 10 a.m. to 4 p.m.; and late May through mid-October, daily 10 a.m. to 5 p.m. Closed Thanksgiving and Christmas. Admission is $11 for adults, $9.50 for seniors, $5 for children ages 7 to 12.

"When the building starts shaking, they've started making," says *USA Today* of **Fly Creek Cider Mill and Orchard**, a turn-of-the-century water-powered mill where visitors can watch apple cider being made and chow down on a host of cider-related products, including hot spiced cider, cider floats, and cider mill donuts. There's also a duck pond, tractorland kids' area, and gift shop selling everything from bagged cheese curds to home accessories. Come hungry to 288 Gloose St., Fly Creek (607-547-9692 or 800-505-6455; www.flycreekcidermill.com) from mid-May until mid-December, daily 9 a.m. to 6 p.m.

Hyde Hall, a New York State Historic Site, unravels the story of one of the state's last great land-owning families right before your eyes. Visitors tour what is considered to be one of the finest examples of a neoclassical country mansion north of the Mason-Dixon Line as it's being restored. It continues to be a work in progress.

The estate's builder, George Clarke, secretary and lieutenant governor of the British Province of New York from 1703 to 1743, wanted to build a home similar to the one he'd left behind in Cheshire, England. He retained Philip Hooker, one of America's foremost early nineteenth-century architects, and kept copious records of the house's construction, furnishing, and decoration, allowing today's restorers to replicate many of the original features as they work. Hyde Hall is a fascinating look into one man's vision, the damage time can render on a once-magnificent dwelling, and the dedication of a small group of people determined to restore the hall to its former glory.

Hyde Hall in Springfield, adjacent to Glimmerglass State Park and overlooking Otsego Lake, is open for tours from 10 a.m. to 4 p.m. on the hour, light permitting. Closed when there are events on site. Admission is $10 for adults, $8 for seniors, and $8 for ages 5 to 12. For information and events contact Linda Van Cleef, director of operations, at lindavancleef@hydehall.org; call (607) 547-5098;, or check their Web site at www.hydehall.org. Special Focus Tours are also available throughout the year; check the Web site for an updated calendar.

At one point in the nineteenth century, 80 percent of the hops produced in America came from within a 40-mile radius of Cooperstown. The **Brewery Ommegang,** on a 135-acre former hops farm alongside the Susquehanna River, carries on the region's proud tradition, using traditional Belgian brewing techniques. For beer laymen who need to brush up on their Belgian brewing knowledge: the brewery utilizes specialty malts, Syrian and Saaz hops, rare spices such as curaçao orange peel and paradise grain, and open fermentation, bottle-conditioning, and warm cellaring. Judge the result for yourself: the brewery is open for free half-hour tours year-round, daily from 11 a.m. to 6 p.m.

Brewery Ommegang is at 656 County Highway 33, paralleling Route 28 and midway between Cooperstown and Milford (800-544-1809 or 607-544-1800; www.ommegang.com).

Central New York's oldest museum, **The Petrified Creatures Museum of Natural History,** was established more than fifty years ago on land that the Devonian Sea covered 300 million years in the past. Visitors climb on the backs of life-size purple and green dinosaurs, learn about life in prehistoric times, and dig for fossils to take home as free souvenirs (tools are provided by the museum). Don't miss the gift shop full of quirky and unusual gifts.

The Petrified Creatures Museum of Natural History, Route 20, Richfield Springs (315-858-2868; www.petrifiedcreatures.com), is open Thursday to Monday in May and June and daily July through September from 10 a.m. to 5 p.m. Admission is $9 adults and $5 children; under 5 free.

In 1816 Eliphalet Remington was 24 years old and in need of a new rifle. He fashioned a barrel at his father's village forge and then walked into the Mohawk Valley town of Utica to have it rifled. Rifling is the series of twisting grooves inside a gun barrel that give the bullet spin, and therefore accuracy, and distinguishes it from the smoothbore muskets of earlier days. His fascination with gun making soon became his life's work and his Remington Arms Company would produce the dependable firearms that would power America's westward expansion.

Learn the history of America's oldest gun maker at the **Remington Arms Museum** in Ilion, housing an impressive collection of rifles, shotguns, and handguns dating back to Eliphalet Remington's earliest flintlocks. Pore over examples of the first successful breech-loading rifles, for which Remington held the initial 1864 patents. You can also view rare presentation-grade guns, bolt-action and pump rifles, autoloading rifles and shotguns, and the Model 32 over-and-under shotgun of 1932.

Other displays include literature on how firearms are built today, advertising, other firearms ephemera, and even antique Remington typewriters—yes, it was the same company.

The Remington Arms Museum, 14 Hoefler Ave. (off Route 5S), Ilion (315-895-3200 or 800-243-9700; www.remington.com), is open year-round, Monday through Friday from 8 a.m. to 4 p.m.; closed major holidays. From Labor Day to Memorial Day, tours are given Monday through Friday at 10 a.m. and 1 p.m. Call ahead for tour information and for information or reservations for large groups. Admission is free. There's also a shop selling clothes and accessories.

"Herkimer diamonds," found just north of Ilion at Middleville, aren't really diamonds, nor are they valuable. But they do provide endless value for an entertaining afternoon while prospecting for a handful at the *Ace of Diamonds Mine and Campground,* once known as the Tabor Estate, where the diamonds were first dug. The friendly staff can provide you with all the tools to begin your hunt.

The "diamonds" are really clear quartz crystals found in a rock formation called dolomite, buried ages ago. Surface water containing silicon seeped down through the earth and got trapped in pockets of dolomite. Tremendous heat and pressure caused the crystals to form, and over the years the effects of erosion, weathering, and water have exposed the strata. The crystals at the Ace of Diamonds are found in pockets in the rock and in soil surrounding the weathered rock. They're primarily used for mineral specimens, but ones of gem quality are used in arts and jewelry.

Ace of Diamonds Mine and Campground, Route 28, Middleville (315-891-3855 or 315-891-3896; www.herkimerdiamonds.com), is open April 1 through October 31 daily from 9 a.m. to 5 p.m. There is a digging fee of $8.50 per adult and $4 for children 7 and under.

From Ilion it's just a short hop down the thruway to Utica and the *Munson-Williams-Proctor Arts Institute,* a multifaceted operation that emphasizes community accessibility and service, with free group tours, a speakers' bureau, and children's art programs, as well as free admission and a modestly priced performing arts series (some performances take place at the nearby Stanley Performing Arts Center).

Their collection of paintings is grounded in nineteenth-century genre work and the Hudson River School. You can also find moderns including Calder,

Picasso, Kandinsky, and Pollock. There are also comprehensive art and music libraries, a sculpture garden, and even a children's room where patrons can leave their kids for supervised play while they peruse the museum. Also on the grounds of the institute is *Fountain Elms,* a beautifully restored 1850 home in the Italianate Victorian style and once the home of the philanthropic Williams family. Four period rooms on the ground floor exemplify Victorian tastes. At Christmastime the house is resplendent with Victorian ornamentation.

The Munson-Williams-Proctor Arts Institute, 310 Genesee St., Utica (315-797-0000; www.mwpai.org), is open Tuesday through Saturday 10 a.m. to 5 p.m. and Sunday 1 to 5 p.m.; closed major holidays.

Children will prefer the Utica *Children's Museum of History & Science,* founded by the city's Junior League. Since 1980 it has occupied its own five-story, 30,000-square-foot building, chock-full of participatory and hands-on exhibits concentrating on natural history, the history of New York State, and technology. Installations designed for children ages 2 to 12 and their families include a Dino Den; Childspace, for children from infant to 12; an Iroquois longhouse and artifacts; a natural history center; and bubbles, architecture, and dress-up areas. The museum also offers special exhibitions on a monthly basis and special programs for families on Saturday beginning at 2 p.m., from October through July. Portions of the permanent Railroad Exhibit, which includes a Santa Fe dining car and diesel locomotive, are on display next to the museum.

The Children's Museum of History & Science, 311 Main St., Utica (315-724-6129; www.museum4kids.net), is open year-round, Monday, Thursday, and Saturday from 9:30 a.m. to 2:30 p.m., and on Friday during holiday and school break weeks. The museum is closed on most major holidays but open when school is closed. Admission is $9 for adults, $8 for seniors, $7 for children 2 to 17; children under age 2 are admitted free.

In 1888 German-born F. X. Matt II opened a brewery in West Utica. Today the *Matt Brewing Company* is the second-oldest family-owned brewery, and twelfth largest in the country. In addition to the Saranac family of beers, it also produces numerous specialty microbrews, including New Amsterdam and Harpoon.

You can tour the brewery and then sample the wares for free in the 1888 Tavern (the brewery makes 1888 Tavern Root Beer for kids and teetotalers). The tour includes a visit to the seven-story brew house, the fermenting and aging cellars, and the packaging plant.

The Matt Brewing Company (now also known as Saranac Brewery), 830 Varick St., Utica (315-732-0022 or 800-765-6288; www.saranac.com), is open for tours year-round. June 1 through Labor Day, tours are given Monday through Saturday from 1 to 4 p.m., every hour on the hour. On Sunday tours are given at 1 and 3 p.m. The rest of the year, tours are given Friday and Saturday at 1 and 3 p.m. (closed major holidays). The gift shop is open Monday through Saturday from 10 a.m. to 5 p.m. Advance reservations are recommended. Admission is $5 for adults and free for children 12 and under. Free parking is available in the Tour Center Concourse at the corner of Court and Varick Streets.

Syracuse and the Erie Canal

Hop aboard a horse-drawn canal boat at **Erie Canal Village,** first opened in Rome in 1973 near the site where the first spadeful of dirt for the Erie Canal was dug on Independence Day in 1817. The short-lived canal era may have been only a prologue to the age of the railroad, but in the 1820s New Yorkers thought the Erie Canal was one of the wonders of the world.

The *Chief Engineer* keeps to a regular schedule of thirty-five-minute trips on the restored section of the original canal at the village. It was built of Mohawk Valley oak to the same specifications as the passenger-carrying packet boats of the canal's early years. The Harden Carriage Museum displays a varied collection of horse-drawn vehicles used on roads and snow. Other buildings in the village are nearly all more than a hundred years old and were moved here from other communities in the area. Visitors can see a tavern, church, smithy, canal store, settler's house, barn, and, my personal favorite, the New York State Museum of Cheese. The Erie Canal Museum explains the technological and social importance of the Erie Canal. Fort Bull, dating from the French and Indian Wars, is also on the premises.

The village presents historical craft demonstrations, interpretive programs, and seasonal festivals, with the primary focus on canal and harvest activities.

Erie Canal Village, 5789 New London Rd., Routes 49 and 46, Rome (315-337-3999 or 888-374-3226; www.eriecanalvillage.net), is open daily from Memorial Day weekend through Labor Day, Wednesday through Saturday from 10 a.m. to 5 p.m. and Sunday noon to 5 p.m. General admission runs $10 for adults, $7 for seniors, and $5 for children. A 40-minute boat excursion only is $6 for all ages. Admission to all attractions is $15 for adults, $12 for seniors and students, and $10 for children 4 to 17.

Back in 1790, the Holland Land Company sent its young agent John Lincklaen to America to scout investment possibilities. Two years later he reached the area around Cazenovia Lake, between present-day Rome and Syracuse, and his enthusiasm led his firm to invest in 120,000 acres here. A village, farms, and small businesses soon sprang up, with Lincklaen remaining in a patriarchal and entrepreneurial role that in 1807 allowed him to build himself a magnificent Federal mansion, today preserved at the **Lorenzo State Historic Site.**

The little fiefdom of Lorenzo offers an instructive glimpse into why New York is called the Empire State. Lincklaen and the descendants of his adopted family lived here until 1968, which was also the same year that the house and its contents were deeded to the state. The family was involved with many of the enterprises that led to the state's phenomenal growth during the nineteenth century including road building, canals, railroads, and industrial development.

The mansion, surrounded by twenty acres of lawns and formal gardens, sits on the shores of a 4-mile-long lake. It is rich with Federal-era furnishings and the accumulated possessions of a century and a half of Lincklaens, including a fine selection of Hudson River School artworks. In the latest renovations Zuber & Cie, of Rixheim, France, used their original nineteenth-century printing blocks to reproduce an 1870 paper originally hung in Lorenzo in 1901. These projects are part of an ongoing process to fully restore the site to its turn-of-the-century beauty.

Lorenzo State Historic Site, 17 Rippleton Rd., Cazenovia (315-655-3200; www.lorenzony.org), is open from early May through October 31, Wednesday through Sunday from 10 a.m. to 4:30 p.m., Sunday 1 to 5 p.m. The grounds are open all year, 8 a.m. to dusk. Admission is $5 for adults, $4 for seniors, and free for children under 12.

Cazenovia is also home to the **Stone Quarry Hill Art Park.** Its 104 acres and hiking trails were one of the country's first outdoor sculpture parks and is a startling reprieve from upstate's wooded pockets and rolling meadows. Founder Dorothy Riester, an established artist, and her husband, Robert, initially bought the land as vacation property before deciding to share it with the public in 1991. They made it their mission to preserve the land while serving as a place for artists to work, exhibit, and perform. There is also an artist-in-residence program in a four-bedroom home on the grounds. Visitors can watch artists work in the Art Barn or hike through five miles of hiking trails while stumbling across large installations of sculpture and art. Take photos and bring a sketch book, it's almost ethereal how the sculptures shoot out of meadows and wildflowers. Many of the outdoor pieces are also designed to eventually decompose back into nature.

An Art in the Sky kite festival is held seasonally, and some of the park's own artwork goes airborne. A renowned Annual Syracuse Ceramic Pottery Fair also takes place on the grounds. Pick up a trail map from the gift shop and bring an extra bag with you. The park is a carry-in, carry-out park and no litter is permitted.

The Stone Quarry Hill Art Park is located at 3883 Stone Quarry Rd., Cazenovia, and is open 365 days a year from dawn until dusk; the offices at the Hilltop House are open Tuesday through Saturday 10 a.m. to 5 p.m.; and the gallery and gift shop are open April to October, 10 a.m. to 5 p.m. There is a suggested donation of $5 per car. Call (315) 655-3196 or visit www.stonequarry hillartpark.org for more information.

Around the turn of the twentieth century, the Arts and Crafts Movement swept America. It was an aesthetic revolution that rejected the superfluous ornamentation of Victorian furniture, advocating a return to clean lines, honest craftsmanship, and sturdy construction. Gustav and Leopold Stickley, leaders of the movement, began making Craftsman, also known as Mission, furniture.

At the beginning of the nineteenth century, a swamp south of Oneida Lake became Syracuse, a city that grew around the salt industry and the Erie Canal. Today, visitors can see the last of the "weighlock" buildings that once dotted the waterway. Built in 1850 in Greek Revival style, this weigh station for canal boats today houses the *Erie Canal Museum.*

Exhibits in the Weighlock Building include a 65-foot replica of a canal boat. The *Frank Buchanan Thomson,* named after a late museum director, offers a look at a typical Erie Canal vessel's crew quarters, immigrant accommodations, and cargo storage. Immigration along the canal is a special focus of the museum's exhibits, particularly with regard to its effects on Syracuse. The museum experience also includes a hands-on display of canal equipment and explanations of the engineering involved in connecting Albany and Buffalo by means of a 363-mile artificial waterway, with eighty-three locks and eighteen aqueducts. The job wasn't easy, but the result was the longest and most successful canal in the world.

The Erie Canal Museum, 318 Erie Boulevard East, Syracuse (315-471-0593; www.eriecanalmuseum.org), is open Monday to Saturday from 10 a.m. to 5 p.m. and Sunday 10 a.m. to 3 p.m.; closed major holidays. Admission is free, but donations are appreciated.

From swamp to canal boomtown, Syracuse was a major commercial and industrial center by the end of the nineteenth century, and ready for a cultural revolution.. The *Everson Museum of Art* was founded by George Fisk Comfort, who had been instrumental in establishing New York City's Metropolitan Museum and who served as founder and dean of the College of Fine Arts at Syracuse University. Comfort established the Syracuse Museum of Fine Arts, which had its the first exhibition in 1900. This initial show featured the work of impressionists Monet, Sisley, and Pissarro, as well as older, more recognized masters.

Renamed the Everson Museum in 1959 following a large bequest from Syracuse philanthropist Helen Everson, the museum moved in 1968 into its present quarters, a massive, modernist concrete structure that was architect I. M. Pei's first museum building. Its three exhibition levels contain nine galleries and a 50-foot-square two-story sculpture court.

The Everson Museum has extensive holdings of American art, including colonial portraits including a famed piece of George Washington. It also showcases the works of nineteenth-century genre and luminist painters, and paintings by twentieth-century artists such as Robert Henri, John Sloan, Grandma Moses, Maxfield Parrish, Reginald Marsh, and Grant Wood. The museum exhibits a reputable graphic-art collection and a small but comprehensive photography section.

The museum's Syracuse China Center for the Study of American Ceramics houses the nation's premier collection in this field, with holdings dating from A.D. 1000 to the present. Find pre-Columbian Native American vessels, colonial and nineteenth-century pieces, and contemporary functional and art pottery, as well as some 1,200 examples of ceramic craftsmanship from cultures outside the Western Hemisphere.

The Everson Museum of Art, 401 Harrison St., Syracuse (315-474-6064; www.everson.org), is open Tuesday and Wednesday noon to 6 p.m., Thursday

onebigoldtree

The sugar maple is New York State's Official Tree. Over in the Camillus Forest Unique Area, just west of Syracuse, there is a sugar maple tree with a diameter of 42 inches believed to be nearly 300 years old.

A Tale of Salt City

Charles Dickens visited Syracuse, once also known as "Salt City," in 1869 to give a reading in the Weiting Opera House. He stayed in the Syracuse Hotel and wrote:

"I am here in a most wonderful out-of-the-world place, which looks as if it had begun to be built yesterday, and were going to be imperfectly knocked together with a nail or two the day after tomorrow. I am in the worst inn that ever was seen, and outside is a thaw that places the whole country under water.

"We had an old buffalo for supper and an old pig for breakfast and we are going to have I don't know what for dinner at 6. In the public room downstairs, a number of men (speechless) with their feet against window frames, staring out the window and spitting dolefully at intervals. And yet we have taken in considerably over 300 pounds for tomorrow night."

and Friday noon to 9 p.m., Saturday and Sunday noon to 6 p.m. Closed holidays. Admission is free, although a suggested donation of $5 is welcome.

At *Clark's Ale House,* 122 West Jefferson St. (315-479-9859; www.clarks alehouse.com), your head may spin over what to drink. They carry thirty-two draughts from around the world, including Michigan Screaming Pumpkin, Saranac Summer Brew, Victory Festbier, Prior Double Dark, Pearl Street Belgian Wit, and more.. Choosing what to eat is far easier, try their specialty hot roast beef on an onion roll, Croghan Bologna, Crumbly Blue Cheese Plate, and Pickled Eggs. The pub is in the Landmark Theatre building and is open from Monday through Saturday from 11 to 2 a.m. Food is served Monday through Wednesday 11 to 1 a.m., Thursday through Saturday until 2 a.m.

If you've always wondered where salt comes from, visit the quirky *Salt Museum* near Syracuse, "The City That Salt Built." At one time the area supplied the entire nation with the "white gold." The museum, constructed of timbers from former salt warehouses, explains the method of turning brine into salt, a process that endured until the 1920s.

rochestermystery

Drive past the old Penfield Manufacturing Company building in Rochester to puzzle over the ornate, Victorian bungalow affixed to its roof. No one seems to really know what it's doing up there. Locals do know the building was once the Moyer Carriage Factory in the late 1800s and the home was actually one of two penthouses that never had a single occupant. The home is reported to be nothing more than a shell and never had a tenant.

The Salt Museum, in Onondaga Lake Park, 106 Lake Dr., Liverpool (315-453-6715; www.onondagacountyparks .com), is open from Mother's Day weekend through Columbus Day, daily 1 to 6 p.m. Admission is free.

Bed & Breakfast Wellington, a National Historic Landmark designed by Ward Wellington Ward, is a 1914 brick and stucco Tudor-style home with canvas flooring, an arched foyer, leaded glass windows, and tile insets. Rates for the five guest rooms (including a housekeeping suite) range from about $105 to $150, including private bath and breakfast. The B&B is at 707 Danforth St. in Syracuse (315-474-3641 or 800-724-5006; www.bbwellington.com).

If you can't dam your insatiable curiosity of canals, you might want to sign on for a grand two- to four-day journey down the Cayuga-Seneca, the Oswego, the Champlain, and the Erie Canals. *Mid-Lakes Navigation Company, Ltd.,* offers escorted, navigated, and catered cruises, with departures from Buffalo, Syracuse, and Albany. During the day passengers travel and dine aboard *Emita II,* a reconverted passenger ferry. At night the boat ties up on shore, and passengers check into a local hotel. It's a perfect blending of the nineteenth and twentieth centuries.

The company also runs weeklong bare-boat charters from Syracuse aboard European-style Lockmaster hire boats, as well as daily cruises on the Erie Canal and Skaneateles Lake.

Mid-Lakes Navigation Company, Ltd., is headquartered at 11 Jordan St., P.O. Box 61, Skaneateles 13152 (315-685-8500 or 800-545-4318; www.midlakes nav.com).

Places to Stay in the Mohawk Valley

ALBANY

Angels Bed and Breakfast
96 Madison Ave.
(518) 426-4104
www.angelsbedand
breakfast.com

Desmond Hotel
660 Albany-Shaker Rd.
(518) 869-8100
www.desmondhotelsalbany
.com

ALTAMONT

Appel Inn
590 Route 146
(518) 861-6557
www.appelinn.com

LITTLE FALLS

Gansevoort House Inn and Galleries
42 West Gansevoort St.
(315) 823-3969
www.gansevoorthouse
.com

ONEIDA CASTLE

Governor's House B&B
50 Seneca Ave.
(800) 437-8177

ROTTERDAM

Malozzi's Belvedere Hotel
1926 Curry Rd.
(866) 4-BELVEDERE or
(518) 630-4020
www.albanynyhotels.com

SCHENECTADY

Parker Inn
424 State St.
(518) 688-1001
www.parkerinn.com

SCOTIA

The Glen Sanders Mansion
1 Glen Ave.
(518) 374-7262
www.glensandersmansion
.com

SYRACUSE

The Craftsman Inn
7300 Genesee St.
(800) 797-4464 or
(315) 637-8000
www.craftsmaninn.com

Places to Eat in the Mohawk Valley

ALBANY

Jack's Oyster House
42 State St.
(518) 465-8854
www.jacksoysterhouse
.com

Miss Albany Diner
893 Broadway
(518) 465-9148
www.missalbanydiner.com

Nicole's Bistro
25 Quackenbush Sq.
(518) 465-1111
www.nicolesbistro.com

COOPERSTOWN

Hoffman Lane Bistro
2 Hoffman Lane
(607) 547-7055
www.hoffmanlanebistro
.com

T.J.'s Place
124 Main St.
(607) 547-4040
www.tjs-place.com

Turncliff Inn Tap Room
34 Pioneer St.
(607) 547-9611
www.cooperstownchamber
.org/tunnicliff

SCHENECTADY

Center Stage Deli at Proctor's
432 State St.
(518) 377-5401

SCOTIA

The Glen Sanders Mansion
1 Glen Ave.
(518) 374-7262
www.glensandersmansion
.com

SYRACUSE

Dinosaur Bar-B-Cue
246 Willow St.
(315) 476-4937
www.dinosaurbarbque.com

SYLVAN BEACH

Harpoon Eddie's
611 Park Ave.
(315) 762-5238
www.sylvanbeach.com/
harpoons

OTHER ATTRACTIONS WORTH SEEING IN THE MOHAWK VALLEY

Historic Cherry Hill
523½ South Pearl St.
Albany
(518) 434-4791
www.historiccherryhill.org

Howe Caverns
255 Discovery Dr.
Howes Cave
(518) 296-8990
www.howecaverns.com

New York State Capitol
Albany
(518) 474-2418
assembly.state.ny.us/Tour

New York State Museum
Empire State Plaza
Albany
(518) 474-5877
www.nysm.nysed.gov

Proctor's Theater
432 State St.
Schenectady
(518) 382-3884 or (518) 346-2604
www.proctors.org

Schenectady Stockade Area
Front Street
Schenectady
(518) 372-5656 or (800) 962-8007
www.historicstockade.com

Ten Broeck Mansion
9 Ten Broeck Place
Albany
(518) 436-9826
http://sites.google.com/site/
tenbroeckmansion

REGIONAL TOURIST INFORMATION— THE MOHAWK VALLEY

**Albany County Convention
& Visitors Bureau**
25 Quackenbush Sq.
Albany 12207
(518) 434-1217 or (800) 258-3582
www.albany.org

**Fulton County Gateway
to the Adirondacks**
2 North Main St.
Gloversville 12078
(800) 676-3858
www.fultoncountyny.org

Otsego County Tourism
242 Main St.
(607) 643-0059
www.thisiscooperstown.com

**Schenectady County Chamber
of Commerce**
306 State St.
Schenectady 12305
(518) 372-5656
www.schenectadychamber.org

**Syracuse Convention
& Visitors Bureau**
572 South Salina St.
Syracuse 13202
(800) 234-4797 or (315) 470-1910
www.visitsyracuse.org

THE FINGER LAKES

Between New York's "northern seaboard" along Lake Ontario and the Pennsylvania border lies the region that many visitors consider to be the most beautiful part of the state. South of the Lake Ontario plain, the Finger Lakes area appears to be furrowed on a vast scale, with hilly farmland descending toward each of the lakes only to rise again before the next. The aptly named elongated lakes extend roughly north and south across an 80-mile swath of the state, offering vistas reminiscent of parts of Switzerland. It's no wonder the city at the northern end of Seneca Lake was named Geneva.

Another distinctly European aspect of the Finger Lakes area is its status as New York State's premier wine-growing region. No longer limited to just the cultivation of native grape varieties, New York's vintners have come a long way. Visits to individual vineyards and the wine museum described in this section will demonstrate their vast history and achievements.

Scenes of well-tended vines in rows along steep hillsides may be reminiscent of Europe, but the Finger Lakes region is rich in Americana with museums of coverlets, Victorian dolls, and horse-drawn carriages. You'll even find Mark Twain's study and a museum devoted to Memorial Day.

THE FINGER LAKES

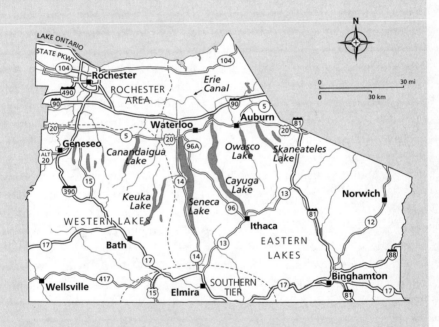

We'll approach this area from the south, beginning near the Pennsylvania border and continuing up toward Rochester, then heading east along the New York State Thruway and the northern Finger Lakes.

The Southern Tier

Mark Twain is revered for his tales of life on the Mississippi, but he wrote many of the stories here in New York from a charming little summer house now located on the campus of Elmira College and preserved as the *Mark Twain Study.*

In 1870 Twain married an Elmira woman named Olivia Langdon, and for years the author and his family took leave of their palatial Hartford home to spend summers with Olivia's sister, Mrs. Theodore Crane. Mrs. Crane and her husband lived on a farm outside Elmira, where in 1874 they built Twain a freestanding octagonal study, with windows on all sides and a massive stone fireplace. Here Twain penned *Tom Sawyer* and completed sections of *Huckleberry Finn, Life on the Mississippi, A Connecticut Yankee in King Arthur's Court,* and other works. Twain said it was "the loveliest study you ever saw."

Difficult to maintain and protect from vandalism, the study was donated to Elmira College by the Langdon family in 1952, whereupon it was relocated to its present site.

The Mark Twain Study, on the Elmira College campus, 1 Park Place, Elmira (607-735-1941), is open from May to Labor Day, Monday through Saturday 9 a.m. to 5 p.m. and Sunday noon to 5 p.m.; Labor Day to mid-October, Saturday 9 a.m. to 5 p.m., and Sunday noon to 5 p.m. To arrange off-season visits e-mail twaincenter@elmira.edu.

The three-story Italianate mansion *Lindenwald Haus,* with twenty-one renovated Victorian guest rooms, has been a popular place to stay for more

AUTHOR'S FAVORITES—FINGER LAKES

Dr. Konstantin Frank Vinifera Wine Cellars

House of Guitars

Letchworth State Park

Mark Twain Study

National Soaring Museum

Paleontological Research Institution

Pat Mitchell's Homemade Ice Cream

Rockwell Museum of Western Art

Willard Memorial Chapel

the year, weather permitting. Even if you don't go up yourself, it's captivating to watch the graceful, silent flights and landings of the sleek sailplanes.

National Soaring Museum, Harris Hill, 51 Soaring Hill Dr., Elmira (607-734-3128 for office or 734-0641 for flight office; www.soaringmuseum.org), is open daily from 10 a.m. to 5 p.m. (closed some holidays). Admission is $6.50 for adults, $5.50 for seniors, and $4 for children ages 5 to 17; family rate, $18. Sailplane flights range from $70 to $80; call for schedules.

Upstream along the Chemung River lies Corning, its famous Steuben Glass Factory, and the Corning Glass Center and Museum. From town, you might notice the striking landmark of Little Joe Tower. Corning once used the tower to stretch hot glass 196 feet high by a cable in what's known as a "vertical draw" process. The result was a smooth, continuous tube of glass, later cut to length into thermometers. The technique has since been abandoned in favor of automatically producing thermometers by a "horizontal process."

A more intimate, and less vertical, environment in which magnificent glass pieces are created by traditional glassblowing techniques is *Vitrix Hot Glass Studio* in Corning's historic Market Street district. Since 1959 Vitrix has been turning out some of the country's finest handblown glass pieces.

Vitrix Hot Glass Studio, 77 West Market St., Corning (607-936-8707; www vitrixhotglass.com), is open Monday through Friday 10 a.m. to 6 p.m., Saturday 10 a.m. to 8 p.m., and Sunday noon to 5 p.m. Glassblowers work on weekends only.

The aptly named *Glass Menagerie* is one of the world's largest dealers in kaleidoscopes. The shop represents more than 100 scope artists, inventories at least 200 examples of their work at all times, and hosts annual summer kaleidoscope shows. But the store has a much broader scope. It carries leaded glass guardian angels made by Carl Goeller, a huge selection of mouth-blown hand-painted Christopher Radko limited edition Christmas ornaments, and unique paperweights. Glass animals, perfume bottles, and both glass and ceramic menorahs are also for sale. One of the owners, Dick Pope, is a professional magician and often gives impromptu performances

As in Life, So in Death

Elmira's Woodlawn Cemetery, burial place of Mark Twain, also holds the graves of Union and Confederate Civil War soldiers. The Confederates are facing south, and the Union graves surround them, exactly as the Union soldiers surrounded their prisoners of war when all died in a nearby railroad accident during the war.

Uncork New York

There are about one hundred wineries, large and small, peppered throughout the Finger Lakes. Visitors can either let serendipity be their guide, taking a leisurely dri through the area and stopping when the spirit moves, or can carefully plan a tastir route with the help of several Web sites: www.fingerlakeswinecountry.com (800-8 2958); www.senecalakewine.com (877-536-2717); www.keukawinetrail.com (800 440-4898); www.cayugawinetrail.com (800-684-5217); and www.newyorkwines. (585-394-3620). You can find listings of wineries as well as places to eat, shop, stay overnight; download the information you need or request maps and brochu

than 115 years since it was built to house widows of the Civil War. nine rooms with private bath, ten with shared bath. The five-acre gro dotted with fruit trees; guests are welcome to walk, bike, or swim.

Lindenwald Haus, 1526 Grand Central Ave., Elmira (607-733-87 440-4287; www.lindenwaldhaus.com), is open year-round. Rates r $85 to $115 for a deluxe suite and include a full breakfast.

When Mark Twain's study was at its original site on the Qu belonging to his in-laws, it commanded a lovely view of the hills along the Chemung River Valley. Little did Twain suspect a few decades after his death, these same hills would attract fl siasts looking beyond the tranquil trails and high above their the 1930s Harris Hill, outside Elmira, had become the "Soarin America." The science and sport of motorless flight is today kep alive at the **National Soaring Museum,** which offers visitors exhibits and the opportunity to go aloft in sailplanes piloted by professionals.

Regardless of whether you agree with the museum's philoso ing is "flying as nature intended," a visit to the facility offers a to this often overlooked aspect of modern aviation. The museu world's largest exhibit of contemporary and historic sailplan displays explaining the development of soaring and its relation fields of meteorology and aerodynamics. You can even climb simulator, similar to those used to teach soaring, and learn what of controlling a motorless plane is like.

But to really understand soaring, you have to get off the gr flight at the museum or at the Harris Hill Soaring Corp. Visitor has a staff of competent pilots licensed by the FAA or check in Gliderport. Rides are available all summer long and on week when he's around. Take time to duck upstairs to **Books of Marvel.** The antiquarian enterprise has one of the world's largest collections of old and rare juvenile series fiction.

The Glass Menagerie, 37 East Market St., Corning (607-962-6300; www .corningmenagerie.com), is open year-round. Hours vary per season; call ahead for an updated calendar.

The **Rockwell Museum of Western Art** owes its existence almost entirely to Robert F. Rockwell, an area native and former proprietor of a small department store chain whose interest in western art dates to his youth spent on a Colorado ranch. He began collecting seriously in the late 1950s, acquiring works by masters of "cowboy" art such as Charles M. Russell and Frederic Remington, as well as by landscapists of the caliber of Albert Bierstadt and Thomas Hill and by animal artists A. F. Tait and Carl Rungius.

Rockwell's protean interests went beyond western art and sculpture to include an area dear to him as a Corning resident: the beautiful art glass created by Frederic Carder, cofounder of the Steuben Glass Works, which was later incorporated into Corning Glass Works, now Corning, Inc. Rockwell even collected antique toys.

By the 1980s, Rockwell's collections were too extensive to be casually shown in his department stores and as part of exhibitions lent to other institutions. He needed his own museum, and found a suitable venue in Corning's old city hall, a Romanesque Revival structure built in 1893. The Corning Company acquired the building from the city for just $1, renovations were undertaken, and in 1982 the Rockwell Museum opened. At present it houses the largest collection of western art on the East Coast, more than 2,000 pieces of Carder Steuben glass, Navajo weavings, antique firearms, Indian artifacts, and the toy collection as well.

The Rockwell Museum of Western Art, 111 Cedar St. at Denison Parkway, Corning (607-937-5386; www.rockwellmuseum.org), is open daily 9 a.m. to 5 p.m. In summer it stays open until 8 p.m. The museum is closed Thanksgiving, Christmas Day, and New Year's. Admission is $6.50 for adults, $5.50 for senior citizens, students and AAA members with cards. Youths 19 and under are free.

Western Lakes

The southern Finger Lakes region is a tranquil, easy-paced corner of the world that simultaneously nurtured one of twentieth-century America's greatest speed demons. At Hammondsport, on the southern tip of Keuka Lake, the **Glenn H. Curtiss Museum** chronicles the lifework of this native son, who was also a serious pioneer in motorcycling and aviation.

ANNUAL EVENTS IN THE FINGER LAKES

MARCH

Central New York Maple Festival
Marathon
www.maplefest.org

MAY

Lilac Festival
Rochester
(585) 256-4960
www.lilacfestival.com

JUNE

Ithaca Festival
Ithaca
(800) 273-3646
www.ithacafestival.org

Strawberry Festival
Owego
(607) 687-2556
www.owegostrawberryfestival.com

Waterfront Festival and Cardboard Regatta
Watkins Glen
(607) 535-3003
www.watkinsglen.com/festival

JULY

Finger Lakes Grassroots Festival
Trumansburg
(607) 387-7764
www.grassrootsfest.org

Finger Lakes Wine Festival
Watkins Glen
(866) 461-7223
www.flwinefest.com

The Great American Antiquefest
Onondaga Lake Park
Liverpool
www.antiquefest.biz

Hill Cumorah Pageant
Palmyra
(315) 597-5851
www.hillcumorah.org/Pageant

Glenn Hammond Curtiss started out, like the Wright brothers, in the bicycle business. He quickly turned his attention to motorcycles and a V-8–powered bike on which he sped more than 136 miles per hour in 1907. He also built engines that powered lighter-than-air craft, and in that same year he became involved with Dr. Alexander Graham Bell and other enthusiasts in the "Aerial Experiment Association." Curtiss's engineering helped lift the association's airplane *Red Wing* off the ice of Keuka Lake on the first public flight (as opposed to the Wrights' secret 1903 experiment) of a heavier-than-air craft in the United States.

Glenn Curtiss's accomplishments over the next twenty years dominated the adolescence of aeronautics. In 1910 he landed a plane on water for the first time, and in 1911 he became the first American to receive a pilot's license. In 1919 a Curtiss "flying boat" made the first transatlantic crossing by air. Meanwhile he had built his Curtiss Aeroplane and Motor Company into an industrial

AUGUST

Empire Farm Days
Seneca Falls
(877) 697-7837
www.empirefarmdays.com

Monroe County Fair
Henrietta
(585) 334-4000
www.mcfair.com

NASCAR Winston Cup at the Glen
Watkins Glen
(607) 535-2486
www.theglen.com

SEPTEMBER

Golden Harvest Festival
Baldwinsville
(315) 638-2519

Grand Prix Festival
Watkins Glen
(607) 535-3003
www.grandprixfestival.com

Great Grape Festival
Naples
(585) 374-2240
www.naplesgrapefest.org

OCTOBER

Letchworth Arts and Crafts Show
Mount Morris
(585) 493-3600 or (585) 237-3517
www.nyfalls.com

NOVEMBER

Lights on the Lake
Onondaga Lake Park
(through early January)
Liverpool
(315) 451-7275
www.lightsonthelake.com

DECEMBER

Dickens Christmas
Skaneateles
www.skaneateles.com

giant, employing 10,000 men at the peak of production during World War I. Sensing the traveling trends of the motor age, he even manufactured the first successful house trailers. Following a merger, the company became Curtiss-Wright, producer of World War II aircraft such as the Navy Helldiver and the P-40 of "Flying Tigers" fame. The museum, founded in 1960, houses seven historic aircraft and three reproductions; one of the latter is a flyable replica of the inventor's 1908 *June Bug*.

The Glenn H. Curtiss Museum, 8419 Route 54, ½ mile south of Hammondsport (607-569-2160; glennhcurtissmuseum.org), is open from May 1 through October 31, Monday through Saturday 9 a.m. to 5 p.m. and Sunday 10 a.m. to 5 p.m.; from November 1 through April 30, it is open Monday through Saturday 10 a.m. to 4 p.m. and Sunday 10 a.m. to 4 p.m. Closed major holidays. Admission is $7.50 for adults, $6 for senior citizens, $5 for students, and free for children ages 6 and under; family rate just $20.

There's hardly anyplace more off-the-beaten-path than **Dr. Konstantin Frank Vinifera Wine Cellars,** on the western banks of Keuka Lake. Yet oenophiles still wind their way through the vineyards to reach the tasting room, eager to sip Pinot Noirs, Gewürztraminers, sparkling wines, and Rieslings. Dr. Frank's wines have won dozens of gold medals and have been ranked among the country's best wines by tastemakers like *Wine Spectator* magazine, finally bringing New York vintages into the national spotlight.

Back in the 1950s, when Dr. Frank arrived from Europe speaking not a word of English, vintners in the Finger Lakes were using indigenous American grapes to make wine that was pretty harsh and unsophisticated. A doctor of viticulture in his native Ukraine, Dr. Frank believed that the *Vitis Vinifera,* the wine grapes of Europe, could be cultivated here, even with the cold winters. He proved it by grafting the varietal vines onto hardy rootstock, and today we can savor the fruits of his labor.

Seek out Dr. Konstantin Frank Vinifera Wine Cellars at 9749 Middle Rd., Hammondsport (800-320-0735; www.DrFrankWines.com), or purchase some of Dr. Frank's finest at your local wine merchant.

Explore winemaking history at the **New York State Wine Museum of Greyton H. Taylor** next door to **Bully Hill Vineyards.**

The museum, at G. H. Taylor Memorial Drive, Hammondsport (607-868-4814; www.bullyhill.com), is open from mid-May through October 31, Monday through Saturday 10 a.m. to 5 p.m. and Sunday 11:30 a.m. to 5 p.m. The visitor center offers wine tastings every half hour and tours every hour. Tastings cost $2 for five wines. A restaurant next door specializes in moderately priced dishes prepared with wine.

The Bully Hill Vineyards can also be visited for tours and tastings; call (607) 868-3610 or visit bullyhill.com.

Want to spend the night on a train? Check into the **Caboose Motel,** 8620 State Route 415N, Avoca (607-566-2216; www.caboosemotel.net). In addition to eighteen standard units, the state's only caboose motel rents five N5 cars equipped with all modern amenities and a speaker that provides train sounds. One unit can accommodate six, the others up to five in upper and lower berths. The cabooses are available spring and summer ranging around $100 a night.

Although far less well known than southeastern Pennsylvania for its Amish and Mennonite populations, the Finger Lakes region attracts such members because of its rich farmland and relative isolation from modern big-city hubbub. One of the most valued and enduring of Amish and Mennonite traditions is quilt making, and at **The Quilt Room** in Penn Yan, more than 200 quilts and wall hangings reveal the meticulous artisanship of women from the surrounding area. In addition to the quilts on display, many of them one-of-a-kind, The Quilt Room can engage quilters to create special-order goods based on any of several thousand traditional designs. Repair work is available as well.

The Quilt Room, 1870 Hoyt Rd., Penn Yan (315-536-5964 or 877-536-5964; www.quiltroom.com), is open year-round; in summer, Monday to Friday 10 a.m. to 4:30 p.m.; after Christmas to the end of April, Monday to Wednesday by appointment only.

If you're looking for seclusion with magnificent mountain views, check out the *Vagabond Inn.* The 7,000-square-foot inn stands in splendid isolation on top of a mountain in the Bristol range. Popular with honeymooners, the inn has a 60-foot-long Great Room with two massive fieldstone fireplaces, a Japanese garden, and an in-ground pool.

Each room boasts individual charm. The Bristol has its own fireplace, a Jacuzzi for two (with views of the mountains), and rents for $225. The Lodge, for $245, has a huge river-stone fireplace and hot-tub chamber. Rates include breakfast.

The Vagabond Inn, 3300 Sliter Rd., Naples (585-554-6271; www.thevagabond inn.com), is open all year.

If you're visiting the area in late September, you might be just in time to sample one of the region's most unusual delicacies—Naples Grape Pie. Local bakeries produce more than 10,000 grape pies six weeks of the year, beginning with the start of the Annual Naples Grape Festival. If you're there any other time of the year, stop in for a slice at *Arbor Hill Grapery & Winery.* They serve them up all year, along with their wines and other wine food products, in a restored eighteenth-century building that once served as the local post office. They also serve light barbecue-style lunches featuring wine soup, wine sausage, and—for dessert—hot grape sundaes. There is also a restaurant on the premises called the *Brown Hound Bistro,* (585) 374-9771.

Arbor Hill Grapery & Winery, 6461 Route 64, South Bristol (Naples; 800-554-7553 or 585-374-2870; thegrapery.com), is open daily from Mother's Day weekend through the first week in January, Monday through Saturday 10 a.m. to 5 p.m. and Sunday 11 a.m. to 5 p.m.; weekends only from January through Mother's Day weekend, Friday and Saturday 10 a.m. to 5 p.m. and Sunday 11 a.m. to 5 p.m. For a dinner schedule, check www.thegrapery.com.

---

extrasyrup
ontheside

Penn Yan is the home to the largest pancake griddle in the world. It's reported to be 27 feet in diameter and was last used in the late 1980s to make, what else? The largest pancake in the world. Find it at 163 Main St. on the side of The Birkett Mills building.

At the southeast corner of the *Alfred University* campus is the *Stull Observatory,* considered to be one of the finest teaching observatories in the Northeast. It exists largely through the efforts of John Stull, who built or rebuilt all of the telescopes and many of the buildings. There are five major telescopes at the observatory: a 9-inch refractor dating from 1863, a 16-inch Cassegrain reflector, and 14-, 20-, and 32-inch Newtonian reflectors.

The Stull Observatory at Alfred University, Alfred (607-871-2208; http://merlin.alfred.edu/stull.html), offers public viewings (weather permitting) at the following times: September, October, November, February, March, and April, Friday from 9 to 11 p.m.; May, June, and July, Thursday from 10 p.m. until midnight.

In July 1937 a freight train pulled into Alfred Station carrying thirty-five bells from Antwerp, Belgium. Eighteen of the bells, which weighed a total of 5,153 pounds (one, called the Bourdon, weighs about 3,850 pounds), were made in 1674 by Pieter Hemony, a famous Netherlands bell founder. They were hung in a wooden tower overlooking the valley and, shortly after, the *Davis Memorial Carillon* rang out over the hills for the first time.

A carillon is a musical instrument built with twenty-three or more cast bronze cup-shaped bells, which are precisely tuned so that many bells can be played together to produce a harmonious effect. The bells are stationary, and only the clappers move. If you're fortunate enough to be in the vicinity on one of the days that the carillonneur is performing, you can hear just how harmonious a sound the carillon can make. Listen for each of its forty-seven bells and see if you can distinguish their rings. Recitals are given Saturday (except over Christmas break and in August) at 4 p.m. throughout the year (except January and August) and on Monday, Wednesday, and Friday from 12:30 to 12:45 p.m. during the academic year. In addition the Wingate Memorial Summer Carillon Recital Series brings guest recitalists to perform Tuesday at 7 p.m. in the month of July.

For information contact the Alfred University Division of Performing Arts, Alfred (607-871-2562; www.alfred.edu/map/carillon.cfm). There is no admission fee.

At the 14,350-acre *Letchworth State Park,* nicknamed the "Grand Canyon of the East," the Genesee River cascades down more than twenty waterfalls as it winds its way north through a series of some 600-feet-high beetling gorges. Visitors can drive through the park on a road that parallels the gorge or hike one of twenty hiking trails of varying difficulty and length.

Accommodations at the park include a campground, cabins, and the yellow-and-white Victorian *Glen Iris Inn* (585-493-2622; www.glenirisinn.com) overlooking Mid Falls, which offers clean, comfortable rooms starting at $50 and suites from $170 from early April to early November. In winter, houses are available from $225 to $350. The inn is the former home of William Pryor Letchworth, who began construction on the building in 1859 and deeded the building and grounds to the state in 1907. They have welcomed guests since 1914. Glen Iris serves three meals a day, and offers a special picnic menu.

Just across from the inn, the **Letchworth Museum** is teeming with exhibits honoring the park's history. On a hill in back of the museum look for the grave of Mary Jemison, the "white woman of the Genesee." A prisoner of the Seneca from the age of 15, she eventually married a chief and later became a leader of her adopted people. Under the Big Tree Treaty of 1797, she was granted a large parcel of land along the river and lived there until she moved to Buffalo Creek Reservation. William Letchworth had her remains brought back and interred here in 1910.

Letchworth State Park, 1 Letchworth State Park, Castile (585-493-3600; www.nysparks.state.ny.us/parks), is open daily year-round from 6 a.m. to 11 p.m. There is an admission fee of $6 per day per car on weekends during off-season. The museum (585-493-2760) is open daily from May through October between 10 a.m. and 5 p.m. A $1 adult and 50 cent child donation is suggested.

Just west of Canandaigua Lake, the little town of Bristol has become renowned for its pottery. A hand-thrown and hand-decorated collection is crafted by "the Wizard of Clay," master potter Jim Kozlowski and his assistants at **The Wizard of Clay Pottery.** Jim's production facilities and retail stores are housed in seven geodesic domes he designed himself.

The potter's wheel and eight kilns are in the workshop. All pieces are fired at a temperature of 2,265° F, which makes them extremely hard and durable, then treated with a specially formulated glaze that gives them a richly colored finish. The Wizard's most original pottery is decorated with delicate imprints from real leaves gathered from the Bristol hills.

The Wizard of Clay Pottery, 7851 Route 20A in Bristol, 3 miles east of Honeoye Lake (mailing address: 7851 Route 20A, Bloomfield 14469; 585-229-2980; www.wizardofclay.com), is open daily from 9 a.m. until 5 p.m.; closed major holidays.

The town of Horseheads got its name in 1789 when settlers coming into the valley happened upon the bleached skulls of pack horses left behind by General John Sullivan after his battle against the Six Nations of the Iroquois. The **Horseheads Historical Society Museum,** in the former train depot at the corner of Broad and Curns Streets, exhibits cartoons and paintings by the nationally renowned humorist Eugene Zimmerman, better known as "Zim." He lived in a home he designed at the corner of Pine and West Mill Streets. It is maintained by Historical Tours and open for tours by appointment. Zim also designed the bandstand in Teal Park.

Horseheads Historical Society Museum is located at the Depot, 312 West Broad St. & Curns Street, Horseheads (607-739-3938; www.horseheadshistorical .com). It is open Tuesday, Thursday, and Saturday from noon to 3 p.m. and by appointment.

Wings of Eagles, formerly known as the National Warplane Museum, houses an impressive collection of aircraft dating from World War II to the present, as well as exhibits tracing the development of flight, ongoing special events, and a flight simulator in which visitors can experience virtual flight and gain an understanding of what it's like to fly in the cockpit of a warplane.

Wings of Eagles, Elmira-Corning Regional Airport, 17 Aviation Dr., Horseheads (607-739-8200; www.wingsofeagles.com), is open Wednesday through Saturday from 10 a.m. to 4 p.m. and Sunday noon to 4 p.m. Closed Christmas, Thanksgiving, Easter, and New Year's Day. Admission is $7 for adults, $5.50 for senior citizens, $4 for children ages 6 to 17, and free for children under 6. A family admission is available for $18.

Rochester Area

"Spend a day in the nineteenth century," reads the invitation of the *Genesee Country Village & Museum,* the state's largest living history museum. It is located in Mumford on the southern outskirts of Rochester. The fifty-plus reconstructed buildings represent different periods in the development of upstate New York, from frontier days to late Victorian times.

The rail-fenced pioneer settlement reveals what rural living was like up near Lake Ontario around 1800. Just twenty-five years later prosperity brought sumptuous Greek Revival homes such as Livingston Manor. Later came the Victorian quirks and fussy comforts of the 1870 Octagon House, with its tidy cupola and broad verandas. Other village buildings include a carriage barn with a collection of forty horse-drawn vehicles, and a Gallery of Sporting Art showcasing paintings and sculpture inspired by wildlife and the hunt. You can also visit the George Eastman birthplace, moved here in homage to the man who made nearby Rochester a "film capital" of an entirely different sort than Hollywood, California. And the John L. Wehle Gallery of Wildlife and Sporting Art exhibits North America's premier collection of wildlife and sporting art.

The Genesee Country Village & Museum, 1410 Flint Hill Rd., off Route 36 in Mumford (585-538-6822; www.gcv.org), is open July through Labor Day Tuesday through Sunday 10 a.m. to 5 p.m.; the rest of the year Tuesday through Friday 10 a.m. to 4 p.m., and weekends and holidays 10 a.m. to 5

On a Pedestal

In 1899 Theodore Roosevelt, governor of New York, came to Rochester to dedicate the country's first public statue to be erected to honor an African American, Frederick Douglass (1807–1895). The escaped slave, abolitionist, and newspaper publisher lived here for seventeen years. His home on Alexander Street was a station on the Underground Railroad. The bronze statue is in Highland Park on Highland Avenue. Douglass is interred in Mt. Hope Cemetery along with other luminaries, including his friend, women's rights champion Susan B. Anthony.

p.m. Closed Monday except on holidays. There is a nature center at the village that is open all year, and special programs are held year-round. Admission is $15 for adults, $12 for seniors and students with ID, and $9 for children ages 4 to 16; under 4, free.

Up near Rochester, in North Chili, Linda Greenfield has assembled an overzealous collection of delicate and elaborately dressed playthings in the **Victorian Doll Museum.** The thousands of dolls lining the museum reflect the tastes of the Victorian era but also show many types of doll construction that have faded from the picture in these days of molded plastic doll faces and bodies.

The Victorian Doll Museum premises are also the home of the **Chili Doll Hospital,** also run by Linda, who is an expert at doll restoration and repair. Antique dolls are appraised by appointment, and a collector's gift shop offers fine modern and period reproduction specimens.

The Victorian Doll Museum & Chili Doll Hospital, 4332 Buffalo Rd., North Chili (585-247-0130; www.chilidollhospital.com), are open mid-February through December, Tuesday through Saturday 11 a.m. to 4:30 p.m. Closed major holidays. Admission to the museum is $3 for adults and $1.50 for children ages 3 to 12.

"Please touch, feel, and explore" is the motto at one of the state's most unusual and engaging museums. The **Strong National Museum of Play,** the legacy of buggy-whip heiress Margaret Woodbury Strong, explores American life and tastes since 1820 with a variety of imaginative permanent and changing exhibits. Explore more than 500,000 objects among the world's largest and most historically significant collection of toys and dolls and the country's most comprehensive collection of homecrafts, souvenirs, and advertising materials. The Time Lab, a hands-on learning lab and interactive warehouse, exhibits thousands of items including lava lamps and political buttons from various periods. Visitors can select a tune from their tabletop jukebox while they dine on burgers and fries at the vintage Skyline Diner or enjoy a sundae at Louie's Sweet Shoppe.

The Strong National Museum of Play, One Manhattan Sq., Rochester (585-263-2700; www.strongmuseum.org), is open Monday through Thursday from 10 a.m. to 5 p.m., Friday and Saturday 10 a.m. to 8 p.m., Sunday from noon to 5 p.m. Closed Christmas and Thanksgiving. Admission is $10 for adults, $9 for senior citizens and students with school ID, and $8 for children ages 2 to 15.

nodistractions?

John D. Rockefeller Sr., Jay Gould, F. W. Woolworth, and George Eastman were among a host of nineteenth- and early twentieth-century tycoons who rose from the obscurity of small-town birthplaces in upstate New York.

The music emporium **House of Guitars,** or HOG, counts Metallica, Aerosmith, Motley Crue, Jon Bon Jovi, and Ozzy Osbourne among its customers. Explore a rambling complex of five warehouses "jam" packed with an array of "musicana" from guitars to amplifiers to concert T-shirts to a pair of Elvis Presley's leather pants.

The House of Guitars was established in 1964 by three brothers named Schaubroeck. Today the musical mecca in Rochester's suburbs calls itself the "World's Largest Music Store" and stocks just about every brand of instrument (if they don't have it, they'll order it), including more than 11,000 guitars ranging in price from $60 to $50,000. Potential customers are invited to test the merchandise in one of several small rooms set aside for that purpose.

Throughout the year the musical brothers Schaubroeck host promotions and in-store appearances, featuring unknown, rising, and well-known performers. The winner of one of their most successful events, the "World's Worst Guitar Player Contest," won a $400 guitar and amp, six free lessons, and a one-way bus ticket to Canada.

The House of Guitars, 645 Titus Ave., Rochester (585-544-3500; www.houseofguitars.com), is open Monday through Saturday from 10 a.m. to 9 p.m. and Sunday 1 to 5 p.m.

South and east of Rochester is a monument to another important development in the history of American popular culture: the shopping mall. Not the steel-and-glass malls of the 1950s, but a sturdy wooden structure erected in 1879 and built by Levi Valentine as an all-purpose market and community center for the settlement he was developing. Thus it lays claim to being the first multistore "shopping center" in the United States.

Today it houses the **Valentown Museum,** a collection of nineteenth-century small-town memorabilia that includes a reconstruction of the first railroad station in the Rochester area and a "Scientific Exhibition," which traveled around the country in a covered wagon from 1825 to 1880.

Valentown Hall, as Valentine called his "mall," had front doors opening into a general store, meat market, cobbler shop, barber shop, bakery, and harness shop. The upstairs contained a Grange lodge with rooms where classes in the arts and trades were held, and a community ballroom. The ambitious scheme lasted only thirty years, since the promised railroad connection never materialized (the restored station interior belonged to an earlier rail operation). The building was saved from demolition and restored in 1940 by J. Sheldon Fisher, a member of the Fisher family that gave its name to the town of Fishers, in which the hall is located. Contact the Valentown Museum, at Valentown Square, Victor (585-924-4170; www.valentown.org).

"Ganondagan, a city or village of bark, situated at the top of a mountain of earth, to which one rises by three terraces. It appeared to us, from a distance, to be crowned with round towers," is how M. L'Abbé De Belmont described a major town of the Seneca people, one of the five original Indian nations that have inhabited central New York since prehistoric times. Shortly afterward the governor general of New France led an army from Canada against the Seneca in an effort to eliminate them as competitors in the international fur trade.

The story of the Seneca people and the Iroquois (Haudenosaunee) Confederacy to which they belonged is recounted at **Ganondagan State Historic Site,** the state's largest Seneca community in the seventeenth century. The 522-acre National Historic Landmark encompasses the palisaded granary M. L'Abbé De Belmont described, a sacred burial ground, and a system of trails. A twenty-seven-minute video in the visitor center relates the history of Ganondagan. A reconstructed bark longhouse similar to ones lived in by the Seneca people is one of the site's high points.

The Visitor Center at Ganondagan State Historic Site, 1488 State Route 444, Victor (585-924-5848; www.ganondagan .org), is open Tuesday through Sunday 9 a.m. to 5 p.m. May through September; Tuesday through Saturday in October. Interpretive trails are open year-round from 8 a.m. to sunset, weather permitting. The bark longhouse is open Tuesday through Sunday 10 a.m. to noon and 1 to 4 p.m. The trails are open

r.i.p.ripper

Rochester is rumored to be the final resting place of Dr. Francis J. Tumuelty, better known as (the suspected) Jack the Ripper. Tumuelty was born upstate, moved to London, and came back while being investigated for the crimes. He was never tried and died of natural causes in 1903. You can find his grave at the Holy Sepulchre Cemetery.

all year. Admission is $3 for adults and $2 for children; tours are $5 for adults and $4 for students and senior citizens.

The early days of vacuum tubes and crystal radios are chronicled in the *Antique Wireless Association's Electronic Communication Museum* south of the thruway in East Bloomfield. The museum's collections, housed in the handsome 1837 quarters of the East Bloomfield Historical Society, have been amassed by AWA members throughout the world. They include nineteenth-century telephones still in working order, some of Marconi's original wireless apparatus, early shipboard wireless equipment, and the crystal radio sets that brought the first broadcast programs into American living rooms. A special attraction is a fully stocked replica of a circa 1925 radio store; another is wireless station W2AN, an actual broadcast operation staffed by AWA members.

The AWA Electronic Communication Museum, on the Village Green just off Routes 5 and 20, Bloomfield (585-657-6260; www.antiquewireless.org), is open May through September on Saturday from 2 to 4 p.m. and Sunday 2 to 5 p.m., closed on the July 4 and 5 and September 5 and 6. Admission is free.

The *Granger Homestead and Carriage Museum* in Canandaigua carries the theme of preserved Americana that is prevalent in upstate New York. "Homestead" is too homespun a term for this grand Federal mansion, which must have been the talk of Canandaigua and all the farms around when it was built in 1816 by Gideon Granger, a lawyer who had served as postmaster general under Jefferson and Madison. Granger came here to live the life of a country squire in his retirement, and his descendants lived here until 1930. Nine restored rooms contain the furniture of the nineteenth century, including Federal, Empire, and Victorian styles. Decorative objects, original artworks, and China Trade porcelain are also displayed.

A distinctive attraction of the Granger Homestead is the Carriage Museum, which exhibits more than fifty horse-drawn vehicles made or used in western New York. The sociological implications of the various conveyances on display are explained in an informative exhibit titled "Sleighs and Surreys and Signs and Symbols."

Forty-five-minute horse-drawn antique carriage rides through the town's historic neighborhoods are offered by reservation on Friday at noon, 1 p.m., 2 p.m., 3 p.m., and 4 p.m. through late October. Adults are $20; children 4 to 12 are $10; under 3 free. The carriage can hold up to three adults or two adults and three children. The museum also gives horse-drawn antique sleigh rides on Sunday from 1 to 3 p.m., mid-January to mid-March, weather permitting. Adults are $5; ages 4 to 12, $3. Call for conditions and availability.

The Granger Homestead and Carriage Museum, 295 North Main St., Canandaigua (585-394-1472; www.grangerhomestead.org), is open mid-May through mid-October on Tuesday and Wednesday from 1 to 5 p.m. and Thursday and Friday 11 a.m. to 5 p.m. During weekends in June through late October, it is open 1 to 5 p.m. The last tour begins at 3 p.m. Guided tours are also available on Tuesday and Wednesday from 1 to 4 p.m., on Thursday and Friday from 11 a.m. to 4 p.m., and weekends from 1 to 4 p.m. from June through October. Admission runs $6 for adults, $5 for seniors, $2 for students, and pre-schoolers are free.

Sonnenberg Gardens are part of a Gilded Age extravaganza, part Tudor Revival, part Queen Anne and were built by the founder of the First National Bank of the City of New York, Frederick Ferris Thompson, in 1887. The forty-room mansion is well worth a tour, but even more impressive than the heavily carved Victorian furniture and fine Oriental rugs contained beneath the house's multicolor slate roof are the gardens themselves.

Frederick Thompson died in 1899, and in 1902 his widow, Mary Clark Thompson, began the extensive formal and informal plantings on the estate as a memorial.

She worked for the next fourteen years, utilizing just about every major mode of horticultural expression. She developed a Japanese garden, a rock garden, an Italian garden, a sunken parterre display in a Versailles-inspired fleur-de-lis motif, an old-fashioned garden, a garden planted entirely in blue and white flowers, and a rose garden containing more than 2,600 magnificent bushes blossoming in red, white, and pink. After the Roman bath, the thirteen-house greenhouse complex with a domed palm house conservatory, the fountains and statuary everywhere, the mansion itself almost seems like an afterthought.

There is no fee to visit the Finger Lakes Wine Center (585-394-9016) in Bay House, which sells gourmet foods and wines from the Finger Lakes region. At the tasting room, visitors can sample ten to fifteen different wines and choose from more than 160.

Sonnenberg Gardens and Mansion State Historic Park, 151 Charlotte Street off Route 21, Canandaigua (585-394-4922; www.sonnenberg.org), is open daily mid-May through October, 9:30 a.m. to 4:30 p.m.; in summer, it is open until 5:30 p.m. Walking tours are offered weekdays at 1 p.m. and on weekends at 10 a.m. and 1 p.m. (no tours before Memorial Day or after Labor Day). Admission is $10 for adults, $9 for senior citizens and AAA members, and $5 for students; children under 12 free. A season pass is available for $20 if purchased after the gardens open, $17 if purchased before. A free tram provides transportation around the grounds.

The 1810 **Morgan Samuels Inn,** nestled on forty-six acres of land, is an 1810 English-style stone mansion with five elegantly furnished bedrooms with fireplaces and one suite, three balconies, and a tennis court. Guests are served breakfast by candlelight. The Victorian porch is a delightful spot to relax and view the gardens. It's at 2920 Smith Rd., Canandaigua (585-394-9232; www .morgansamuelsinn.com). Rates range from $195 to $395 a night, depending on season.

The craftsmanship of women is often undervalued throughout history, but Mrs. Merle Alling of Rochester appreciated skilled hand work. For over thirty years she amassed the country's largest collection of homespun coverlets, which are now displayed at the **Alling Coverlet Museum,** part of Historic Palmyra. The heirlooms represent both the simple spreads hand-loomed by farmwives and the somewhat more sophisticated designs woven on multiple-harness looms by professionals during the nineteenth century. The collection also includes a number of handmade nineteenth-century quilts and antique spinning equipment.

The Alling Coverlet Museum (Historic Palmyra, Inc.), 122 William St., Palmyra (315-597-6981; www.historicpalmyrany.com), is open daily June through mid-September, 1 to 4 p.m. and by appointment. Admission is $2 per museum or $5 for all three for adults, $1 per museum or $2 for all three for children 2 and older, and $1.50 per museum or $2 for all three for senior citizens.

You can find another facet of Historic Palmyra is the **William Phelps General Store & Home Museum.** Erected in 1825, this commercial build-ing was purchased by William Phelps in 1867 and remained in his family until 1977. Having remained practically unchanged over the past 130 years, the store, along with its stock, furnishings, and business records provides a time capsule of Palmyra in the nineteenth and early twentieth centuries. The gaslight fixtures in the store and upstairs residential quarters were used by a Phelps family member until 1976, electricity never having been installed in the building.

The William Phelps General Store & Home Museum, 140 Market St., Palmyra (315-597-6981), is open from late spring to fall, Tuesday through Saturday from 11 a.m. to 4 p.m.; from fall to spring, Tuesday through Thursday 10 a.m. to 4 p.m. or by appointment.

Historic Palmyra, Inc.'s final holding is the **Palmyra Historical Museum,** erected about 1900 as a hotel. It is now a museum housing a unique display of elegant furniture, children's toys and dolls, household items, tools, gowns, and other artifacts of bygone ages.

The Palmyra Historical Museum, 132 Market St., Palmyra (315-597-6981), is open from late spring to fall, Tuesday through Saturday from 11 a.m. to 4 p.m.; from fall to spring, Tuesday through Thursday 10 a.m. to 5 p.m. or by appointment.

Eastern Lakes

To see if the fish are biting, head for **Sodus Bay** on the shore of Lake Ontario. In season more than twenty-five charter boat companies offer their services in this small fishing paradise. Stop for a bite at **Papa Joe's Restaurant** on Sodus Point. The only restaurant open here year-round, it has a children's menu and entertainment on the deck on summer weekends. Lunch and dinner are served from 11:30 a.m. until 10 p.m. A two-bedroom apartment overlooking the bay is available for rent on a nightly basis. Call (315) 483-6372.

The lighthouse at **Sodus Bay Lighthouse Museum** (7606 N. Ontario St., Sodus Point 14555; 315-483-4936; www.soduspointlighthouse.org) was built in 1871 and remained in use until 1901. Museum displays include ship models, dioramas, shipboard equipment, a lens repair shop, and other maritime exhibits. There's a wonderful view of the lake from the tower. It is open May 1 through October 31, Tuesday through Sunday 10 a.m. to 5 p.m. Admission is $3 for adults, $1 for children ages 11 to 17.

The 1870 Victorian **Carriage House Inn** (corner of Ontario and Wickham Boulevard, Sodus Point; 315-483-2100; www.carriage-house-inn.com) charges around $150 for rooms and suites with a private bath, cable TV, and full breakfast. Rooms are also available in the stone carriage house, which overlooks the lake and lighthouse. Two efficiencies, which sleep up to four, have outdoor decks and picnic tables.

Bonnie Castle Farm Bed & Breakfast, on fifty acres of landscaped grounds overlooking Great Sodus Bay, is a three-story Victorian with private balconies and bilevel decks. Each of the eight rooms has its own bath; the Bonnie Castle Suite has a kitchen. If you need three bedrooms, there's also an 1890 Victorian summer home, the Aldrich Guest House, whose balcony and porch overlook the water. Locust Grove Cottage, overlooking the meadow, can accommodate three to six people.

Bonnie Castle Farm Bed & Breakfast, 6603 Bonnie Castle Rd., Wolcott (315-587-2273), is open year-round. Rates range from $120 to $200 for rooms to $1,500 a week for the three-bedroom guest house and include a full breakfast buffet with such dishes as apple knocker sausages, seafood pasta, and Mexican frittatas. There's also a private beach.

The northern Finger Lakes region serves as New York State's dust covered attic, filled with an eclectic range of collections. In Newark the **Hoffman Clock Museum** comprises more than a hundred clocks and watches collected

No Passengers, Please

If you're planning to put a boat into any of the Finger Lakes, make sure the trailer, hull, and external motor or drive apparatus have been thoroughly cleaned. It's especially important if the vessel has been in the Great Lakes, St. Lawrence River, Lake Champlain, or connected waters. Zebra mussels and the aquatic weed milfoil are invasive, non-native pests whose spread you can help prevent by scrubbing down hulls, motors, and trailers with hot water.

by local jeweler and watchmaker Augustus L. Hoffman. Housed in the Newark Public Library, the collection includes timepieces from Great Britain, Europe, and Japan. Although the majority of the clocks and watches are of nineteenth-century American manufacture, more than a dozen were made in New York State. Each summer the museum's curator mounts a special exhibit devoted to a particular aspect of the horologist's art.

The Hoffman Clock Museum, Newark Public Library, 121 High St., Newark (315-331-4370; www.hoffmanclockmuseum.org), is open Monday through Thursday 9:30 a.m. to 9 p.m., Friday 9:30 a.m. to 6 p.m., and Saturday 9:30 a.m. to 5 p.m.; closed Sunday and holidays. Admission is free.

If your interest in antiques extends beyond timepieces, head south a few miles to Geneva for a tour of *Rose Hill Mansion,* the Geneva Historical Society's National Historic landmark property overlooking the east shore of Seneca Lake. Built in 1839, the twenty-six-room mansion is one of the nation's premier examples of the Greek Revival style at its peak of refinement and popularity. Formal, symmetrical, and serene within its boxwood garden, Rose Hill Mansion has been exquisitely restored and furnished with as many pieces original to the house as it has been possible to collect. The twenty-one-room tour highlights the dining room, with its 5-foot-long 1815 Portuguese crystal chandelier; the front parlor, containing a seven-piece Rococo rosewood ensemble; and the Green Bedroom, decorated in the Empire style that paralleled the Greek Revival architectural trend. Rose Hill's formality is offset by its airy, spacious character—all of its front windows open from the floor, making a seamless link between ground-floor rooms and the colonnaded front porch.

Rose Hill Mansion, Route 96A, just south of Routes 5 and 20, Geneva (Geneva Historical Society, 315-789-5151; www.genevahistoricalsociety.com/rose_hill.htm; Rose Hill, 315-789-3848), is open May through October, Tuesday through Saturday 10 a.m. to 4 p.m. and Sunday 1 to 5 p.m. Admission is $7 for adults, $6 for seniors, $4 for students age 10 to 18. Children under 10 are free.

Two of the Finger Lakes' most elegant inn-restaurants overlook its deep-est lake, Seneca, in Geneva, the self-proclaimed "Trout Capital of the World."

It took fifty men more than four years to build the turreted red Medina stone **Belhurst Castle,** overlooking Seneca Lake. When it was finally completed in 1889, the cost of construction exceeded $475,000. Today the Richard-sonian Romanesque inn is on the National Register of Historic Places and has a reputation as one of the finer places in the region at which to stay and/or dine.

There are fourteen period mansion rooms in the castle (including one with a private balcony and one in the castle turret, with a widow's walk) and several houses on the grounds behind the castle. These include the Carriage House, with a four-poster bed and private patio, and the Ice House, with a loft bedroom; both of these offer more private accommodations. A three-bedroom ranch house adjacent to Belhurst is also available.

White Springs Manor, sister property to Belhurst Castle, was once owned by a wealthy lawyer and land baron. The imposing 1806 Georgian Revival mansion, perched on a hilltop in the middle of eighteen acres, affords guests a panoramic view of Seneca Lake and beyond. Each of the twelve guest rooms and the "playhouse" (a detached house) has a private bath, gas fireplace, and queen- or king-size bed. Belhurst's new Vinifera Inn, opened in summer 2004, offers rooms with lake views, opulent appointments, fireplaces, and two-person Jacuzzis. Rates range from $75 to $355 depending on the room and season.

Belhurst Castle, 4069 Lochland Rd. (Route 14S), Geneva (315-781-0201; www.belhurst.com), is open year-round.

"An oasis, a little island of beauty, peace, and friendliness in a busy world" is how **Geneva On The Lake** describes itself. However, American Historic Inns describes it as "One of the 10 most romantic inns in the United States." The inn, with its terra-cotta tile roof, Palladian windows, Ionic columns, clas-sical sculptures, and magnificent formal gardens, was built in 1910 by Byron Nester, who was inspired by the summer residences around northern Italy's Lakes Garda and Maggiore. All rooms are suites and range in price, depending on time of year, from upwards of $300 to $1,293 for special packages . Rates include wine, fresh fruit and flowers, the New York Times delivered to your door, a wine and cheese party on Friday evening, and continental breakfast, weather permitting, on the terrace overlooking the gardens and lake.

Geneva On The Lake, 1001 Lochland Rd., Route 14S, Geneva (315-789-7190; www.genevaonthelake.com), is open all year.

"To honor in perpetuity these women, citizens of the United States of America, whose contributions to the arts, athletics, business, education, government, the humanities, philanthropy and science have been the great-est value for the development of their country." Thus were the parameters for entry outlined when the women of Seneca Falls created the ***National Women's Hall of Fame*** in 1969, believing that the contributions of American women deserved a permanent home.

The list of members reads like a "Who's Who" in women's history. Marian Anderson, Pearl S. Buck, Rachel Carson, Amelia Earhart, Billie Jean King, Sally Ride, Dorothea Dix, and a host of others who left their mark on American history and the American psyche are honored.

Exhibits are housed in the bank building in the heart of the Historic District II and include a panel celebrating Elizabeth Cady Stanton, who led the way to rights for women, and artifacts and mementos about the members, events, and activities significant to women's history.

The National Women's Hall of Fame, 76 Fall St., Seneca Falls (315-568-8060; www.greatwomen.org), is open from May through September, Monday through Saturday from 11 a.m. to 5 p.m. and Sunday noon to 5 p.m.; October through April, Wednesday through Saturday 10 a.m. to 5 p.m. Closed Thanksgiving, Christmas, and the month of January. Admission is $3 for adults, $1.50 for senior citizens and students. There is a family rate of $7.

The ***Hubbell House Bed & Breakfast*** overlooking Van Cleef Lake was built in the 1850s as a Gothic Revival cottage and later enlarged and remodeled in the Second Empire style. It also holds recognition of being a stop on the Underground Railroad. The delightfully eccentric building with scrolled bargeboards, wooden pinnacles, windows of all sizes, and a rear mansard roof with diamond-shaped slate tiles is furnished with an eclectic mix of antiques, including an 1860s Eastlake dresser, armchair, and rocker, and has four guest rooms (two with private bath). The wrap-around porch overlooks the lake.

Hubbell House Bed & Breakfast, 42 Cayuga St., Seneca Falls (315-568-9690; www.hubbellhousebb.com), is open all year. Rates range from $135 to $155 a night and include a full breakfast. Guests can swim and use paddleboats from the inn's private dock.

A Snake in the Grass

Just outside the town of Geneva lies Bare Hill, sacred to the Seneca. According to legend, it was here the Creator opened up the earth and allowed their ancestors to enter into the world. But a giant serpent lay in wait, eating the newborns as they appeared. Finally, a warrior, acting upon a dream in which the Creator told him to fear not, slew the snake with a magic arrow, and the snake, in its death throes, disgorged all those he'd eaten.

In the summer of 1865 in the village of Waterloo, a patriotic businessman named Henry C. Welles put forward the idea of honoring the fallen soldiers of the Civil War by placing flowers on their graves on a specified day of observance. On May 5 of the following year, the village was draped in mourning, thanks to the efforts of Welles and Civil War veteran General John B. Murray. A contingent of veterans and townspeople marched to the local cemeteries and decorated their comrades' graves. Thus Memorial Day was born.

In 1966 President Johnson signed a proclamation officially naming Waterloo the birthplace of Memorial Day. On May 29 of that same Memorial Day centennial year, Waterloo's ***Memorial Day Museum*** opened in a reclaimed mansion in the heart of town. The once-derelict, twenty-room brick structure is itself a local treasure and distinguished by the ornate ironwork on its veranda. Although built in the early Italianate Revival era of 1836–50, the house has undergone renovations to restore its appearance circa 1860–70, the decade of the Civil War and the first Memorial Day observances.

The museum's collections cover the Civil War and the lives and era of the originators of the holiday, as well as memorabilia from all other U.S. wars.

The Memorial Day Museum, 35 East Main St., Waterloo (315-539-9611; www.waterloony.com/mdaymus.html), is open from Tuesday through Saturday 10 a.m. to 5 p.m. from April 15 through May 22 and September 8 through December 15. From May 23 until September 4, the museum is open from Tuesday through Sunday 10 a.m. to 5 p.m. and by appointment only. Admission is by donation, and tours by appointment only.

Just a block from the Memorial Day Museum is the ***Waterloo Terwilliger Historical Museum,*** where the "antique and elegant" combine with the "long-lasting and functional" to tell the story of Waterloo and surrounding areas. The collection includes everything from Native American artifacts to Roaring Twenties fashions. Authentic full-size vehicles and a replica of a general store offer a slice of life as it used to be; five rooms, decorated down to the last detail, each depict a specific era.

The Waterloo Library & Historical Society and Terwilliger Museum, 31 East Williams St., Waterloo (315-539-0533; www.waterloony.com/library), is open year-round, from 11 a.m. to 8 p.m. Monday through Wednesday; 11 a.m. to 5 p.m. Thursday to Friday; and 9 a.m. to noon on Saturdays from September to June only. Tours are given by appointment.

Between 1942 and 1946, Sampson Naval Training Station prepared 411,429 sailors and Waves to serve in World War II. The ***Sampson WW-2 Navy Museum,*** established in the station's original Navy brig facility, is filled with military artifacts donated by members of the Sampson WW-2 Navy Veterans organization and the U.S. Navy Department. The museum, in Sampson

Bloomers and Suffragists

Although Amelia Jenks Bloomer didn't invent "bloomers" (they were invented by Elizabeth Smith Miller), she was instrumental in making them the uniform of nineteenth-century suffragists. The *New York Tribune* described Mrs. Bloomer's outfit: ". . . a kilt descended just below the knees, the skirt of which was trimmed with rows of black velvet. The pantaloons were of the same texture and trimmed in the same style. She wore gaiters. Her headdress was cherry and black. Her dress had a large open corsage with bands of velvet over the white chamesette in which was a diamond stud pin. She wore flowing sleeves, tight undersleeves, and black lace mitts. Her whole attire was rich and plain in appearance."

Mrs. Bloomer and her fellow suffragists abandoned their costume when they became objects of ridicule and children would follow them, chanting:

"Hi Ho,

In sleet and snow,

Mrs. Bloomer's all the go.

Twenty tailors to take the stitches,

Plenty of women to wear the britches."

State Park, 6096 Route 96A, Romulus (315-585-6392; http://www.dmna .state.ny.us/forts/fortsQ_S/sampsonNavalTrainingBase.htm), is open Tuesday through Saturday 10 a.m. to 4 p.m. and Sunday noon to 4 p.m. and closed on Monday and all New York State holidays. Admission is free, but there is a park entrance fee of $7 per vehicle ($6 until mid-June) from mid-June through Labor Day.

The *Cayuga Museum* in Auburn is really two museums combined in one, unraveling the rich history of Auburn, "the village that touched the world," and surrounding Cayuga County. Located in the 1836 Willard-Case Mansion, the museum was founded in 1936. On display are business timekeeping devices including the "Thousand Year Clock," manufactured by Auburn's Bundy brothers. Their Binghamton, New York, operation evolved into IBM, as well as an exhibit on the early history of the now-giant corporation. Other notables from Cayuga County highlighted at the museum include President Millard Fillmore; E. S. Martin, founder of the original, pre-Luce *Life* magazine; prison reformer Thomas M. Osborne; and Ely Parker, the Seneca Indian who penned the surrender at Appomattox.

The Stanton Gallery once served as the dining room in the Willard-Case mansion and holds the Dyckman Collection of period furnishings that typify the decor found in upper-class European and American homes in the mid- to late 1800s.

In 1911 Theodore W. Case proved that recording sound on film was possible, and in late 1922 he made it a reality with the assistance of E. I. Sponable. Restored in 1993 after being forgotten for sixty years, the *Case Research Lab Museum* opened its doors to the public on the second floor of the Cayuga Museum's carriage house. Exhibits include the laboratory building, the soundstage, and many examples of the early history, inventions, and laboratory equipment developed to commercialize sound on film. The building where Theodore Case developed the first "talkies" now houses an exhibit telling the story of how this medium was developed in the museum's backyard.

The Cayuga Museum and the Case Research Lab Museum, 203 West Genesee St., Auburn (315-253-8051), are open February through December, Tuesday through Sunday; the Cayuga Museum hours are noon to 5 p.m., and Case Research Lab Museum hours are noon to 4:30 p.m.; closed major holidays. Admission is free; however, there is a suggested donation $3.

The "Woman Called Moses" is remembered at the *Harriet Tubman Home* in Auburn, where she settled after making nineteen trips to the South to rescue more than 300 enslaved persons. A guided tour includes a visit to the Tubman House, the Home for the Aged, the ruins of the John Brown Infirmary, the former Thompson Memorial A.M.E. Zion Church building, and Mrs. Tubman's grave at Fort Hill Cemetery.

The Harriet Tubman Home, at 180 South St., Auburn (315-252-2081; www .nyhistory.com/harriettubman), is open Tuesday through Friday 11 a.m. to 4 p.m. and Saturday by appointment. There are extended hours in February, Black History Month. Admission is $5 for adults, $3 for seniors, and $2 for children.

The *Willard Memorial Chapel* is all that remains of the Auburn Theological Seminary campus, which thrived here from 1818 to 1939. Experts believe it is the only extant example of a complete Louis Comfort Tiffany interior. The handsome gray limestone and red sandstone Romanesque Revival building was designed by A. J. Warner of Rochester and houses a magnificent interior designed and handcrafted by the Tiffany Glass and Decorating Company. Among the highlights are a three-paneled stained-glass window of "Christ Sustaining Peter on the Water," nine leaded-glass chandeliers, and fourteen opalescent nave windows.

"The Tiffany Treasure of the Finger Lakes" hosts numerous concerts throughout the year, including the Tiffany Summer Concert Series on Wednesday at noon in July and August. Admission is by donation. For a complete concert schedule, contact the Community Preservation Committee, Inc., at the number below.

The Willard Memorial Chapel, 17 Nelson St., Auburn (315-252-0339; www .willardchapel.org), is open Tuesday through Friday 10 a.m. to 4 p.m. year-round, and on Sunday from 1 to 4 p.m. in July and August, or by appointment; closed holidays. Suggested donation is $3 per person.

"Quando mangiate da Rosalie sembra mangiare in Italia" (When you eat at Rosalie's, it's like eating in Italy), proclaims the menu at **Rosalie's Cucina.** Most of the dishes are northern Italian, and many are family reci-pes, such as Braciole, Vitello Piccata, Cappa Santa al Prosciutto e Basilico. The restaurant is at 841 West Genesee St., Skaneateles (315-685-2200; www .rosaliescucina.com) and is open for dinner nightly. Closed major holidays and Super Bowl Sunday.

Classic cars, historic race cars, and racing memorabilia are all exhibited at the **D.I.R.T. Motorsports Hall of Fame & Classic Car Museum,** along with a "Hall of Fame" of legendary race car drivers.

Among the classic cars on display are a 1926 Duesenberg, the 1929 Dodge Roadster that won first place in a cross-country race in 1993, and a 1969 Dodge Charger Hemi 4-speed. For stock car enthusiasts, there's the Buzzie Reutimann "00" coupe, which won the first two Schaefer 100s, and "Batmobile" #112 driven by Gary Balough in 1980. In the Jack Burgess Memorial Video Room, the "master of the microphone" recounts exciting racing events of the past. The Northeast Classic Motorsports Extravaganza is held each August.

Also here is Cayuga County Fair Speedway, home of Drivers Independent Race Tracks (D.I.R.T.), the second-largest race-sanctioning body in the nation (races every Sunday night May through September).

D.I.R.T. Motorsports Hall of Fame and Classic Car Museum, 1 Speedway Dr., Weedsport (315-834-6606), is open May through October, Saturday and Sunday 10 a.m. to 5 p.m. Admission is $5 for adults and $3 for children under 12 years and senior citizens over age 60.

Beaver Lake Nature Center, an Onondaga County park, incorporates several different ecosystems connected by 9 miles of well-maintained hiking trails. A 200-acre lake offers beautiful vistas but no recreational facilities and is a migration-time magnet for up to 30,000 Canada geese. Guided canoe tours of the lake are available during the summer. Rental canoes are avail-able for these tours, and you must pre-register. The entire center is a great place for birders; nearly 200 species have been sighted here over the years. The informative Beaver Lake Visitor Center is the starting point for a regular schedule of hour-long guided tours of the trails, given by professional natu-ralists each weekend.

Beaver Lake Nature Center, 8477 East Mud Lake Rd., Baldwinsville (315-638-2519; www.onondagacountyparks.com/parks/beaver), is open all year, daily from 7:30 a.m. to dusk; closed Thanksgiving and Christmas. Admission is $2 per car.

Ithaca is home of the ***Paleontological Research Institution*** (PRI), whose Museum of the Earth houses more than two million fossils. It is one of the premier collections in the Western Hemisphere and tells the story of the planet's 4.6-billion-year history through exhibits, hands-on activities, and audiovisual presentations that tend to focus on the Northeast. The institution, located in a former orphanage on the southwest shore of Cayuga Lake, was founded by Gilbert D. Harris, a professor of geology at Cornell University from 1894 to 1934.

Among the fossils exhibited are single-celled microfossils, ancient plants, the remains of ancient vertebrates including dinosaurs, whales, and woolly mammoths, and a magnificent 425-million-year-old trilobite. The Hyde Park Mastodon Fossil skeleton is one of the most complete in the world.

Museum of the Earth, 1259 Trumansburg Rd., Route 96, Ithaca (607-273-6623; www.museumoftheearth.org), is open from Labor Day through Memorial Day, Monday and Thursday through Saturday 10 a.m. to 5 p.m., Sunday 11 a.m. to 5 p.m. (closed major holidays); and after Memorial Day until Labor Day, Monday through Saturday, 10 a.m. to 5 p.m. and Sunday from 11 a.m. to 5 p.m. Admission is $8 for adults, $5 for seniors and students with ID, $3 for youths 4 to 17, and free for children 3 and under.

Thanks to a poor boy who grew up to be a wealthy shoe manufacturer and benefactor, six of approximately 170 carved wood ***carousels*** remaining in this country are located in Broome County. Between 1919 and 1934 George F. Johnson donated six carousels manufactured by the Allan Herschell Companies of North Tonawanda to the county. Remembering his poor childhood, he put one stipulation on the gift. He felt that everyone should be able to ride and insisted that the municipalities never charge a fee.

Today, gorilla chariots, pigs, and horses with lions hidden in saddle blankets transport riders on their backs to magical realms. And at two of the carousels—Recreation and Ross Parks—the

sundaespecialty

While other cities may lay claim to the invention of the sundae, Ithaca has the earliest documentation. A newspaper advertisement announcing the "Cherry Sunday, a New 10 cent Ice Cream Specialty Served only at Platt & Colt's Famous day and night Soda Fountain" dates back to April 5, 1891.

Bright Lights Binghamton

If you've already seen the Hollywood Walk of Fame, you can add Binghamton's to your celebrity sidewalk repertoire. Shortly after WWII, the city proudly called a handful of celebrities locals. In today's terms, we probably would have called them "B" list. Among the motley crew is Richard Deacon, boss on the *Dick Van Dyke Show* and Lumpy's dad on *Leave it to Beaver,* and Rod Serling from the *Twilight Zone.* Find the stars in the heart of downtown on Court Street between Water and State Streets.

animals twirl to the sounds of the original Wurlitzer band organs. Riders who take a spin on all six merry-go-rounds receive a special button.

The carousels are located at C. Fred Johnson Park, Johnson City (607-797-9098); George W. Johnson Park, Endicott (607-757-2427); West Endicott Park, Endicott (607-786-2970); Recreation Park, Binghamton (607-722-9166 or 607-662-7017); Ross Park, Binghamton (607-724-5461); and Highland Park, Endwell (607-786-2970). They operate from Memorial Day to Labor Day, and riders are asked to donate a piece of litter collected along the way. An exhibit at Ross Park explores the history of carousel making. For general information contact the Broome County Chamber of Commerce at (800) 836-6740.

For more than sixty-five years, Endicott has been home to ***Pat Mitchell's Homemade Ice Cream.*** Founded in 1920 by Joseph Travis, the store began to thrive in 1948 when Raymond "Pat" Mitchell bought the business. Using a vintage 1920s batch freezer, he began making ice cream that has become legendary in these parts. Today's owners continue to make thousands of gallons, three gallons at a time, filling orders from coast to coast and around the globe.

What makes Pat Mitchell's ice cream so good? Everyone has a different opinion, as the store offers more than 250 flavors. Choose from treats such as banana delight, made with fresh banana ice cream, cashews, and a chocolate weave; fresh cantaloupe; coconut almond fudge; and chocolate chip.

Pat Mitchell's Homemade Ice Cream shops are at 231 Vestal Ave. in Endicott, and on Vestal Avenue in Binghamton. For information call (607) 785-3080 or (607) 786-5501.

Places to Stay in the Finger Lakes

To receive a copy of the Finger Lakes Bed & Breakfast Association brochure, contact the organization at:
Finger Lakes Bed & Breakfast Association
56 Cayuga St.
Seneca Falls 13148
(877) 422-6327
www.flbba.org

AURORA

Aurora Inn
391 Main St.
(315) 364-8888
www.aurora-inn.com

CORNING

Hillcrest Manor
227 Cedar St.
(607) 936-4548
www.corninghillcrestmanor
.com

ELMIRA

The Painted Lady B&B
520 Water St.
(607) 846-3500
www.thepaintedlady.net

GENEVA

Belhurst Castle
4069 Route 14 South
(315) 781-0201
www.belhurst.com

HAMMONDSPORT

Elm Croft Manor Bed & Breakfast
8361 Pleasant Valley Rd.
(607) 569-3071 or
(800) 506-3071
www.elmcroftmanor.com

ITHACA

Hilton Garden Inn
130 East Seneca St.
(607) 277-8900
www.ithaca.gardeninn.com

Statler Hotel
130 Statler Dr., Cornell University
(800) 541-2501
www.statlerhotel.cornell
.edu

OTHER ATTRACTIONS WORTH SEEING IN THE FINGER LAKES

Elizabeth Cady Stanton Home
32 Washington St.
Seneca Falls
(315) 568-2991
www.nps.gov

George Eastman House/International Museum of Photography & Film
900 East Ave.
Rochester
(585) 271-3361
www.eastmanhouse.org

Richardson-Bates House Museum
135 East Third St.
Oswego
(315) 343-1342
www.rbhousemuseum.org

Seward House
33 South St.
Auburn
(315) 252-1283
www.sewardhouse.org

Susan B. Anthony Home
17 Madison St.
Rochester
(585) 235-6124
www.susanbanthonyhouse.org

Watkins Glen International Raceway
2790 County Route 16
Watkins Glen
(607) 535-2486
www.theglen.com

REGIONAL TOURIST INFORMATION— THE FINGER LAKES

Cayuga County Office of Tourism
131 Genesee St.
Auburn
(800) 499-9615
www.tourcayuga.com

Chemung County Chamber of Commerce
400 East Church St.
Elmira
(607) 734-5137
www.chemungchamber.com

Corning Area Chamber of Commerce
1 West Market St.
Corning
(607) 936-4686
www.corningny.com

A Finger Lakes Visitors Connection
(Ontario County)
25 Gorham St.
Canandaigua
(877) FUN-IN-NY
www.visitfingerlakes.com

Finger Lakes Trails Visitor Center
6111 Visitor Center Rd.
Mount Morris
(535) 658-9320
www.fingerlakestrail.org

Finger Lakes Tourism Alliance
309 Lake St.
Penn Yan
(800) 548-4386
www.fingerlakes.org

Hammondsport Chamber of Commerce
47 Shethar St.
Hammondsport
(607) 569-2989
www.hammondsport.org

Ithaca/Thompkins County Convention and Visitors Bureau
904 East Shore Dr.
Ithaca
(800) 284-8422
www.visitithaca.com

Seneca Falls Heritage Area Visitor Center
115 Fall St.
Seneca Falls
(315) 568-2703
www.senecafalls.com

Watkins Glen & Schuyler County Chamber of Commerce
100 North Franklin St.
Watkins Glen
(607) 535-4300
www.watkinsglenchamber.com

SENECA FALLS

John Morrison Manor
2138 Route 89
(866) 484-4218
www.johnmorrismanor.com

SKANEATELES

Sherwood Inn
26 Genesee St.
(800) 374-3796
www.thesherwoodinn.com

WATKINS GLEN

Idlewood Inn
1 Lakeview Ave.
(607) 535-3081
www.idlewildeinn.com

Places to Eat in the Finger Lakes

CANANDAIGUA

Bristol Harbour's Lodge Restaurant
5410 Seneca Point Rd.
(800) 288-8248
www.bristolharbour.com

London Underground
69 East Market St.
(607) 962-2345

ELMIRA HEIGHTS

Pierce's 1894 Restaurant
228 Oakwood Ave.
(607) 734-2022

HAMMONDSPORT

Crooked Lake Ice Cream Parlor
Village Square
(607) 569-2751

Village Tavern Restaurant & Inn
30 Mechanic St.
(607) 569-2528
www.villagetaverninn.com

ITHACA

Moosewood Restaurant
215 North Cayuga St.
DeWitt Mall
(607) 273-9610
www.moosewood
restaurant.com

LODI

Dano's Heuriger on Seneca
9564 Route 414
(607) 582-7555
www.danosonseneca.com

Suzanne Fine Regional Cuisine
9013 Route 414
(607) 582-7545
www.suzannefrc.com

SKANEATELES

Doug's Fish Fry
8 Jordan St.
(315) 685-3288
www.dougsfishfry.com/
dff_skaneateles

The Krebs 1899
53 West Genesee St.
(315) 685-5714
www.thekrebs.com

TRUMANSBURG

Taughanock Farms Inn
2030 Gorge Rd.
(607) 387-7711
www.t-farms.com

WATKINS GLEN

Veraisons Restaurant
Glenora Wine Cellars
5435 Route 14
(607) 243-9500 or
(800) 243-5513
www.glenora.com

THE NIAGARA–ALLEGANY REGION

Ever since the Erie Canal opened nearly a century and a half ago, New York City became the Empire State's gateway to the world, a capital of international shipping and finance. Meanwhile, the docksides and rail yards of Buffalo were the portals through which the industrial output and raw materials of the Midwest flowed into the state. Buffalo became an important "border" city between the East Coast and the hinterlands, a center of manufacturing and flour milling whose fortunes have risen and fallen with the state of the nation's smokestack economy.

While many dismiss Buffalo for its cold and sleepy demeanor, it has some impressive architecture ranging from Louis Sullivan's splendid Prudential Building and the art deco City Hall downtown to the Frank Lloyd Wright houses. South Park, with its conservatory, and Riverside Park on the Niagara offer welcome open spaces, and there are even culinary treasures like Buffalo chicken wings and beef on 'weck (hot sliced roast beef on a pretzel-salt–coated kimmelweck or Kaiser roll).

The countryside at the western tip of New York provides further evidence as to why Niagara Falls isn't the only reason

THE NIAGARA–ALLEGANY REGION

to drive to the end of the thruway. The Pennsylvania border country boasts the expansive Allegany State Park, a hiking and camping paradise, and the byways along the Lake Erie shore wander through a picture-pretty territory dotted with vineyards, cherry orchards, and roadside stands selling delicious goat's milk fudge. It's the little serendipities that make traveling all that much sweeter.

Buffalo-Niagara Region

Only 40 miles northeast of Buffalo is a pristine tract of some 19,000 acres, the core of which (11,000 acres) makes up the federal *Iroquois National Wildlife Refuge,* managed by the U.S. Fish and Wildlife Service. On either side of the refuge are the *Oak Orchard* (east) and *Tonawanda* (west) *Wildlife Management Areas,* operated by the state of New York's Department of Environmental Conservation.

Roughly two-thirds of Iroquois National Wildlife Refuge is made up of freshwater marshes and hardwood swamps that are fed by Oak Orchard Creek as it meanders east to west through the refuge. Forests, meadows, and fields slope up gently from the wetland's edge, attracting a wide variety of wildlife. The refuge maintains four scenic overlooks and three nature trails, which are open from sunrise to sunset year-round for self-guided visits and wildlife watching.

Both the Oak Orchard and the Tonawanda areas are primarily wetlands, with some grassland and forest habitat. The dikes surrounding the man-made impoundments, as well as several overlooks and parking areas, provide access that offers superb opportunities not only for hunters (during designated seasons) but for hikers and birders as well.

AUTHOR'S FAVORITES—NIAGARA–ALLEGANY REGION

Burchfield-Penney Art Center	Panama Rocks Scenic Park
Griffis Sculpture Park	Pedaling History Bicycle Museum
Herschell Carrousel Factory Museum	The Roycroft Inn
Lucy-Desi Museum	Theodore Roosevelt Inaugural National Historic Site
Old Fort Niagara	

Stage One

The handsome French Renaissance home at 484 Delaware Ave. in Buffalo was built in 1894 for S. Douglas Cornell, the successful owner of a lead foundry. Cornell, an avid amateur actor, had architect Edward A. Kent install a theater in the attic story of his new mansion. Here, he and his prominent Buffalo friends staged frequent performances. Among the amateur players' most enraptured fans was Cornell's little granddaughter, Katherine. Years later, when she was one of the great ladies of the American stage, Katherine Cornell credited those Delaware Avenue theatricals with kindling her ambition to become an actress.

The best time for birders to visit the area is from early March to mid-May when more than 100,000 Canada geese and ducks, including black, pintail, mallard, American widgeon, teal, shoveler, and ring-necked, pause on their northward migration, with some staying to nest. The transitional habitat along the borders of the marsh attracts shore and wading birds and migrating spring warblers.

The Iroquois National Wildlife Refuge headquarters, 1101 Casey Rd., Basom (585-948-5445), is open year-round Monday through Friday from 7:30 a.m. to 4 p.m., except holidays, and March through mid-July, Saturday and Sunday 9 a.m. to 5 p.m. Maps and other information are available here and on the Internet at http://iroquoisnwr.fws.gov. There are self-guided exhibits and an observation tower at the Oak Orchard Education Center on Knowlesville Road, just north of the town of Oakfield. The center is open daily from sunrise to sunset and is the starting point for four nature trails. For information about Oak Orchard and Tonawanda WMA, contact the New York State Department of Environmental Conservation, P.O. Box 422, Basom 14013; (585) 948-5182.

The *Asa Ransom House* is an 1853 farmhouse on the site of one of the country's early gristmills. All but one of the ten guest rooms have fireplaces, and several have private front porches and balconies. The inn is also a full-service restaurant and serves a "country dinner" Sunday and Tuesday through Thursday, with specialties such as herb-crusted flounder with crab and roasted red pepper sauce, and sauerbraten roast with spaetzle and sour cream, as well as a five-course fixed-price dinner ($40-$50) on Saturday. Lunch is served Wednesday, and afternoon tea is served Tuesday, Thursday, and Saturday from 1 to 4 p.m. Dinner is served daily except Monday.

The Asa Ransom House is at 10529 Main St., Clarence (716-759-2315 or 800-841-2340; www.asaransom.com). A double room, including full breakfast, ranges from $230 to $330 MAP (or Modified American Plan, i.e., with breakfast and dinner included in the rate) or $170 to $275 B&B for Saturday night; Sunday through Friday a B&B rate of $120 to $190 is available, as well as an MAP rate of $180 to $250. Prices do not include service and tax.

Thirty Mile Point Lighthouse, more than 60 feet high, was built in 1875 from hand-carved stone near the mouth of Golden Hill Creek to warn vessels of the sandbar and shoals jutting out into Lake Ontario. Visitors can climb the circular steel staircase to the top of the tower for magnificent views of the lake and across to Canada. Tours of the lighthouse, now part of *Golden Hill State Park,* costs $1 for adults and 50 cents for children with the park's $6 entrance fee. It's open daily, July 4 through Labor Day 10 a.m. to 6 p.m. The park is located at 9691 Lower Lake Rd., Barker (716-795-3885; www.nysparks .state.ny.us/parks).

You can only drive a few miles in this state before encountering one of the string of forts that once defended the thirteen colonies' northwestern frontier, playing a role not only in the struggles between the British and the French for North American supremacy but in the War of Independence as well. The state's westernmost of these is *Old Fort Niagara* located downstream from the falls at *Fort Niagara State Park* at the point where the Niagara River flows into Lake Ontario.

Fort Niagara occupies what was one of the most strategic locations in all of North America's interior. The great "French Castle" erected here in 1726 served as the core of Fort Niagara's defenses through nearly a century of intermittent warfare and was in use as officers' housing as recently as World War I. Now restored to its eighteenth-century appearance, it is the focal point of Old Fort Niagara.

Restored between the years 1927 and 1934, the older buildings of Fort Niagara are maintained by the private, nonprofit Old Fort Niagara Association in cooperation with the State of New York. Beyond the silent military structures are the broad vistas of Lake Ontario and the rising mists of Niagara Falls 14 miles to the south.

Old Fort Niagara, off the Robert Moses Parkway North, Youngstown (716-745-7611; www.oldfortniagara.org), is open year-round daily from September to June 9 a.m. to 5 p.m. and July and August 9 a.m. to 7 p.m. Closed Thanksgiving, Christmas, and New Year's Day. During the summer there are frequent costumed reenactments of military drills, with musket and cannon firings. Admission is $10 for adults, $9 for senior citizens and AAA members, and $6 for children ages 6 to 12.

Scottish émigré Allan Herschell carved a place for himself in America's history in 1883when he produced the first steam-driven "riding gallery,"(known today as a merry-go-round). By 1891, one machine a day was being shipped to places around the world; later the Herschell-Spillman Company became the world's largest producer of carousels and amusement park devices. And because merry-go-rounds need music, North Tonawanda also became a major producer of band organs.

The **Herschell Carrousel Factory Museum** is housed in a historic factory building and traces the history of Herschell, his hand-carved wooden animals, and the finished carousels. There are ongoing woodcarving demonstrations, and, best of all for all us kids, an antique, hand-carved wooden carousel to ride. "Super Sunday" family performances are held at 2 p.m. from mid-June through mid-September.

The Herschell Carrousel Factory Museum, 180 Thompson St., North Tonawanda (716-693-1885), is open April through mid-June, Wednesday through Sunday noon to 4 p.m.; mid-June through August, from Monday to Saturday 10 a.m. to 4 p.m., and Sunday noon to 4 p.m.; and September through December, Wednesday through Sunday noon to 4 p.m. Closed major holidays. Admission is $5 for adults, $4 for seniors, and $2.50 for children ages 2 to 12 and includes one carousel ride. Extra rides cost just 50 cents.

Heading upriver you'll find Buffalo, the terminus town of the Erie Canal and gateway to the Midwest. For a quick introduction to this sprawling inland port, head downtown to reconnoiter the city and Lake Erie from City Hall's twenty-eighth-floor observation deck (open weekdays from 8 a.m. to 4 p.m.) and then visit the nearby historic neighborhood of **Allentown.**

thegoats weregot

According to legend, Goat Island is named for the only survivor of a herd that was left to winter there in 1779 by a settler named John Stedman.

The works of a number of important architects and the homes of several famous people are tucked into the compact Allentown neighborhood. Representative of the district's myriad building styles are the Kleinhans Music Hall on Symphony Circle, designed in 1938 by Eliel and Eero Saarinen. You'll also find the 1869 Dorsheimer Mansion at 434 Delaware Ave., an early work of the peerless Henry Hobson Richardson; Stanford White's 1899 Butler Mansion (672 Delaware) and 1895 Pratt Mansion (690 Delaware). There's also a lovely example of the Flemish Renaissance style at 267 North St. As for the haunts of the famous, find the childhood home of F. Scott Fitzgerald at 29 Irving St.; the home of artist Charles Burchfield (once a designer for a Buffalo wallpaper company) at 459 Franklin St.; and, at 472 Delaware Ave., the carriage house formerly attached to the home of Samuel Langhorne Clemens, who was once the editor and part-owner of the *Buffalo Morning Express* (though he always hated Buffalo). For information call the Allentown Association at (716) 881-1024 or see www.allentown.org.

The Greek Revival house at 641 Delaware Ave. is important not for its architecture, but its history. On September 14, 1901, the home of prominent Buffalo lawyer Ansley Wilcox became part of American history after a vigorous young man, rushed from a vacation in the Adirondacks, stepped into the library to take the oath of office as president of the United States. William McKinley was dead, the victim of an assassin; and the era of Theodore Roosevelt was about to begin.

The story of that fateful day and the tragic event that preceded it is told at the ***Theodore Roosevelt Inaugural National Historic Site,*** as the Wilcox House has been known since its restoration and opening to the public in 1971. Perhaps the most interesting aspect of the tale depicts the mad dash Roosevelt made from the Adirondacks to Buffalo. He had gone to the city and stayed for a few days at the Wilcox House after McKinley was shot by an anarchist at the Pan-American Exposition. He had left to join his family at their mountain retreat after being assured by the president's doctors that his condition had stabilized. Notified several days later of McKinley's worsening state, the vice president made an overnight journey by horse and wagon to the nearest train station, where he learned that the president was dead. Roosevelt and his party then raced to Buffalo in a special train. Within two hours after his arrival, he was standing in Wilcox's library, wearing borrowed formal clothes as he took the oath of office as the nation's twenty-sixth president.

On September 6, 1901, President McKinley was in Buffalo attending the Pan-American Exposition. While he was shaking hands with the public, Leon F. Czolgosz walked up and shot him with a revolver he had hidden under a handkerchief. Today the site where McKinley was assassinated is marked with a bronze plaque. It's on the traffic island on Fordham Drive between Elmwood Avenue and Lincoln Parkway. (Czolgosz was put to death the following October.)

Visitors can also see artifacts and memorabilia from McKinley and the expo at the ***Buffalo & Erie County Historical Society.*** Check out the resource center at 459 Forest Ave. to see an artifact of the Pan-American Exposition. The oversized head of what appears to be a Victorian woman, donning pearls, drapes the front door to the building. Dubbed the "Dreamland" sculpture, she was part of the display at the exposition and guards the exhibits from the expo. It is open Tuesday through Saturday from 10 a.m. to 5 p.m. and Sunday noon to 5 p.m. Admission runs $6 adults, $4 seniors ages 60 and over, $4 for students 13 to 21, and children 7 to 12, $2.50. Visit www.bechs.org or call (716) 873-9695, extension 302, for more information.

The Theodore Roosevelt Inaugural National Historic Site, 641 Delaware Ave., Buffalo (716-884-0095; www.nps.gov/thri), is open by tour only, Monday through Friday 9:30 a.m. to 3:30 p.m., weekends 12:30 to 3:30 p.m. Closed major holidays. Admission is $10 for adults, $7 seniors and students, and $5 for children 6 to 8; family rate, $25.

The residential neighborhoods north of the downtown and Allentown areas of Buffalo boast five examples of the work of America's greatest architect, Frank Lloyd Wright. Wright's residential architecture is generally distributed within the central and upper Midwest, where he brought his "prairie style" to maturity. He had formerly designed a house in Oak Park, Illinois, for the brother of John D. Larkin, founder of the Larkin Soap Company of Buffalo. Larkin admired his brother's house and brought Wright to Buffalo to design the company headquarters. The Larkin Building, a light, airy masterpiece of commercial architecture, stood on Seneca Street from 1905 until it was unconscionably demolished in 1950. But fate was kinder to the five Buffalo houses built for Larkin Soap Company executives following Wright's arrival in town, all of which survive to this day. Here is a list of the *Frank Lloyd Wright houses* in Buffalo and their locations:

William Heath House, 76 Soldiers Place, corner of Bird Avenue, completed in 1906 and landscaped by Frederick Law Olmsted. (Private; not open to visitors.)

Darwin D. Martin House, 125 Jewett Parkway, corner of Summit Avenue (www.darwinmartinhouse.org). Also completed in 1906, this expansive home was unfortunately left vacant for seventeen years prior to the mid-1950s, during which time half of the original Wright windows were lost. It was restored in 1970 by the State University of New York at Buffalo, which uses it for offices. For information regarding tours contact the School of Architecture and Planning, Hayes Hall, 125 Jewett Parkway, Buffalo (716-947-9217). Tour schedules vary with seasons. Tours last one hour, except for two-hour in-depth tours offered on the fourth Saturday of each month at 11 a.m. Tour prices are contingent on the scope and specialty of the tour, but generally start at $26; tours run from April through November. The George Barton House is included in all tours.

George Barton House, 118 Summit Ave., is a smaller brick structure with distinctive top-story casement windows and a broad roof overhang built in 1903–4.

Gardener's Cottage, Martin Estate, 285 Woodward Ave. Constructed in 1906, the cottage is one of the few surviving service buildings of the Martin Estate. (Private; not open to visitors.)

ANNUAL EVENTS
IN THE NIAGARA–ALLEGANY REGION

FEBRUARY

Olmstead Winterfest
Buffalo
(716) 838-1249
www.buffaloolmstedparks.org

APRIL

Buffalo in Bloom
Buffalo and Erie County
Botanical Gardens
(716) 851-5344
www.buffaloinbloom.com

MAY

Falls Fireworks and Concert Series
Niagara Falls, Ontario
(877) 642-7275
www.niagaraparks.com
(through mid-September)

JUNE

Shakespeare in Delaware Park
Buffalo
(716) 856-4533
www.shakespeareindelawarepark.org
(through mid-August)

JULY

Can-Am Arts Festival
Sackets Harbor
(315) 646-2321
www.sacketsharborny.com

AUGUST

National Buffalo Wing Festival
Buffalo
(716) 565-4141
www.buffalowing.com

SEPTEMBER

Niagara County "Fall Classic" Fishing Derby
Lake Ontario
(800) 338-7890
www.ilovenyfishing.com

NOVEMBER

Lights in the Park
Buffalo
(716) 856-4533

Winter Festival of Lights
Niagara Falls, Ontario
(800) 563-2557
www.wfol.com
(till early January)

DECEMBER

First Night Buffalo
Buffalo
(716) 635-4959
www.firstnightbuffalo.org

Walter Davidson House, 57 Tillinghast Place. With the exception of Darwin Martin's 1926 summer house, built south of the city on a bluff above Lake Erie, the 1909 Davidson House is the last of Wright's Buffalo residences. (Private; not open to visitors.)

Just minutes from downtown the *Buffalo Museum of Science* houses an extensive collection of natural science exhibits. The museum was built in the 1920s and features a blend of classic dioramas and modern museum exhibits.

A glass-enclosed atrium connects the museum to the Charles R. Drew Science Magnet School, one of the first science magnet schools in the nation to be physically and programmatically linked to a museum.

The museum's main exhibit hall is filled with temporary exhibitions. A visit to the permanent "Dinosaurs & Co." exhibit provides a look at some of the favorite prehistoric giants. "Insect World" features insects six times life-size in two vastly different ecosystems—the cloud forest in the coastal Andean highlands of north central Venezuela and the Niagara frontier region of New York State. Two halls of space provide detailed information about our world and the worlds around us, and observatories provide views of stars, planets, and our sun. The museum also features exhibits on endangered species, zoology, flora and fauna, gems and minerals, and technology. "Camp Wee Explorers," for kids 2 to 7, offers interactive exhibits focused on discovering the natural world.

The Buffalo Museum of Science is located at 1020 Humboldt Parkway (Best Street exit off the Kensington Expressway), Buffalo (716-896-5200; www .sciencebuff.org). Open Wednesday through Saturday from 10 a.m. to 4 p.m., and on Monday of Presidents Day and Columbus Day weekends, from 10 a.m. to 5 p.m., and Sunday noon to 5 p.m. Closed January 1, July 4, Thanksgiving, and Christmas. Admission is $7 for adults, $6 for seniors, and $5 for military personnel, students and children 3 to 18.

The Buffalo Museum of Science also operates *Tifft Nature Preserve* just 3 miles from downtown. Billed as an "Urban Nature Sanctuary," the preserve is a 264-acre habitat for animal and plant life, dedicated to environmental education and conservation. With miles of hiking trails, three boardwalks, and a self-guided nature trail, it's a wonderful place to spend the day hiking or fishing. For bird-watchers there's a 75-acre freshwater cattail marsh with viewing blinds. In winter the preserve rents snowshoes. "Wellness Walks" are offered on Thursday at 10 a.m. The Makowski Visitor Center has some wonderful exhibits on ecology, animals, and plant life.

The Tifft Nature Preserve, 1200 Fuhrmann Blvd., Buffalo (716-825-6397 or 716-896-5200; www.sciencebuff.org/tifft-nature-preserve), is open daily from dawn to dusk; the Makowski Visitor Center is open Wednesday through Saturday 10 a.m. to 4 p.m. Closed major holidays. There is no admission charge, but donations are appreciated.

The *Burchfield-Penney Art Center* exhibits the largest and most comprehensive collection of the works of Charles E. Burchfield, one of the country's foremost watercolorists, as well as the works of other western New York artists. The center serves the community as a multifaceted cultural and educational institution and hosts numerous special exhibitions throughout the year.

One of the center's exhibits, "Access to Art," uses a unique assortment of interpretive tools such as hands-on art activities, interviews with artists, tactile works, and library resources to give visitors of all ages the skills to enjoy a museum without feeling intimidated.

The Burchfield-Penney Art Center, Buffalo State College campus, 1300 Elmwood Ave., Buffalo (716-878-6011; www.burchfield-penney.org), is open Tuesday through Saturday from 10 a.m. to 5 p.m. and Sunday from 1 to 5 p.m.; closed Monday and major holidays. Admission is $7 for adults, $4 for seniors, and $4 for students and children over 6 years old.

Cemeteries are not often thought of as places to go to for fun, but **Forest Lawn** is not a typical cemetery, but more a city park. It's known as the final

The "Real Thing"?

The Buffalo chicken wings recipe below is reputed to be the genuine Anchor Bar version—but only they know for sure, and they're not talking.

6 tablespoons Durkee's Hot Sauce

½ stick margarine

1 tablespoon white vinegar

⅛ teaspoon celery seed

⅛ to ¾ teaspoon cayenne pepper

¼ teaspoon Worcestershire sauce

1 to 2 teaspoons Tabasco sauce

dash of black pepper

Mix ingredients in a small saucepan over low heat until margarine melts, stirring occasionally.

Fry wings at 375° F for 12–15 minutes in vegetable or peanut oil.

Drain for a few minutes on a brown paper bag or paper towels, then put them in a bowl. Pour the sauce over them, cover the bowl, and shake it to coat the wings. (An option here is to put the wings on a baking sheet and bake a few minutes for an extra-crispy coating.) Serve with carrot and celery sticks and blue cheese dressing.

Here's a second "authentic" recipe:

1 tablespoon butter

¼ cup Durkee Red Hot Cayenne Pepper Sauce

Melt the butter and combine it with the hot sauce, then follow the directions above. This recipe, however, calls for baking the wings at 350° F for 11–12 minutes.

resting place of prominent Buffalonians such as Red Jacket, the Seneca orator, and Millard Fillmore, the country's thirteenth president. But it's also a nature sanctuary with 6,000 trees and 157 species of birds.

Upon request, cemetery attendants will ring the 6-foot, 3,000-pound solid bronze Oishei bell cast in France. Other highlights include the Blocher monument, with life-size figures carved in Italian marble, and numerous unique monuments and mausoleums.

Sundays from June to September, the staff offers walking and motor-coach tours. Several of the interred, such as President Fillmore, make guest appearances during the 1½-hour-long tours that relate the cemetery's history. (Tours are not given in inclement weather.) Advance reservations are required. Walking tours are $15 and motor-coach tours run $25.

Forest Lawn Cemetery & Garden Mausoleums, 1411 Delaware Ave. at Delavan, Buffalo (716-885-1600; www.forest-lawn.com), is open daily 8 a.m. to 7 p.m. from April to October; closing time changes with Daylight Savings, call for hours.

Mark Twain aficionados will want to visit the **Buffalo & Erie County Public Library's Grosvenor Rare Book Room.** The original manuscript of *The Adventures of Huckleberry Finn* is just one of its thousands of manuscripts and first editions dating back to the fifteenth century. The room also contains other mementos of Twain, a one-time Buffalo resident.

Buffalo & Erie County Public Library, 1 Lafayette Sq., Buffalo (716-858-8900; www.buffalolib.org); call for hours.

Those buffalo-style chicken wings really were invented in Buffalo. The **Anchor Bar and Restaurant** has been serving them up with celery and blue cheese dip since 1964. The restaurant has a reputation for good food, moderate prices, and large portions. Find your next serving of wings at 1047 Main St. (716-886-8920; www.anchorbar.com).

Sample the city's other local specialty, beef on 'weck, at **Anderson's** or at **Charlie the Butcher;** both have several branches in the area.

More than 400 rare and unique bicycles and thousands of cycling-related collectibles span more than 185 years of bicycling history at the **Pedaling History Bicycle Museum,** the world's largest of its kind.

Among the exhibits are a reproduction of the very first bicycle dating back to 1817, an Irish Mail four-wheel velocipede, some "boneshakers" dating back to the 1860s, a pneumatic high wheel safety American Star, an 1881 Marine bicycle, and an electric bike from the year 2000. There are also extensive bicycle stein and lamp collections and ample photo opportunities.

The Pedaling History Bicycle Museum, 3943 North Buffalo Rd. (Routes 277 and 240), Orchard Park (716-662-3853; www.pedalinghistory.org), is open

Monday through Saturday 11 a.m. to 5 p.m. and Sunday 1:30 to 5 p.m.; closed Tuesday through Thursday from January 15 to April 1 and major holidays. Admission is $7.50 for adults, $6.75 for seniors, $4.65 for children ages 7 to 15, and $22 for a family of up to eight people. Call for a listing of special free events, including antique bike parades on July 4 and other occasions.

Lake Erie Shore

The southwestern tip of New York State is packed with an eclectic mix of off-the-beaten-path treasures. Remember kazoos? Those quirky little musical instruments played by just humming into them? They're still being made in Eden, at *The Original American Kazoo Company Factory, Museum, and Gift Shop.* Established in 1916, it's now the only metal kazoo factory in the world, and it's still making them the same way they were made in 1916. The company used to produce everything from toy flutes and fishing tackle boxes to metal dog beds and peanut vending machines, but in 1965 the demand for kazoos became so great that the firm stopped manufacturing everything else.

The "working museum" at The Original American Kazoo Company, Factory, Museum, and Gift Shop shows how "America's only original musical instrument" is made, chronicles kazoo history, and regales visitors with such fascinating trivia as "'Far, Far Away' is the most requested tune played on the kazoo."

The Original American Kazoo Company, Factory, Museum, and Gift Shop, 8703 South Main St., Eden (716-992-3960 or 800-978-3444; www.edenkazoo .com), is open Tuesday through Saturday 10 a.m. to 5 p.m., Friday 10 a.m. to 7 p.m., Sunday noon to 5 p.m. Self-guided tours are available for free guided tours for groups of six or more. Closed during major holidays. Admission is free.

Although it's now just a short hop off I-90, it's easy to evoke how isolated the *Dunkirk Historical Lighthouse* must have looked when the lantern in the square, 61-foot tower first began guiding ships into Dunkirk Harbor in 1876. Today an automated light in the tower shines, and the two-story stick-style keeper's dwelling has been converted into a *Veterans' Park Museum.*

Five of the museum's rooms are devoted to displays of each branch of the military; five are preserved to show how the lighthouse keeper used to live; and one is a memorial to the Vietnam era. An exhibit of maritime history and lake freighters is on display in the souvenir store and a separate building displays artifacts from the submarine service and Coast Guard.

Displays on the grounds include a 45-foot lighthouse buoy tender, a 21-foot rescue boat, and Civil War cannons. Visitors can take a tour of the lighthouse tower. An admission fee is charged for grounds tours and tours of the museum.

Dunkirk Historical Lighthouse and Veterans' Park Museum, off Point Drive North, Dunkirk (716-366-5050; www.dunkirklighthouse.com), are open May through June and September through October, daily from 10 a.m. to 2 p.m. with the last tour at 1 p.m.; closed Wednesday and Sunday. In July and August the complex is open from 10 a.m. to 4 p.m., with the last tour at 2:30 p.m. Admission is $6 for adults and $2.50 for children ages 4 to 12; $1 per person for entry to the grounds only.

Stop at the stately **White Inn in Fredonia.** Duncan Hines did, back in the 1930s, and was so taken with the food that he included it in his "Family of Fine Restaurants." Although the restaurant/inn has since undergone several transformations, it still proudly displays the Duncan Hines sign out front. And the building itself encompasses the original Victorian mansion built in 1868 and operated as an inn since 1919. Today it serves the local delicacy beef on 'weck, Dijon-grilled salmon, and filet mignon with bacon and smoked gouda.

The White Inn, 52 East Main St., Fredonia (716-672-2103 or 888-FREDO-NIA for reservations; www.whiteinn.com), is open daily year-round. Breakfast and lunch are served Monday through Saturday, and dinner is served nightly. Inn rates, from $69 to $199, include breakfast.

Locals dubbed the sixteen-room mansion completed by James McClurg in 1820 "McClurg's Folly." He designed it, made and baked his own bricks, prepared local timber for the interior woodwork, and landscaped the spacious grounds with ornamental trees and shrubs and a water fountain stocked with goldfish.

Today the Chautauqua County Historical Society operates the restored frontier mansion as a museum and library and has filled it with furnishings, fine art, and local artifacts from its collection.

McClurg Museum, Moore Park, Routes 20 and 394, Westfield (716-326-2977; mcclurgmuseum.org), is open Tuesday through Saturday from 10 a.m. to 4 p.m. Admission is $5 for adults, children free.

At the northern tip of Chautauqua Lake in Mayville, the people at the **Webb's Candies** factory have been making goat's milk fudge since 1942. The goats are no longer out back and the milk now comes from cans, but the confection is just as rich and creamy as ever, and the chocolate fudge with pecans is a regional taste treat not to be missed. Webb's makes all its candies by hand, using the old-fashioned copper-kettle method, and has added a host of other treats to its repertoire, including "frogs," hard suckers, chocolate bars, divinity, and chocolate clusters. If you own a goat and want to start production, take a short tour of the candy factory between 10 a.m. and 4 p.m. Monday through Friday.

Webb's Candies factory, Route 394, Mayville (716-753-2161; www .webbscandies.com), is open daily year-round. In summer the hours are 10 a.m. to 9 p.m.; in winter noon to 5 p.m. Call for holiday hours.

Chautauqua Lake is also the home of a 133-year-old enterprise that exemplifies the American penchant for self-improvement. The **Chautauqua Institution** gave its name to an endless array of itinerant tent-show lyceums around the turn of the century. A lot of us have forgotten that the original institution is still thriving right where it was founded in 1874. Bishop John Heyl Vincent and industrialist (and father-in-law of Thomas Edison) Lewis Miller originally founded Chautauqua with the modest goal of establishing a school for Sunday-school teachers. **Chautauqua** grew to become a village unto itself, offering not only religious instruction but a program of lectures and adult-education courses.

The largely secularized Chautauqua of today bears little resemblance to the Methodist camp meeting of more than a hundred years ago, although services in the major faiths are held daily. The Chautauqua emphasis on culture and mental and spiritual improvement has led to an extensive annual summer calendar of lectures, classical and popular concerts, dramatic performances, and long- and short-term courses in subjects ranging from foreign languages to tap dancing to creative writing. It has its own 30,000-volume library.

To put it simply, Chautauqua is a vast summer camp of self-improvement, a place where you can rock (in chairs) on broad verandas, walk tree-lined streets that have no cars, and listen in on a chamber music rehearsal on your way to lunch.

The season at Chautauqua lasts for nine weeks each summer, but admission is available on a daily, weekend, or weekly basis.

For complete information on facilities and programs, contact Chautauqua Institution, 1 Ames St., Chautauqua (716-357-6200 or 800-836-ARTS; www .ciweb.org).

Head south along the lake for a few miles to catch a ride on the **Bemus Point–Stow Ferry.** The cable-drawn ferry has traversed the "narrows" of the lake at these points since 1816. The oxen that once pulled the ferry with the aid of a treadmill and manila rope retired, but the pace and charm of the primitive open barge still remain. The six-minute ride debarks from North Harmony.

The Bemus Point–Stow Ferry, Stow (mailing address: 15 Water St., Mayville 14757; 716-753-2403; www.bemuspoint.com/ferry.html), is open from 11 a.m. to 9 p.m. Saturday and Sunday in June, and daily in July and August. Admission is $4 per car, $2 for motorcycles, and $1 for walk-ons.

The same folks who run the Bemus Point–Stow ferry also offer tours on the **Chautauqua Belle,** one of only six authentic stern-wheel steamboats operating east of the Mississippi. The *Belle* cruises Chautauqua Lake daily from May 23 through October 25, with departures at 11 a.m., 1 p.m., 3 p.m., and 5 p.m.; limited schedule in May, June, and September. The trips last one hour and 45 minutes. Fares are from $15 for adults, and $10 for ages 3 to 12; children under 3 are free. For information, call (716) 269-BELL, or visit www .chautauquabelle.com.

Geologists believe that more than 300 million years ago *Panama Rocks*—reputed to be the world's most extensive outcropping of glacier-cut, ocean-quartz conglomerate rock—were islands of gravel and sand amid a vast inland sea that extended west toward what is now Utah. As a multitude of layered materials were deposited, the weight forced the water out, and a natural form of concrete called quartz conglomerate, or pudding stone, was created.

Approximately 165 million years ago, earthquakes and other geological upheavals raised what was to become Panama Rocks to its present altitude of 1,650 feet. The layers fractured, and water, carrying minerals such as iron and lead, seeped into the openings. A scant 10,000 years ago, during the last ice age, a passing glacier widened these fractures, creating thousands of crevices and alley passageways.

Today visitors can thread through these crevices and passageways along a mile-long trail that winds through a world of towering rocks, past cavernous dens and small caves. Most hikers take one-and-a-half hours to follow the route, although the more adventurous can leave the trail and explore at their own pace. Because there are no railings, adults are required to sign a waiver of liability and are warned that the upper part of the trail can be dangerous for children. If you're not looking for adventure, stick to the lower trail, which has the most dramatic scenery. Persons under the age of 18 must be with an adult to enter the rock area. No pets are allowed.

Panama Rocks Scenic Park, 11 Rock Hill Rd. (County Route 10), Panama (716-782-2845; www.panamarocks.com), is open mid-May through late October, 10 a.m. to 4 p.m.; grounds close at 5 p.m. Admission is $6 for adults, $5 for ages 13 through 22, $4 for children ages 6 to 12, and $5 for seniors and military personnel. There is a picnic area with grills for guests. For more information check the Web site.

Jamestown, birthplace of one of the country's leading naturalists, is home to his *Roger Tory Peterson Institute of Natural History,* housed in a handsome wood and stone building designed by architect Robert A. M. Stern on twenty-seven acres of woods and meadows.

The institute's mission is to train educators to help children discover the natural world around them. The program houses changing exhibitions of wildlife art and nature photography at the institute, and the public is invited to visit, hike the surrounding trails, and stop in the Butterfly Garden and gift shop.

The Roger Tory Peterson Institute of Natural History, 311 Curtis St., Jamestown (716-665-2473 or 800-758-6841; www.rtpi.org), is open Tuesday through Saturday 10 a.m. to 4 p.m. and Sunday 1 to 5 p.m. Admission is $5 for adults, $3 for students, and $12 for families. The grounds are open daily dawn to dusk.

In Jamestown, the **Lucy-Desi Museum** stands in the heart of the city's theater district, between the Lucille Ball Little Theatre of Jamestown—the largest community theater in New York—and the former Palace Theater (now the Reg Lenna Civic Center), where little Lucy went with her grandfather to see vaudeville.

Among the exhibits are a computer program with Lucy trivia questions, an audio clip from the *My Favorite Husband* radio show, which preceded *I Love Lucy,* and exclusive clips from *Lucy and Desi: A Home Movie* produced by their daughter, Lucie Arnaz. The gift shop carries over 600 *I Love Lucy* licensed products.

The Lucy-Desi Museum, 10 West Third St., Jamestown (877-LUCY FAN [582-9326] or 716-484-0800; www.lucy-desi.com), is open Monday through Wednesday and Saturday 10 a.m. to 4 p.m., Thursday and Friday 10 a.m. to 5:30 p.m., and Sunday 1 to 5 p.m.; closed major holidays. Admission is $10 for adults, $9 for seniors, and $7 for children ages 6 to 18.

Jones Bakery, across the street from the museum, still makes Lucy's cherished Swedish limpa bread. Stroll through downtown Jamestown and look for the three outdoor wall murals depicting scenes from *I Love Lucy,* all within walking distance of the museum.

Ellington encompasses several towns to the north and east and borders on **Amish Country.** The Amish first came to Cattaraugus County from Ohio in 1949. Although they usually keep to themselves, they're friendly people who generally welcome questions about their way of life. (However, they do request that you not photograph them.) There are a number of small shops on Route 62 in the town of Conewango Valley that offer products made by, or about, the Amish. **Franklin Graphics** sells Amish photos, books, and postcards. Stop at **Mueller's Valley View Cheese Factory** to sample Swiss cheese and forty other varieties made in Amish country. **Amish Country Fair** carries furniture and crafts.

Allegany Heartland

Salamanca is the only city in the United States located on a Native American reservation and is also home to the largest park in the state's park system. The **Seneca-Iroquois National Museum** on the Allegany Indian Reservation traces the cultural and historical heritage of the Seneca, known as "Keeper of the Western Door of the Iroquois Confederacy." The museum exhibits collections of artifacts beginning with prehistoric times and re-creates the culture and history of the Seneca people.

The Seneca-Iroquois National Museum, 814 Broad St., Salamanca (716-945-1760; www.senecamuseum.org), is open year-round, Thursday through Monday 9 a.m. to 5 p.m. and Sunday noon to 5 p.m. Admission is $5 for adults, $3.50 for senior citizens and college students with ID, and $3 for military personnel and children ages 7 to 17.

With 65,000 acres, two 100-acre lakes, and 80 miles of hiking trails, **Allegany State Park,** "the wilderness playground of western New York," is the largest of the state parks. It's a mecca for both summer and winter outdoor enthusiasts. There are lakes for boating and swimming, ball fields, tennis courts, picnic areas, playgrounds, bike paths, and miles of cross-country and snowmobile trails. Rowboats and paddleboats can be rented at the Red House boathouse. You can also find a tent and trailer area, and bicycle rental. The park has archery seasons for small game, turkey, and deer. There's an extensive campground as well as more than 370 cabins, with163 winterized. Some are "turn-key," offering many amenities.

Allegany State Park, 2373 ASP, Route 1 (off Route 17), Salamanca (716-354-9121; www.nysparks.state.ny.us/parks), is open daily year-round. There is an entrance fee of $7 per car when the lake is open for swimming, and $6 per car when the lake is closed. The gate is closed weekdays off-season.

Before you leave Salamanca, stop at the **Salamanca Rail Museum,** a fully restored passenger depot constructed in 1912 by the Buffalo, Rochester, and Pittsburgh Railroad. The museum uses exhibits, artifacts, and video presentations to re-create an era when rail was the primary means of transportation from city to city.

Salamanca Rail Museum, 170 Main St., Salamanca (716-945-3133; mysite .verizon.net/bixyrad/salamancarailmuseumassociation), is open Tuesday through Saturday from 10 a.m. to 5 p.m. and Sunday from noon to 5 p.m. in April and from October through December; Monday through Saturday from 10 a.m. to 5 p.m. and Sunday from noon to 5 p.m. from May through September. Admission is free, but donations are welcomed.

Nannen Arboretum is home to Roanji Temple Stone Garden (an abstract garden of stone and sand) and Amano-Hashidate Bridge (bridge to heaven) along with over 260 species of rare and unusual trees, herbs, and perennial gardens. The arboretum (716-699-2377 or 800-897-9189; www.nannenarboretum .org) is at 28 Parkside Dr., directly behind Cornell Cooperative Extension, in Ellicottville. It is open daily from dawn to dusk. Donations are welcomed.

Head north on Route 219 a short distance to Ashford Hollow to see one of the most unconventional sculpture "gardens" around. For almost forty years, local sculptor Larry Griffis has been integrating his art with nature, placing his monumental abstract/representational creations throughout a 400-acre woodland setting/nature preserve. More than 200 of his pieces, most made of steel and between 20 and 30 feet high, are on exhibit at *Griffis Sculpture Park.* Ten nudes ring a pond, sharing the banks with live swans and ducks. A towering mosquito awaits unwary hikers along one of the 10 miles of hiking trails. Giant toadstools grow in a field, waiting to be climbed on. Watch as seemingly fluid statues come to life as they skip down the banks and fly through the water. Well-known artists like Ken Payne and Laura Feldberg are exhibited at the park, as well as the work of new and emerging talent.

Griffis Sculpture Park, on Ahrens Road off Route 219 South, Ashford Hollow (mailing address: 6902 Mill Valley Rd., East Otto 14729; 716-667-2808; www.griffispark.org), is open daily, May through October, from sunup to sundown; closed November through April. Admission is $5 for adults and $3 for seniors and students. Tours are given by appointment.

About 320 million years ago, river and delta sediments were deposited on the eroded surface of Devonian shoals. Crystalline igneous and metamorphic rocks with milky quartz veins were exposed, and long transportation of the sediments selectively weathered and eroded the nonquartz minerals.

Rock City Park is one of the world's largest exposures of quartz conglomerate (pudding stone), a place where you can wander through crevices and past towering, colorfully named formations like Fat Man's Squeeze, Tepee Rock, and Signal Rock, with its 1,000-square-mile view. Hike along a three-quarter-mile natural trail or visit the 4,200-square-foot building with museum, rock shop, video room, and rock room.

Rock City Park, 505A Route 16 South, Olean (716-372-7790 or 866-404-ROCK; www.rockcitypark.com), is open daily May through October from 9 a.m. to 6 p.m. Admission is $4.50 for adults (12 years and older), $3.75 for seniors, $2.50 for ages 6 to 12, children 5 and under are free; a season pass is $9.95. Last hiking tickets are sold at 5 p.m.

If you were heading off to a summer at Chautauqua three generations ago, you would have gotten there by a steam-hauled train of the Erie, Pennsylvania, or New York Central Railroad. Of course, Amtrak can get you there today (nearest station: Erie, Pennsylvania), but if you want steam, you'll have to head to a nostalgia operation like the ***Arcade and Attica Railroad,*** headquartered just southeast of Buffalo in Arcade.

The company's passenger operation is an unabashed throwback, relying for motive power on a pair of circa 1920 coal burners pulling old, open-window steel coaches that once belonged to the Delaware, Lackawanna, and Western. Arcade and Attica passengers enjoy a ninety-minute ride through some of upstate's loveliest farm country, ending right where they started by way of a trip back through time.

The Arcade and Attica Railroad, 278 Main St., Arcade (585-492-3100; www .arcadeandatticarr.com), operates weekends from Memorial Day through the end of October; in July and August there are 2 p.m. steam trips on Friday, and noon steam trips and 2:30 p.m. diesel trips on Saturday, Sunday, and Wednesday. There are special excursions using a diesel engine, including an Easter Bunny run, a Santa Claus Express, and nature ride/hikes scheduled off-season. Call for information. Tickets cost $12 per person; children 2 and under ride free if sitting on a parent's lap. No reservations except for special events.

Horse lovers roll out of bed and onto a mount for a trail ride through the Colden Hills at ***Pipe Creek Farm B&B,*** a working equine farm. The four-bedroom inn has shared baths (private baths available on request) and an in-ground pool. Rates range from $75 to $125 and include a continental breakfast. In addition to trail rides, owners Phil and Kathy Crone give lessons in hunt seat, stock seat, and saddle seat. In the winter there are 200 acres of cross-country ski trails to enjoy.

Pipe Creek Farm B&B, 9303 Falls Rd., West Falls (716-652-4868; www.pipe creekfarm.com), is open year-round.

One of the most interesting personalities of turn-of-the-century America was a self-made philosopher named ***Elbert Hubbard.*** He was famous for writing what he called a little "preachment" titled "A Message to Garcia" dealing with the themes of loyalty and hard work and publishing his views in a periodical called the *Philistine.* Hubbard was also celebrated for importing the handcrafts design aesthetic fostered in England by the artist and poet William Morris. Elbert Hubbard became the chief American proponent of the Arts and Crafts movement, touting, the virtues of honest craftsmanship in the face of an increasing tendency in the late nineteenth century toward machine production of furniture, printed matter, and decorative and utilitarian household objects.

Visually, the style absorbed influences as diverse as art nouveau and American Indian crafts and is familiar to most of us in the form of solid, oaken, slat-sided Morris chairs and the simple "Mission" furniture of Gustav Stickley.

Elbert Hubbard not only wrote about such stuff but also set up a community of craftspeople to turn out furniture, copper, leather, even printed books. He called his operation The Roycrofters, and it was headquartered on a "campus" in East Aurora.

There are several ways the modern traveler can savor the spirit of Elbert Hubbard in modern-day East Aurora. One is by visiting the **Roycroft Campus,** on South Grove Street. The campus grounds, now a National Historic Site, feature a gift shop, working pottery, art gallery, and several antiques dealers, all housed in Hubbard-era buildings. The site also includes the East Aurora Town Museum, housed in the Town Hall Building—the former Roycroft Campus chapel. For information contact the Greater East Aurora Chamber of Commerce, 431 Main St., East Aurora 14052 (716-652-8444; www.eanycc.com).

Another window on the Roycroft era is the **Elbert Hubbard–Roycroft Museum,** recently located in a 1910 bungalow built by Roycroft craftsmen. It's now on the esteemed list of the National Register of Historic Places. Part of the furnishings, including the superb Arts and Crafts dining room, are original and were the property of centenarian Grace Scheide Mantel when she turned the house over to the museum in 1985. Scheide Mantel's husband, George, once headed the Roycroft leather department. Other Roycroft products on display include a magnificent stained-glass lamp by Roycroft designer Dard Hunter and a saddle custom-made for Hubbard just prior to his death on the torpedoed *Lusitania* in 1915.

There is also a period garden, complete with a sundial and a "gazing ball," maintained by "The Master Gardeners" of the Erie County Cooperative Extension Service.

The Elbert Hubbard–Roycroft Museum (Scheide Mantel House), 363 Oakwood Ave., East Aurora (716-652-4735; www.roycrofter.com/museum.htm), is open from June 1 through October Wednesday, Saturday, and Sunday 1 to 4 p.m.; by appointment the rest of the year. Admission is $5 for adults; free for children under 12. Private or group tours also can be arranged, year-round, by appointment.

Elbert Hubbard opened **The Roycroft Inn** in 1903 to accommodate the people who came to visit his community of craftsmen. When Hubbard and his wife died in 1915, their son, Elbert II, assumed leadership of the Roycroft enterprises. In 1938, the ownership of the inn passed from the Hubbard family through a series of owners. By 1986 the inn was granted National Landmark status, and it reopened in 1995 after extensive restorations by the Margaret L. Wendt Foundation.

All of the inn's charm and history have been preserved. Although the suites have all of the modern-day amenities, each has been meticulously restored and furnished with historically accurate elements, including Stickley furniture, Roycroft lamps and wall sconces, and wallpaper in the style of William Morris.

The Roycroft Inn, 40 South Grove St., East Aurora (716-652-5552; for reservations only, 877-652-5552; www.roycroftinn.com), rents three-, four-, and five-room suites ranging from $130 to $280 a night.. The restaurant is open for lunch Monday through Saturday, for dinner nightly, and for Sunday brunch.

Stop in at the home of one of our least-appreciated presidents, Millard Fillmore. Fillmore, who was born in the Finger Lakes town of Genoa in 1800, came to East Aurora to work as a lawyer in 1825. He built this house on Main Street with his own hands, and it is the only presidential residence to make that claim. He moved it to its present Shearer Avenue location the same year and lived here with his wife until 1830. As restored and furnished by previous owners and the Aurora Historical Society, the *Millard Fillmore House National Landmark* contains country furnishings of Fillmore's era, as well as more refined pieces in the Greek Revival, or "Empire," style of the president's early years. A high desk to be used while standing was part of the furnishings in Fillmore's law office; the rear parlor, added in 1930, showcases furniture owned by the Fillmores in later years, when they lived in a Buffalo mansion. The large bookcase was used in the White House during the Fillmore presidency.

The Millard Fillmore House National Landmark (Aurora Historical Society), 24 Shearer Ave., East Aurora (716-652-8875; www.nps.gov), is open from June through October, Wednesday, Saturday, and Sunday 1 to 4 p.m. or by appointment.

The village of *Wyoming,* settled in the early 1800s, has more than seventy buildings on the Historic Register. Gaslight Village Shops, in the historic landmark district, include the *Gaslight Christmas Shoppe, Silas Newell's Provisions, Eccentricities,* and *Carney's Antiques.* Stop for a cappuccino at the *Gaslight Village Cafe and Pub* or for lunch, dinner, or the night at *Wyoming Inn B&B.*

The village of Le Roy's claim to fame is the birthplace of Jell-O. There is even a museum enthusiastically celebrating the invention in the oldest house in town. In 1897 Le Roy was already known as the Patent Medicine Capital of the world. But it was the gelatinous creation of P. B. Waite, which his wife named Jell-O, that earned it a place in history. Two years later, Mr. Waite sold his recipe to the Genesee Pure Food Company for $450, but it was not until 1964, when Jell-O was sold to the Postum Company (which later became General Foods), that Le Roy ceased its production of Jell-O.

Today, the *Jell-O Gallery,* situated just behind the Historic Society's Le Roy House, documents the creation and rise of the gelatinous dessert. Seven rooms of the 1823 building are furnished with period pieces of the nineteenth century, and there's an extensive exhibit of Morganville redware pottery made here by Fortunatus Gleason Jr., in the nineteenth century.

The Jell-O Gallery, behind the Le Roy House, 23 East Main St., Le Roy (585-768-7433; www.jellogallery.org), is open April through December, Monday through Saturday 10 a.m. to 4 p.m., Sunday 1 to 4 p.m.; January through March, Monday through Friday 10 a.m. to 4 p.m. Admission is $4 for those 12 years of age and older, and $1.50 for children 6 through 11.

OTHER ATTRACTIONS WORTH SEEING IN THE NIAGARA–ALLEGANY REGION

Amherst Museum
3755 Tonawanda Creek Rd.
Amherst
(716) 689-1440
www.amherstmuseum.org

Artpark
450 South 4th St.
Lewiston
(716) 754-437
www.artpark.net

Broadway Market
999 Broadway
Buffalo
(716) 893-0705
www.broadwaymarket.com

Buffalo Harbor Cruises
Erie Basin Marina
Buffalo
(716) 856-6696
www.buffaloharborcruises.com

Colonel William Bond House
143 Ontario St.
Lockport
(716) 434-7433

Davis Memorial Carillon
Alfred University
Saxon Drive
Alfred
(607) 871-2562
www.alfred.edu/map/carillon.cfm

Fredonia Opera House
9–11 Church St.
Fredonia
(716) 679-1891
www.fredopera.org

Lily Dale Assembly
5 Melrose Park
Lily Dale 14752
(716) 595-8721
www.lilydaleassembly.com

Lockport Cave and Underground
Boat Ride
21 Main St.
Lockport
(716) 438-0174
www.lockportcave.com

Maid of the Mist Boat Tour
151 Buffalo Ave.
Niagara Falls
(716) 284-4233
(in season) or (716) 284-4122
www.maidofthemist.com

Places to Stay in the Niagara–Allegany Region

ALBION

Tillman's Historic Village Inn
14369 Ridge Rd.
(585) 589-9151
www.tillmansvillageinn.com

BUFFALO

Beau Fleuve
242 Linwood Ave.
(800) 278-0245
www.beaufleuve.com

Hampton Inn
220 Delaware Ave.
(716) 855-2223
www.hamptoninn.hilton
.com

The Mansion on Delaware
414 Delaware Ave.
(716) 886-3300
www.mansionondelaware
.com

Red Coach Inn
2 Buffalo Ave.
Niagara Falls
(866) 719-2070 or
(716) 282-1459
www.redcoach.com

CHAUTAUQUA

Athenaeum Hotel
South Lake Drive
(800) 821-1881
www.ciweb.org/
athenaeum-home

Brasted House B&B
4833 West Lake Rd.
(888) 753-6205
www.brastedhouse.com/
article.php

The Spencer Hotel
25 Palestine Ave.
(800) 398-1306`
www.thespencer.com

DUNKIRK

Clarion Hotel Marina and Conference Center
30 Lake Shore Dr. East
(716) 366-8350
www.clariondunkirk.com

ELLICOTTVILLE

Ellicottville Inn
8 Washington St.
(716) 699-2373

WESTFIELD

Brick House B&B
7573 East Route 20
(716) 326-6262
www.brickhousebnb.com

The William Seward Inn
6645 South Portage Rd.
(716) 326-4151
www.williamsewardinn.com

REGIONAL TOURIST INFORMATION— THE NIAGARA–ALLEGANY REGION

Buffalo-Niagara CVB
617 Main St.
Buffalo, NY 14203
(800) BUFFALO
www.visitbuffaloniagara.com

Niagara County Tourism
345 Third St., Suite 605
Niagara Falls, NY 14303
(877) FALLS-US
www.niagara-usa.com

Wyoming County Tourist Promotion Agency
30 North Main St.
P.O. Box 502
Castile 13327
(800) 839-3919
www.wyomingcountyny.com

Places to Eat in the Niagara–Allegany Region

ALBION

Tillman's Historic Village Inn
14369 Ridge Rd.
(585) 589-9151
www.tillmansvillageinn.com

BUFFALO

Chef's
291 Seneca St.
(716) 856-9187
www.ilovechefs.com

Left Bank
511 Rhode Island St.
(716) 882-3509
www.leftbankrestaurant
.com

Mother's Restaurant
33 Virginia Place
(716) 882-2989

Red Coach Inn
2 Buffalo Ave.
(800) 282-1459 or
(716) 282-1459
www.redcoach.com

EAST AMHERST

La Scala Ristorante
9210 Transit Rd.
(716) 213-2777
www.lascalaristorante.net

KENMORE

O'Connell's Hourglass Restaurant
981 Kenmore Ave.
(716) 877-8788
www.oconnellsamerican
bistro.com

TONAWANDA

Saigon Bangkok
512 Niagara Falls Blvd.
(716) 837-2115
www.saigonbangkok.net

WILLIAMSVILLE

Tandoori's
7740 Transit Rd.
(716) 632-1112
www.tandooris.com

Trattoria Aroma
5229 Main St.
(716) 631-2687
www.vinoaroma.com/
trattoria.htm

THE CATSKILLS

To past generations of New Yorkers, the Catskills were once the "Borscht Belt," summers filled with shuffleboard and table tennis at sprawling vacation colonies like the Nevele, Grossinger's, and the Concord. While some of these resort hotels survive as golf destinations, the era of highballs and "Bésame Mucho" evoked in the movie *Dirty Dancing* is but a memory.

Today towns along the New York State Thruway like Kingston, New Paltz, Woodstock, Hudson, and Saugerties are rife with chic shops and fine dining, and the expanse is dotted with wineries, organic food co-ops, inns, and spas.

Clearly, what draws so many ex-urbanites, many of whom migrated to their former weekend homes, is the area's incredible natural beauty, largely unspoiled despite 300-odd years of European incursion. This is mostly thanks to the creation of the Catskill Park and Forest Preserve, 700,000 acres of mountains and valleys, forests and farms, rivers, streams, and waterfalls. The park is not only ground zero for fly-fishing, but it is a vital watershed, supplying half the state, including New York City, with clean drinking water.

With thirty-five peaks topping out at more than 3,500 feet, the Catskills have long attracted skiers, and now they are

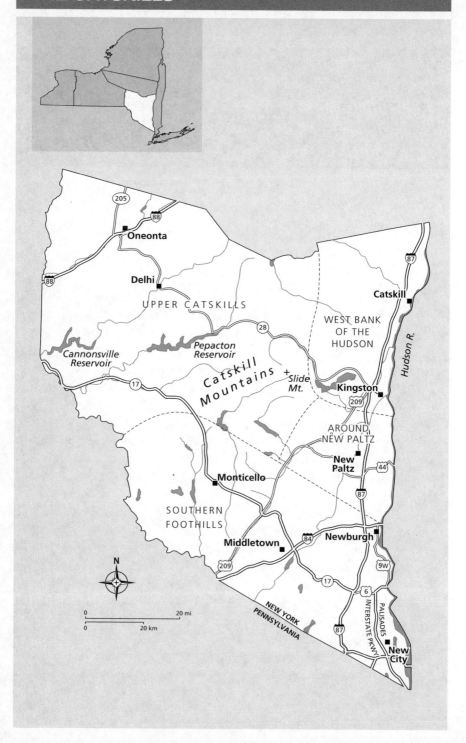

Oneonta

Delhi

UPPER CATSKILLS

Cannonsville
Reservoir

Pepacton
Reservoir

Catskill

WEST BANK
OF THE
HUDSON

Hudson R.

Catskill
Mountains

Slide
Mt.

Kingston

AROUND
NEW PALTZ

New
Paltz

Monticello

SOUTHERN
FOOTHILLS

Middletown

Newburgh

NEW YORK
PENNSYLVANIA

PALISADES INTERSTATE PKWY

New
City

N

0   20 mi
0   20 km

fast becoming a haven for mountain bikers, rock climbers, and other extreme sports fans.

Southern Foothills

During World War II more than 1.3 million soldiers shipped out from Camp Shanks to fight in North Africa and Europe. They lived and trained in 2,500 buildings sprawled across 1,300 acres; today a small exhibit, vintage training films, and memorabilia at **Camp Shanks WWII Museum** tell the story of the men and women who passed through here on their way to the front. The museum, on South Greenbush Road State Routes 303/340, Orangeburg (845-638-5419), is open Memorial Day to Labor Day, Saturday and Sunday 10 a.m. to 3 p.m.

The **Edward Hopper House,** birthplace and boyhood home of the realist painter famous for works such as *Night Hawk,* is now a New York State Historic Site. One room of the home, built in 1858, documents his life and work in Nyack. Three other rooms exhibit works by local artists. Jazz concerts are presented in the restored garden in the summer. The house and gallery, at 82 North Broadway, Nyack (845-358-0774), is open Thursday through Sunday from 1 to 5 p.m. Admission is $2 for adults, $1 for students and retirees, free for children.

Manitoga, Algonquin for "Place of the Great Spirit," was the home of Russel Wright, one of the country's foremost designers of home furnishings and a proponent of American design. His designs reflected his love of natural, organic shapes, and he would extend this respect for the earth and nature to the grounds where he built his home, Dragon Rock.

When he bought the property for his home in 1942, it had been damaged by 150 years of logging and quarrying. Over the next 30 years, Mr. Wright worked

AUTHOR'S FAVORITES—CATSKILLS

Catskill Fly Fishing Center and Museum/Hall of Fame

Gomez Mill House

Inn at Lake Joseph

Minnewaska State Park Preserve

Mohonk Mountain House

Onteora Mountain House

Saugerties Lighthouse

Slabsides

Sugar Loaf Arts and Craft Village

to restore the land, designing a living theater—a carefully designed backdrop of native trees, ferns, mosses, and wildflowers that appears as if it grew naturally.

The designer-naturalist opened his land to the public a year before he died and today's programs at Manitoga teach ecology, science, art, and design. Visitors are invited to wander several one-way paths that Mr. Wright designed as journeys into the secrets of the forest. Wright studied the landscape and the land's natural contour to determine its direction when building. The main path passes by his home, designed to blend into the landscape of the quarry.

The grounds of Manitoga, the Russel Wright Design Center, Route 9D, Garrison (four miles south of Cold Spring), (845-424-3812; www.russelwright center.org), are open from May through October, Monday through Friday 9 a.m. to 4:30 p.m. and Saturday and Sunday 10 a.m. to 6 p.m. The grounds are open the rest of the year on weekdays only. House and landscape tours are offered select weekdays at 11 a.m. and weekends at 11 a.m. and 1:30 p.m. Visitors can take self-guided hikes on weekdays during daylight hours April through October. A donation of $5 is suggested if visitors hike the grounds. Admission for the tour is $15 for adults, $13 for senior citizens, and $5 for children 12 and under (call to confirm times).

In the 1830s John Jaques emigrated from Europe to the small town of Washingtonville. Trained as a shoe and bootmaker, he planned to support himself with his trade. To augment his income he purchased ten acres of land on Main Street and planted grapes in the rich, loamy Hudson Valley soil to sell at market. When he became a church elder, he used some of his grapes to make sacramental wine.

Today **Brotherhood** is America's oldest winery, and the church where Mr. Jaques's wine was first served is the winery's gift shop. Brotherhood has been making wine continuously since 1839, having survived Prohibition by

A Magnifico's Bequest

The town of Harriman and Harriman State Park, a unit of the Palisades Interstate Park system, are now just names on the map to most travelers, though some New Yorkers may remember the late diplomat and one-time New York governor W. Averell Harriman. But the town and the park were named for the governor's father, E. H. Harriman, at one time the most powerful railroad baron in the United States. Edward Henry Harriman (1848–1909) controlled some 60,000 miles of American railways, including the Union Pacific. The present-day park consists of much of the 20,000-acre estate he acquired northwest of New City, and which he left to his wife with the intention that it would one day be transferred to state ownership.

once again reverting to the sale of sacramental wine. Its vast underground cellars, comparable to those of famous European wineries, are the largest in the country and, in addition to sacramental wine, Brotherhood now makes specialty, table, dessert, and premium vintage wines, including Grand Monarque champagne. A tour of the winery includes a visit to the underground cellars and a sampling of a half-dozen wines.

Brotherhood, 100 Brotherhood Plaza, Washingtonville (845-496-3661; www.brotherhoodwinery.net), offers guided half-hour tours daily at 11:30 a.m. with the last tour at 2:30 p.m.; weekends only January through March. The tasting room is open April through December, Sunday through Friday from 11 a.m. to 6 p.m., and January through March on Saturday and Sunday 11 a.m. to 5 p.m. A tour and tasting pass is $10 per person, a tasting flight is $5, and a tour pass is $6 per person. Call for a calendar of weekend events.

westpoint washouts

Not everyone is cut out for the rigors of cadet life at West Point. In 1831, after eight months, Edgar Allan Poe was dismissed for insubordination. Artist James A. McNeill Whistler washed out in his third year when he failed chemistry. He later commented, "Had silicon been a gas, I would have been a major general."

Orange County is known for its fine standard bred horses, the horses of the harness track. Hambletonian, sire of practically all of today's trotters, was born here. For years it has been home to the Trotting Horse Museum, Home of the Hall of Fame of the Trotter, now officially the *Harness Racing Museum & Hall of Fame.*

Visitors to the museum can experience the thrill of harness racing with the museum's permanent exhibit, the "Ready to Ride Racing Simulator," which invites participants to sit on a twelve-seat motion-based platform. There are six stationary seats for those who want to see the film but not experience the motion. Regardless of where you sit, guests watch a film that utilizes a variety of advanced techniques to create what amounts to a virtual harness race.

There are a host of other activities and exhibits, including the opportunity to call and judge a race, and a historic collection of photographs, ephemera, and fine art.

The Harness Racing Museum & Hall of Fame, 240 Main St., Goshen (845-294-6330; www.harnessmuseum.com), is open daily from 10 a.m. to 5 p.m.; closed major holidays. Admission is free.

Across the way is *Goshen Historic Track,* the oldest active harness track in the country and the first sporting site in the nation to be designated a National Registered Historic Landmark by the National Park Service.

ANNUAL EVENTS IN THE CATSKILLS

JANUARY

Hudson Valley Rail Trail Winterfest
New Paltz
(845) 691-8151
www.hudsonvalleyrailtrail.com

FEBRUARY

Winter Carnival Weekend
Monticello
(845) 796-3161
www.holidaymtn.com

MARCH

Women's History Month
New Paltz
(845) 255-1403

APRIL

Pennsylvania Dutch Festival
Port Ewen
(845) 338-0356

MAY

Hudson Valley Mayfaire
New Paltz
(845) 331-1957
www.hudsonvalleymayfaire.com/

Irish Festival
East Durham
(518) 634-2224
www.irishvillageusa.com

JUNE

Arts on the Bridge Festival
New Paltz
(845) 255-2871
www.newpaltzchamber.org

JULY

Belleayre Music Festival
Highmount
(800) 254-5600
www.belleayremusic.org
(through August)

Hurley Stone House Tour
Hurley
www.stonehouseday.org

New Paltz Gardens Plus Tour
New Paltz
(845) 255-0243
www.newpaltzchamber.org

Peaceful Valley Bluegrass Festival
Shinhopple
(607) 363-2211

Windham Chamber Music Festival
Windham
(518) 734-3868
www.windhammusic.com
(through August)

The hamlet of Sugar Loaf has enjoyed a reputation as a crafts community for more than 250 years. Today more than fifty artisans live and work in the original barns and buildings, creating a variety of goods ranging from stained glass to pottery to hand-tooled leather products. Visitors are invited to watch the artists at work in their studios and browse through a variety of specialty and gift shops peppered throughout the town.

AUGUST

Colonial Street Festival
New Paltz
(845) 255-1660
www.newpaltz.org

Daniel Nimham International Pow Wow
Carmel
(800) 470-4854
www.nimham.com

International Celtic Festival
Hunter
(518) 263-4223
www.huntermtn.com

Maverick Concert Series
Woodstock
(845) 679-8348
www.maverickconcerts.org
(through early September)

SEPTEMBER

Great Catskill Mountain Quilt Show
Windham
(800) SKI-WINDHAM
www.windhammountain.com

Hudson River Valley Ramble
Two weekends, various locations
(800) 453-6665
www.hudsonrivervalleyramble.com/

Turn-of-the-Century Day
Roxbury
(607) 326-3722
www.roxburyny.com

OCTOBER

Hudson Valley Fall Festival
Milton
(845) 464-2789

Oktoberfest
Hunter
(518) 263-4223
www.huntermtn.com

NOVEMBER

Annual Greek Festival
Kingston
(845) 331-3522
www.ulstercountyalive.com

Rosendale International Pickle Festival
Rosendale
(845) 658-9649
www.picklefest.com

DECEMBER

Woodstock's Holiday Open House
Woodstock
(845) 679-6234
www.woodstockchamber.com

There is an extensive program of concerts, festivals, and special events at *Sugar Loaf Arts and Craft Village* throughout the year. The 700-seat theater, Lycian Centre for the Performing Arts (www.lyciancentre.com), offers a venue for performances by national and international touring companies in Broadway musicals, drama, dance, concerts, and children's shows.

Sugar Loaf Arts and Craft Village, Sugar Loaf Chamber of Commerce, Inc., P.O. Box 125, Sugar Loaf 10981 (845-469-9181; www.sugarloafnychamber .com), is open year-round. Days and hours vary from shop to shop, but most are open from Wednesday through Sunday 11 a.m. to 6 p.m.; request a brochure from the Chamber of Commerce or visit www.sugarloafartsvillage.com.

The next time you eat an onion, consider this: it might well have been grown in black dirt formed 12,000 years ago in a glacial lake in an area now known as *Pine Island.* As the glaciers melted and the climate warmed, vegetation grew, died, and sank to the bottom of the lake. The lake area earned the nickname "the drowned lands" and remained a swamp until the early 1900s, when immigrants came, bought the land cheap, drained the lake by hand, built drainage ditches, and then planted onions in the rich black dirt. Today, with thousands of acres planted, the "black dirt" region is one of the country's leading producers of onions.

The cream of onion soup at *Ye Jolly Onion Inn* is made from Pine Island onions. So are the deep-fried onion blossoms, the onion rings, and the onion gravy on the Pine Island steak. And the vegetables on the salad bar are all from farms in the area (in season).

If your interest in horses has been piqued by the Harness Racing Museum & Hall of Fame, head over to *New Hope Farms Equestrian Park* in Port Jervis. With eighty acres it's one of the largest equestrian facilities in the nation and features indoor and outdoor arenas and permanent stabling for one hundred horses. Visitors are invited to stop by at any time to watch thoroughbreds and warmbloods being trained for show jumping competitions.

Throughout the year there are events such as a tri-state rodeo, a family festival, polo matches, and a championship dressage; musical events are also presented. The indoor arena, which seats 2,500, is one of the largest in the country.

New Hope Farms Equestrian Park is at 517 Neversink Dr., Port Jervis (845-856-8384; www.frontiernet/~nhfarms). For a list of events, check the Web site.

Black Tie, No Tails

Toward the end of the nineteenth century, in the gated community of millionaires' estates called Tuxedo Park in the Ramapo Mountains near the New Jersey border, daring young fashion plates scandalized their elders by abandoning traditional full evening dress with its cutaway tailcoats in favor of a shorter black jacket cut like a daytime suit coat. Despite initial resistance the new style caught on, and the new semiformal men's uniform came to be known as the tuxedo.

The ***Inn at Lake Joseph*** is a Victorian country estate high in the Catskill Mountains. It nestles against a 250-acre lake and is surrounded by thousands of acres of forest and wildlife preserve.

Built by Thomas Hunt Talmadge in the latter part of the nineteenth century, the estate served as a retreat for the Dominican Sisters, as a vacation home of Cardinals Hayes and Spellman of New York, and finally as a sumptuous inn.

Rooms are available in the Manor, the Carriage House, and The Cottage. Several of the inn's ten guest rooms in the Manor have working fireplaces and whirlpool baths. If you require even more privacy, request a room in the recently restored turn-of-the-century Adirondack-style Carriage House. Pets are also welcome. Each has its own entrance, a working fireplace, and a whirlpool bath. Some have lofted ceilings and private sundecks. Pets are also welcome in The Cottage with three rustic, Adirondack–style guest rooms with stone fireplaces, full kitchens, whirlpool baths, and private sundecks. Meals are served, and there are plenty of outdoor sporting activities, including paddling around in a Victorian-style swimming pool. Lake Joseph has a reputation as one of the finest largemouth bass lakes in the state.

Inn at Lake Joseph, 162 St. Joseph Rd., Forestburgh (845-791-9506, www .lakejoseph.com), is open year-round. Rates range from $210 to $460. There is pet fee of $6.25 per leg per day (no cats allowed). I wonder if they would hold up their per leg fee for the three-legged rescue dogs roaming my neighborhood.

From December through March, Sullivan County becomes home to a large concentration of migrant ***bald eagles***—mostly from Canada. A few of their favorite nesting places include Mongaup Falls Reservoir and Rio Reservoir in Forestburgh and the Rondout Reservoir in Grahamsville. For an update and complete list of sites, contact the Audubon Society of New York State, P.O. Box 111, Eldred 12732, (845) 557-8025 or visit http://ny.audubon.org.

Established in 1927, the ***Wurtsboro Airport*** bills itself as the oldest soaring site in the nation. The airport's Flight Service is currently the largest soaring school in the United States, offering lessons for people with no flight experience as well as for those licensed to fly power planes. For the casual visitor, however, the big attraction is the demonstration rides. After being towed aloft by a single-engine Cessna, you'll glide high above the Catskills with an FAA-rated commercial pilot at the stick. A demonstration ride or an introductory lesson costs $75 plus tax. Be sure to call in advance for a reservation.

Wurtsboro Airport and Flight Service, Route 209, Wurtsboro (845-888-2791; www.wurtsboroairport.com), is open daily all year from 9 a.m. to 5 p.m. or dusk (weather permitting), whichever comes first. Closed major holidays.

According to the folks at **Memories,** buyers searched five states and three countries to fill their 20,000-square-foot building with more than 25,000 unique items covering every style and taste from the early 1800s to the 1950s. Stock includes furniture, lamps, clocks, rocking horses, decoys, glass, china, magazines, and, as they say, "who knows what's coming in?"

Memories, 7126 Route 17, Parksville (845-292-4270 or 800-ABC-TIME; www.memoriesantiques.com), is open daily year-round from 10 a.m. to 5 p.m.

Many devotees of fly-fishing believe that, in North America, the sport began in the Catskills. And seeing the streams that run along the Beaverkill and Willowemoc Valleys, it's hard to imagine a more suitable location for a center devoted to preserving the heritage and protecting the future of fly-fishing in the United States. That's the mission of the **Catskill Fly Fishing Center and Museum/Hall of Fame,** on the shores of the Willowemoc River between Roscoe and Livingston Manor.

Founded in 1891, the new facility, which opened in May 1995, illuminates the contributions and lives of the great names associated with the Catskill era—Gordon and Hewitt, Dette and Darbee, LaBranche and Flick—as well as Lee Wulff, Poul Jorgensen, and others from the world of fly-fishing. Interpretive exhibits on the evolution of the sport, as well as hundreds of meticulously crafted rods, flies, and reels are on display. Special guest fly tyers demonstrate their craft every Saturday afternoon throughout the season. The center offers a variety of educational and recreational programs year-round, including courses in stream ecology and angling, fly tying, and rod building.

Catskill Fly Fishing Center and Museum/Hall of Fame, 1031 Old Route 17, Livingston Manor (845-439-4810; www.cffcm.net), is open daily 10 a.m. to 4 p.m. from April through October; Tuesday through Friday 10 a.m. to 1 p.m., and Saturday 10 a.m. to 4 p.m. November through March. Closed holidays. Varying donations are requested during special events and programs, including $10 for their "In the Catskills. Hidden spots, secret techniques" session.

Consider escaping the stresses of everyday life for a peaceful weekend at **Dai Bosatsu Zendo,** a Zen Buddhist monastery on 1,400 acres in the Catskill Mountain Forest Preserve. All are welcome here, whether it be for a three-day weekend for novices who want to learn basics, such as sitting, breathing, and chanting; a longer stay for those steeped in the way of Rinzai Zen Buddhism; or even those just looking for an overnight retreat. The grounds are open to day visitors March through November.

As expected, accommodations are simple but comfortable and include three vegetarian meals a day. Rooms with private and shared baths are available. Rates for the three-day weekend begin at under $200.

Dai Bosatsu Zendo, 223 Beecher Lake Rd., Livingston Manor (845-439-4566; www.daibosatsu.org). The accommodations are for like-minded travelers, as the staff notes, "As we are a practicing religious community and a private property, we cannot accommodate casual visitors who wish to enjoy our grounds."

More than one hundred varieties of cheese and fifty flavors of jelly beans make *The Cheese Barrel* a popular stop for kids of all ages. The shop specializes in gourmet goodies and breads from Bread Alone. The old stockroom has been turned into an ice-cream parlor, and the dining area serves continental breakfasts and light lunches with homemade soups, salads, and sandwiches.

The Cheese Barrel, 798 Main St. at Bridge Street, Margaretville (845-586-4666; www.cheesebarrel.com), is open daily.

Around New Paltz

The 90,000-acre Northern Shawangunk mountain range, whose cliffs, summits, and plateaus are home to almost forty rare plant and animal species, has been designated a "Last Great Place on Earth" by the Nature Conservancy.

Minnewaska State Park Preserve, high in the Shawangunk Mountains, is an outdoor paradise of hiking trails, waterfalls, and scenic vistas. A network of carriageways accessible to bicyclists, hikers, and horseback riders links many of the park's major highlights. You'll need to hike nearly 3 miles to reach Lake Awosting, a mile-long swimming lake rimmed by pine trees and one of the park's greatest draws. Although it's a popular spot on a hot summer day (a lifeguard is on duty), those accustomed to the crowds at ocean beaches will feel almost as if they're at a private party. For the less ambitious there's also swimming at the more accessible Lake Minnewaska, nestled amid white sandstone cliffs (it's easy to see why the Indians named it "floating waters").

Minnewaska State Park Preserve, off Route 44/55 near New Paltz (845-255-0752; www.lakeminnewaska.org), is open year-round. There is a $7 parking fee.

Not far from Minnewaska lies *Sam's Point Dwarf Pine Ridge Preserve,* a 4,600-acre tract of land that contains one of the world's best examples of a ridgetop dwarf pine barrens. According to the Nature Conservancy, managers of the barrens, one of Earth's most endangered ecosystems thrives here for several reasons: "limited water during the growing season; exposure to direct sun and wind; shallow, highly erodible soils; and the regular occurrence of fires. All of these processes, and perhaps yet unknown factors, have historically worked together to shape the plant and animal communities that thrive there today."

Several trails wind throughout the preserve. One of the most popular, Verkeerderkill Falls/Long Path, meanders through the barrens to the falls and offers panoramic views to the southeast.

For information contact the Nature Conservancy, Eastern New York Chapter, 265 Chestnut Ridge Rd., Mt. Kisco 10549; (914) 244-3271; www.nature.org/samspoint.

In 1714 Louis Moses Gomez, a refugee from the Spanish Inquisition, purchased 6,000 acres of land along the Hudson highlands and built a fieldstone blockhouse. Today the **Gomez Mill House** is the earliest surviving Jewish residence in North America.

Over the ensuing years subsequent owners of the house made changes to the original structure. The most famous twentieth-century owner was the Craftsman-era designer Dard Hunter, who rebuilt the old gristmill on "Jew's Creek" into a paper mill and then made paper by hand, cut and cast type, and hand printed his own books.

Today the house, continuously inhabited for almost 300 years, is preserved by the Gomez Foundation for Mill House. The foundation is made up of friends and descendants of families who lived here.

The Gomez Mill House, 11 Mill House Rd., Marlboro (845-236-3126; www.gomez.org), is open from the Wednesday after Easter and Passover through October, Wednesday through Sunday 10 a.m. to 4 p.m., with tours at 10 and 11:30 a.m. and 1 and 2:30 p.m. Admission is $7.50 for adults, $5 for seniors, and $2 for children. On Sunday the museum sponsors a lecture series.

The **Buttermilk Falls Inn and Spa** in Milton is a seventy-acre estate overlooking the Hudson River just 75 miles north of New York City. Dating from 1764, the sophisticated inn has thirteen rooms, three carriage houses, the North Cottage, and a two-story, 3,500-square-foot spa.

"The spa at Buttermilk Falls Inn embraces a total holistic philosophy," says spa director Heidi Weaver. Guests unwind with a stroll on the estate's tranquil grounds past cascading waterfalls, winding brooks, flowering terraces, a peacock and chicken rookery, and a pre-Revolutionary cemetery. The spa lunch, prepared from organically grown produce from the estate's garden and from local farms and orchards, is served up with a charming river view.

The spa offers deep-tissue and hot-stone massages and purifying facials using organic skin care products. Buttermilk Spa's couples massage and spine-realigning "raindrop technique" are two of its signature treatments. Various sixty-minute sessions are priced from $90 and higher. Four spacious massage rooms even have river views. The spa is also adding a saltwater pool, a steam room, and a Jacuzzi.

For more information call (845) 795-1310 or 877-7-INN-SPA, or visit www .buttermilkfallsinn.com.

Back in the old Hudson Valley town of New Paltz, ***Historic Huguenot Street*** is the oldest street in America that still has its original houses. Think about it: find a street where each building lot has had only one house upon it, and chances are you're in a modern subdivision. But the stone houses on Huguenot Street were built between 1692 and 1712, and they'll look good for at least another 300 years.

Persecuted by the Catholic majority in their native France, many Huguenots came to New York in pursuit of freedom and tolerance. In 1677 twelve of their number purchased the lands around present-day New Paltz from the Esopus Indians and built log huts as their first habitations.

As the twelve pioneers and their families prospered, they decided to build more permanent dwellings. And permanent they were. Five perfectly preserved houses, with additions that were built by the settlers' descendants over the years still stand today. All of the houses are maintained by the Huguenot Historical Society, which gives standard and deluxe tours Tuesday through Sunday from May 1 through October 31, and standard tours in April and from November through December.

Standard tours of the houses are available for $9 for adults; $8 for students, seniors, and AAA members; $3 for ages 6 to 17; free for under 6. Family rate is $24. Deluxe tours are $12 for adults; $11 for students, seniors, and AAA members; $5 for ages 6 to 17; free for under 6. Family rate is $30. For information contact the Huguenot Society, 18 Broadhead Ave., New Paltz (845-255-1660; http://huguenotstreet.org).

Just north of New Paltz, at High Falls, is a museum dedicated to a great work of engineering brought about by an energy crisis—a disruption in coal supply brought about by America's 1812–14 war with Great Britain. Two brothers, Maurice and William Wurts, envisioned a canal to bring Pennsylvania anthracite (hard coal) from the mines to New York City and vicinity. In 1825, they formed the Delaware and Hudson Canal Company with the goal of linking Honesdale, Pennsylvania, with the Hudson River port of Eddyville, New York.

The surveying and engineering of the 108-mile route was handled by Benjamin Wright, chief engineer of the Erie Canal. The Delaware and Hudson Canal, completed in 1828, was the first million-dollar enterprise in America. Between 1847 and 1852 it was enlarged and deepened to accommodate heavier traffic. A lot of coal barged along that route, yet in 1829, the company also began to work its gravity-operated rail line between Honesdale and Carbondale, Pennsylvania, with a new English steam locomotive. Except for a few weedy stretches, the canal is gone, but the Delaware and Hudson Railroad survives to this day as the oldest transportation company in the United States.

The **Delaware and Hudson Canal Museum** is a private institution established to tell the story of the old canal, and it does so not merely through glassed-in exhibits but by preserving the extant structures, channel, and locks in the High Falls vicinity. Visitors learn about the canal through sophisticated dioramas, photos, and technological exhibits, including models of a working lock and gravity railroad. There are five locks at High Falls. The Delaware and Hudson Canal Historical Society has done whatever restoration and preservation work is possible on them and has linked canal sites in the area with a system of hiking trails. Self-guided tours take in nearby canal segments as well as the remains of John Roebling's suspension aqueduct.

The Delaware and Hudson Canal Museum, 23 Mohonk Rd., High Falls (845-687-9311; www.canalmuseum.org), is open May through October, Saturday and Sunday 11 a.m. to 5 p.m. Admission is $5 for adults, $3 for children.

Originally built to serve canal workers, the **Depuy Canal House** is a 1797 stone tavern right on the Delaware and Hudson Canal. It still has its original fireplaces and wooden floors, and diners can watch meals being prepared from a second-floor balcony that overlooks the kitchen.

From these dizzy heights, foodies revel in watching chef John Novi, whom *Time* magazine called "The Father of Nouvelle Cuisine," prepare beef short ribs barbecue and German style Pork Choucroute.

The menu might come with a warning about over-indulging in the multi-course prix fixe. But that's no problem if you've planned to overnight at the **Locktender's Cottage** right next door. The variety of comfortable accommodations includes the Chef's Quarters, a suite with a hot tub and, of course, a kitchenette. Reservations are recommended for both dining and overnight stays; contact the Depuy Canal House, Route 213, High Falls at (845) 687-7700 or www.depuycanalhouse.net. Dinner is served Friday through Sunday; breakfast and brunch are also offered on Saturday and Sunday.

Even as canals and railroads were changing the face of America, the first conservationists started speaking out against the dangers of the Industrial Revolution. Among them was John Burroughs, a native New Yorker who wrote twenty-five books on natural history and the philosophy of conservation. In 1895 Burroughs built a rustic log hideaway in the woods outside the village of West Park, barely 2 miles from the west bank of the Hudson. He called it **Slabsides,** and it is a National Historic Landmark today.

Burroughs, whose permanent home was only a mile and a half away, came to his little retreat to write and quietly observe his natural surroundings. John Muir came here to talk with Burroughs, as did Theodore Roosevelt and

Thomas Edison. They sat around the fire on log furniture of Burroughs's own manufacture, much of it still in the cabin.

Slabsides, which was deeded to the John Burroughs Association after the author's death in 1921, now stands within the 191-acre *John Burroughs Sanctuary,* a pleasant woodland tract that forms a most fitting living monument to his memory. The sanctuary is open all year; on the third Saturday in May and the first Saturday in October, the John Burroughs Association holds an open house from noon to 4:30 p.m. In addition to an opportunity to see the cabin, the special days include informal talks and nature walks. Admission is free. The sanctuary has 2½ miles of hiking trails open to the public daily from dawn to dusk.

For further information write the association at 15 West 77th St., New York, NY 10024, or call (212) 769-5169, or visit www.research.amnh.org/burroughs.

Nestled in the heart of a 24,000-acre natural area in the Shawangunk Mountains, overlooking Lake Mohonk, is a sprawling Victorian castle resort called *Mohonk Mountain House.* Built in 1869, the castle is a National Historic Landmark. Above the Mohonk Mountain House stands *Sky Top Tower,* an observation tower built in 1923 of Shawangunk conglomerate that was quarried at its base. On a clear day from the top of Sky Top Tower, you can see as far as the Rondout and Wallkill valleys, New Jersey, Connecticut, Vermont, Pennsylvania, and Massachusetts. (The tower is also known as the Albert K. Smiley Memorial Tower in tribute to the cofounder of the Mohonk Mountain House.) Guests have use of the resort's spacious grounds and many amenities, but even if you're not an overnight guest, you can purchase a guest pass for $15 that will give you access to the tower; 85 miles of hiking trails, paths, and carriage roads; and the lovely landscaped grounds with their formal show gardens, herb garden, and new Victorian maze.

Day visitors are also invited to visit the *Barn Museum,* in one of the largest barns in the Northeast. Built in 1888, it houses more than fifty nineteenth-century horse-drawn vehicles and many working tools made more than one hundred years ago.

Mohonk Mountain House, 1000 Mountain Rest Rd., New Paltz (845-255-1000 or 800-772-6646; www.mohonk.com). Overnight rates vary according to view and decor, but all include three meals. They range from $510 a night for a double in one of the traditional-style rooms to $940 for a tower room.

West Bank of the Hudson

When mayonnaise king Richard Hellmann was told, at the age of 55, that he had only six months to live unless he moved to the country, he promptly built a magnificent estate on the side of Mount Ticetonyk overlooking the Esopus River valley, moved there with his family, and lived to be 94.

Now a B&B, *Onteora Mountain House* (Onteora is the Mohican name for the Catskills, which translates to "the land and the sky") is surrounded by 225 acres of forest and features a magnificent multi-windowed 20- by 30-foot Great Room with a massive stone fireplace; a 40-foot covered dining porch with Adirondack-style tree-trunk columns and railings; and a 60-foot southwest deck. All five guest rooms have private baths. The house is filled with an eclectic collection of antiques and Japanese and Korean art.

Onteora Mountain House, 96 Piney Point Rd., Boiceville (845-657-6233; www.onteora.com), is open year-round. Rates, which include a full breakfast (with items such as crepes with three fillings and Eggs Hellmann), range from the mid $100s a weekday night to upwards of $300 a weekend night; there is a two-night minimum on weekends.

Totem Indian Trading Post is a New York State Historic Site and one of, if not *the* oldest, trading posts in the state. It's also the site of numerous megalithic sculptures done by Emil Brunel, founder of the New York Institute of Photography, who died in Boiceville in 1944. The ashes of the man who perfected the one-hour film developing process seventy years before it became popular are interred in one of his cement pieces here.

Totem Indian Trading Post, Sacred Ground, Route 28, Boiceville (845- 657-2531), is open daily from 10 a.m. to 6 p.m.

Floating down Esopus Creek on a lazy afternoon as it winds through the Catskill Mountains is the ultimate vacation: relaxing, scenic, and fun. The *Town Tinker* rents tubes, helps chart your course, provides instruction as needed, and arranges transportation. There are separate 2½-mile routes for beginner and expert tubers. Each route takes approximately two hours, and transportation is provided by either Town Tinker Tube Taxis on weekdays or the Catskill Mountain Railroad on weekends.

The Town Tinker, 10 Bridge St. (Route 28), Phoenicia (845-688-5553; www .towntinker.com), is open daily Memorial Day weekend through September from 9 a.m. to 6 p.m. (last rentals are at 4 p.m.). Basic inner tubes rent for $12 a day. A full-gear package for $30 includes a tube with seat, life vest, wetsuit, and helmet as well as one-time transportation. Children must be 12 years old and good swimmers. Taxi transportation is around $5 per trip.

On weekends and holidays *Catskill Mountain Railroad* transports novice tubers back to Phoenicia at the end of their run (one-way fare is $6 for adults and $4 for children ages 4 to 11 years). But if you'd rather tour Esopus Creek by rail, the railroad offers a 6-mile round-trip ride, stopping at Phoenicia at a circa 1900 train depot.

Catskill Mountain Railroad Company, Route 28, Mt. Pleasant (845-688-7400; www.catskillmtrailroad.com), operates weekends and holidays Memorial Day weekend through late October with trains running hourly 11 a.m. to 5 p.m. Fare is $14 for adults, $8 for children ages 4 to 11. Call ahead to verify schedules.

Housed in an old farm silo, *Emerson Kaleidoscope,* the world's largest kaleidoscope, is more than 60 feet high with three 38-foot mirrors, creating a total immersion in color and light. Three specially designed shows are presented throughout the year: "America, The House We Live In," is a history in music and light; "Hexagon Holiday" is a winter wonder that is shown from Christmas through Presidents Day weekend; and "Metamorphosis" is a show that opens in early spring, just as the buds are popping, and traces the progress of the seasons through the Catskills. Entry is $5 per person; children under 12 get in free. You can find it at Emerson Place, an upscale hotel and spa complex on Route 28 in Mt. Tremper.

Emerson Place also offers a country store and other shops, including the *Kaleidoscope,* where handmade, one-of-a kind kaleidoscopes are on sale. The rebuilt *Emerson Resort and Spa* now has twenty-five new suites in addition to the Adirondack-style accommodations at the old *Lodge at Emerson Place.* Rates for a standard double start at $190 a night; call (877) 688-2828 or go to www.emersonresort.com for more information.

Head to *Catskill Rose* for hot smoked salmon with scallion cheesecake appetizers and entrees like smoked duckling with peach rhubarb marmellata. The restaurant, on Route 212 in Mt. Tremper (845-688-7100; www.catskillrose .com), begins serving dinner at 5 p.m. Thursday through Sunday. Reservations are encouraged.

One of the country's first art colonies was founded in Woodstock in 1903, and today Ulster County is still a haven for artists. The *Woodstock Byrdcliffe Guild,* a multi-arts center, displays and sells works of some of the area's best. It's at 34 Tinker St., Woodstock (845-679-2079; www.woodstockguild.org), and has varying hours by season and events.

The baguette is a work of art at *Bread Alone,* 22 Mill Hill Rd., Woodstock (845-679-2108). Workers at the European-style bakery shape the breads by hand and then bake the loaves in the wood-fired ovens. Among the house specialties: brioche, challah, and sourdough currant buns. The bakery is open daily from 7 a.m. to 6 p.m.; visit www.breadalone.com for locations in Boiceville and Rhinebeck.

There are numerous excellent restaurants in the Woodstock area. Among the more unusual is *New World Home Cooking Company,* 1411 Route 212, Saugerties (845-246-0900; www.ricorlando.com), featuring "New Wave" cooking, boasting an eclectic assortment of ethnic dishes often pepped up with hot peppers and Asian spices. House specialties include Jamaican jerk chicken, Cajun-peppered shrimp, and ropa vieja. There's also an outdoor patio and a varied selection of beers to extinguish the fire. From May through October, dinner is served seven days a week Sunday through Thursday 5 p.m. to 10 p.m. and Friday and Saturday from 5 to 11 p.m. From October to May, dinner is served on Sunday and Monday through Thursday from 5 to 10 p.m. and Friday and Saturday from 5 to 11 p.m. They are closed on Tuesday and Wednesday during the off season. Reservations are highly recommended.

For almost forty years until his death in 1976, Harvey Fite created a monumental environmental sculpture out of an abandoned Saugerties blue-stone quarry. **Opus 40,** made of hundreds of thousands of tons of finely fitted stone, covers more than six acres. Visitors can walk along its recessed lower pathways, around the pools and fountains, and up to the nine-ton monolith at the summit. To create his Opus, Fite worked with traditional tools that were used by quarrymen here. The **Quarryman's Museum** houses his collection of tools and artifacts.

Opus 40 and the Quarryman's Museum, 50 Fite Rd., Saugerties (845-246-3400; www.opus40.org), is open Memorial Day weekend through Columbus Day weekend, Friday, Saturday, and Sunday and most Monday holidays (call in advance) 11:30 a.m. to 5 p.m. Admission is $10 for adults, $7 for students and senior citizens, and $3 for children.

Stay in an authentic lighthouse at the **Saugerties Lighthouse,** an 1869 stone structure at the mouth of Esopus Creek on the Hudson River.

Deactivated by the U.S. Coast Guard in 1954, the lighthouse has since been restored by the Saugerties Lighthouse Conservancy, which operates it as a museum and inn. In 1990 the Coast Guard installed a fourth-order solar-powered light, and the lighthouse once again aids mariners.

Two second-floor bedrooms are for rent and guests share a kitchen and bath. Guests travel to the lighthouse via a half-mile nature trail (at low tide only) or by private boat. From March through January the rooms rent for $200, based on double-occupancy. Reservations are essential.

The museum at Saugerties Lighthouse Conservancy, 168 Lighthouse Dr., Saugerties (845-247-0656; www.saugertieslighthouse.com), is open Saturday, Sunday, and holidays from noon to 3 p.m. Memorial Day through Labor Day, and no tours during the Between the Tides festival. There is a suggested dona-tion of $5 for adults and $2 for children.

New York's highest waterfall is actually 3 miles east of Tannersville at **Kaaterskill Falls.** Kaaterskill Falls leaps from a rock ledge as a narrow curtain of white water, plunging past a natural grotto to a second scooped-out shelf at which it gathers force to finish its plunge toward the floor of Kaaterskill Clove. To get there, drive along Route 23A up the winding road, watch for the vehicle pullout and park there. Follow the sign that says TRAIL back down the road a short distance to the bridge to view the falls. Little known outside of hikers' guidebooks, the falls were once the Catskills' most celebrated natural wonder. Thomas Cole, founder of the Hudson River School of art, immortalized the falls in his painting *View of Kaaterskill Falls* in the early 1800s. Washington Irving described the cove as "wild, lonely, and shagged, the bottom filled with fragments from impending cliffs, and scarcely lighted by the reflected rays of the setting sun."

The path to the base of the falls is not particularly difficult. Step gingerly during spring when its snow cover has melted and refrozen into splintering ice. Follow along the short ravine gouged by Kaaterskill Creek for less than a mile before reaching the base.

Over in the Broncks, named for the family of one of the original clans of Swedish settlers in New Amsterdam and the Hudson Valley, lies the ***Bronck Museum.*** The farmstead of Pieter Bronck, who settled on the west bank of the Hudson near what is now Coxsackie, today makes up the museum grounds.

Eight generations of Broncks lived in the seventeenth-century house before it passed to the Greene County Historical Society, along with the entire farm settled in those early years. The Broncks' property had come down practically intact until Leonard Bronck Lampman willed the acreage and buildings to the historical society. Visitors appreciate not only the oldest of the farm buildings, but also all of the barns, utility buildings, and furnishings acquired over two centuries of prosperity and familial expansion. What it all amounts to is an object lesson in the changes in style, taste, and sophistication that took place between the seventeenth and nineteenth centuries.

The Bronck Museum, 45 Lafayette Ave., Coxsackie (518-731-6490; www .gchistory.org/barns.php), is open from Memorial Day weekend to mid-October, noon to 4 p.m. On Wednesday through Friday, Saturday and Monday holidays, 10 a.m. to 4 p.m. and Sunday 1 to 4 p.m. On Memorial Day, Labor Day, and Columbus Day, hours are 1 to 4 p.m. The last tours are 3:30 p.m. daily. Admission runs $5 for adults, $3 for youth ages 12 to 15, $2 for children 5 to 11, and children under 5 are free.

Upper Catskills

The clear, cold streams of the Catskills from Beaver Kill, Esopus Creek, the east and west branches of the Delaware River are among the most hallowed waterways in the history of American trout fishing. Consequently, the Catskills have a rich tradition of handcrafted trout flies. If you're headed up this way to do some fishing, stop in at Mary Dette's home, where she sells flies hand-tied by artisans from around the Catskills region. (Mary also ties some herself, but we hear the wait for these is up to a year.) *Dette Trout Flies,* a local institution, is at 68 Cottage St., Roscoe (607-498-4991). Look for the sign out front: DETTE TROUT FLIES: WALT, WINNIE, MARY. It's open daily from 8 a.m. until 8 p.m.

If you're heading west from the Hudson Valley into the upper Catskills, stop at the *Durham Center Museum* in East Durham, which is housed in a circa 1825 one-room schoolhouse and several newer adjacent buildings. The collections run to Indian artifacts, portions of local petrified trees, old farm tools, and mementos of the 1800 Susquehanna Turnpike and the 1832–40 Canajoharie-Catskill Railroad, both of which passed this way.

There is also a collection of Rogers Groups, those plaster statuette tableaux that decorated Victorian parlors and played on bourgeois heartstrings before Norman Rockwell was born. Finally, don't miss the collection of bottled sand specimens from around the world, sent by friends of the museum. If you're planning a trip to some exotic spot not represented on these shelves, don't hesitate to send some sand.

The Durham Center Museum, Route 145, East Durham (518-239-8461), is open by appointment.. Admission is $2.50 for adults and $1 for children under 12. Genealogical researchers are welcome year-round by appointment.

Two 1876 Queen Anne boarding houses were restored and joined to create *Albergo Allegria,* a luxurious sixteen-room inn with an elegant Victorian flavor and modern-day amenities. There is also a carriage house with five suites. Rates, which range from $93 for a weekday room in the inn to $299 (in high season) for the Millennium Suite, include a gourmet breakfast, with stuffed French toast, Belgian waffles, and honey-cured bacon. The B&B is on Route 296, Windham (518-734-5560; www.albergousa.com).

In 1824 Zadock Pratt came to a settlement called Schoharie Kill to establish a tannery. He bought some land, surveyed it, and set up his factory. Over the next twenty years, more than 30,000 employees tanned a million sides of

The Bridges of Delaware County

Three historic covered bridges are among the rural attractions of Delaware County. The Hamden and Fitches Bridges span the west branch of the Delaware River, while the Downsville Bridge, crossing the Delaware's east branch, is at 174 feet the longest covered bridge still in use in New York State.

The Long Good Night

Literature's most famed napper, Rip Van Winkle, hailed from Palenville and took his twenty-year snooze in a ravine halfway up Catskill Mountain. Hikers still search for the spot where Rip sat, drank from a keg offered to him by an old man with thick, bushy hair and a grizzled beard, and watched odd-looking fellows playing ninepins before he drifted off. If a stranger offers you any hooch, just keep walking.

sole leather with the use of hides imported from South America. They were shipped down the Hudson River to New York City. And in the meantime Mr. Pratt established Prattsville, one of the earliest planned communities in New York State.

Mr. Pratt went on to become a member of the U.S. Congress elected in 1836 and 1842. He sponsored a bill that created the Smithsonian Institution. But one of the most enduring legacies he left behind was *Pratt Rocks Park* (518-299-3395), on Main Street, which he donated to the town in 1843. Carved into the park's cliffs are symbols of Mr. Pratt's life, including a huge bust of his son who was killed in the Civil War, a horse, a hemlock tree, an uplifted hand, his tannery, a wreath with the names of his children, and an unfinished tomb where Pratt was to be buried overlooking the village. He was actually buried in a conventional grave at the other end of town. There's also a grave site with a stone bearing the names of his favorite dogs and horses.

While you're in Prattsville, take time to visit the *Zadock Pratt Museum* (518-299-3395; www.prattmuseum.com), located in Zadock Pratt's restored homestead in the center of town. The museum, on the National Register of Historic Places, is just a half mile from the rocks and focuses on the history and culture of the northern Catskills in the mid-nineteenth century. It's open on Saturday and Sunday from 11 a.m. to 4 p.m. with the last tour through the museum by 4 p.m. There is a $5 admission fee. Nearby, the National Register *Reformed Dutch Church,* with its handsome three-tiered tower, was built in 1804.

Naturalist John Burroughs may have spent much of the last decades of his life at Slabsides, down on the Hudson, but he was born in Roxbury in 1837 and spent the last ten summers of his life at Woodchuck Lodge. He was also buried here, in a field adjacent to the lodge, on April 2, 1921. The grave site and the nearby "Boyhood Rock" that he had cherished as a lad are now part of *John Burroughs Memorial State Historic Site.*

The Burroughs Memorial lies in a field surrounded by forests and the rolling Catskill hills. This is as restful a memorial as one could possibly imagine

Breaking "Legs"

The tiny town of Acra was once home to one of Prohibition's most infamous criminals. Jack "Legs" Diamond heard about a potent applejack that the locals made from cider and decided to move in and "organize" the stills. He bought a farmhouse just north of the village for his gang headquarters and began calling on the mountain bootleggers. Unfortunately for "Legs," the locals didn't want to be organized, and he was gunned down. Wounded, he had the trunks of the trees around his house painted white to hinder a possible ambush and was eventually killed in an Albany rooming house.

for a man who once said about the Catskills, "Those hills comfort me as no other place in the world does—it is home there."

John Burroughs Memorial State Historic Site, off Route 30 (take Hardscrabble Road to Burroughs Road), north of Roxbury, is open during daylight hours. Admission is free. For information call (518) 827-6111 or visit www.nysparks .state.ny.us/historic-sites.

Many of John Burroughs's modern-day spiritual descendants use the term *appropriate technology* to refer to renewable, nonpolluting sources of energy. Over in the northwestern Catskills town of East Meredith, the **Hanford Mills Museum** celebrates one of the oldest of these so-called alternative-energy sources, the power of running water harnessed to a wheel. Kortright Creek at East Meredith has been the site of water-powered mills since the beginning of the nineteenth century, and the main building on the museum site today was built in 1846.

The old mill became the Hanford Mills in 1860, when David Josiah Hanford bought the operation. During the eighty-five years in which it owned the mill, the Hanford family expanded its output to include feed milling and the manufacture of utilitarian woodenware for farms and small industries. The mill complex grew to incorporate more than ten buildings on ten acres, all clustered around the millpond and it continued in operation until 1967.

Much of the original nineteenth-century equipment at Hanford Mills is still in place and in good working order. Today's visitors can watch lumber being cut on a big circular saw and shaped with smaller tools, all powered by the waters of Kortright Creek. At the heart of the operation is a 10-by-12-foot waterwheel evoking what traditional waterwheels have done for more than 2,000 years. Visitors may explore at their leisure, or take a guided tour.

The Hanford Mills Museum, intersection of County Routes 10 and 12, East Meredith (607-278-5744 or 800-295-4992; www.hanfordmills.org), is open May 15 to October 15, Tuesday through Sunday and Memorial Day, Labor Day, and Columbus Day from 10 a.m. to 5 p.m. Admission is $8.50 for adults, $5 for senior citizens, and free for children 12 and under. Group rates are available.

Places to Stay in the Catskills

GREENVILLE

Greenville Arms 1889 Inn
11135 State Route 32
(888) 665-0044
www.greenvillearms.com

HIGH FALLS

Captain Schoonmaker's 1760 House
913 Route 213
(845) 687-7946
www.captainschoonmakers
.com

HIGHLAND

Jingle Bell Bed & Breakfast
302 Swartekill Rd.
(845) 255-8458
www.jinglebellbandb.com

MONROE

Roscoe House
45 Lakes Rd.
(845) 782-0442

NEWBURGH

Morgan House
12 Powelton Rd.
(845) 561-0326

SAUGERTIES

The Villa at Saugerties
159 Fawn Rd.
(845) 246-0682
www.thevillaatsaugerties
.com

WALDEN

My Saddle Brook Farm
163 Berea Rd.
(845) 778-3420
www.mysaddlebrookfarm
.com

WALKILL

Audrey's Farmhouse
2188 Brunswyck Rd.
(800) 501-3872
www.audreysfarmhouse
.com

REGIONAL TOURIST INFORMATION— THE CATSKILLS

Catskills Tourism
(800) NYS–CATS
www.visitthecatskills.com

Delaware County Chamber of Commerce
5½ Main St.
Delhi, NY 13753
(607) 746-2281
www.delawarecounty.org

Greene County Promotion Department
700 Route 23B
Leeds, NY
(800) 355-CATS
www.greenetourism.com

Sullivan County
100 Sullivan Ave., Box 248
Ferndale, NY 12734
(800) 882-2287
www.scva.net

OTHER ATTRACTIONS WORTH SEEING IN THE CATSKILLS

Byrdcliffe Historic District
Glasgow Turnpike and Lark's Nest Road
Woodstock
(845) 679-2079
www.woodstockhistory.org

Fort Delaware Museum of Colonial History
6615 Route 97
Narrowsburg
(845) 252-6660
www.scgnet.us

Hudson River Cruises
Rondout Landing
Kingston
(845) 340-4700
www.hudsonrivercruises.com

Hunter Mountain Skyride
Route 23A
Hunter
(518) 263-4223
www.huntermtn.com

Knox's Headquarters State Historic Site
Forge Hill Road, Route 94
Vails Gate
(845) 561-5498
www.nysparks.state.ny.us

Last Encampment of the Continental Army
Route 300
Vails Gate
(845) 561-5073
http://co.sullivan.ny.us

Museum Village in Orange County
1010 Route 17M
Monroe
(845) 782-8247
www.museumvillage.org

New Windsor Cantonment State Historic Site
374 Temple Hill Rd., Route 300
Vails Gate
(845) 561-1765
www.nysparks.com

Rondout Lighthouse
One Rondout Landing
Kingston
(845) 338-0071
www.hrmm.org/rondout/light.htm

Thomas Cole House
218 Spring St.
Catskill
(518) 943-7465
www.thomascole.org

Tomsco Falls
Mountaindale
(845) 434-6065
www.scva.net

Trolley Museum
Route 89 East Strand
Kingston
(845) 331-3399
www.tmny.org

Washington's Headquarters State Historic Site
84 Liberty Street
Newburgh
(845) 562-1195
nysparks.state.ny.us

West Point Museum
Main Street
USMA Visitor Center
West Point
(845) 938-3590
www.usma.edu/museum

WINDHAM

Hotel Vienna
107 Route 296
(518) 734-5300
www.thehotelvienna.com

WOODSTOCK

Woodstock Inn on the Millstream
48 Tannery Brook Rd.
(800) 420-4707
www.woodstock-inn-ny.com

Places to Eat in the Catskills

DELHI

Quarter Moon café
53 Main St.
(607) 746-8886
www.quartermooncafe.com

HIGHLAND

The Would Restaurant
120 North Rd.
(845) 691-9883
www.thewould.com

KINGSTON

Armadillo Bar and Grill
97 Abeel St.
(845) 339-1550
www.armadillos.net

Le Canard Enchainé
278 Fair St.
(845) 339-2003

Ship to Shore
15 West Strand
(845) 334-8887
www.shiptoshorehudsonvalley.com

PHOENICIA

Sweet Sue's
49 Main St.
(845) 688-7852

ROSENDALE

Rosendale Cement Company
419 Main St.
(845) 658-3210

SAUGERTIES

Cafe Tamayo
89 Partition St.
(845) 246-9371
www.cafetamayo.com

WALTON

Miller's Barbecue and Apple Place
29735 State Highway 10
(607) 865-4721

WOODSTOCK

The Bear Café
295 Tinker St. (Route 212)
(845) 679-5555
www.bearcafe.com

Joshua's Cafe
51 Tinker St.
(845) 679-5533
www.joshuascafe.com

Mountain Gate Indian Restaurant
4 Deming St.
(845) 679-5100
www.mountaingaterestaurant.com

The Prince and the Pauper
24 Elm St.
(802) 457-1818
www.princeandpauper.com

Violette
85 Mill Hill Rd.
(845) 679-5300
www.violettewoodstock.com

Index